T[…]
and us[…] advantage. Today's topography is one of signs and symbols, information and communication. Jason Del Gandio is an indispensable guide for any activist seeking to navigate this ephemeral ground, and his *Rhetoric for Radicals* promises to be as essential for this generation of political organizers as Saul Alinsky's *Rules for Radicals* was for previous ones.

— Stephen Duncombe, author of
Dream: Re-Imagining Progressive Politics in an Age of Fantasy

Jason Del Gandio has written a courageous, original and provocative book of the importance of rhetoric and communication for radical social change. For those inside the revolution, this is must reading. For those outside the revolution, read this book and see a world you never imagined.

— Robert W. McChesney, author of
The Political Economy of Media

Jason Del Gandio *is* radical — he believes we who work for change can change ourselves! His optimism, affection and respect for the diversity of activist work invite our confidence and boldness. In a brilliant book that works well for both theory and practice, he gives us tools that show us how to be more powerful *and* more consistent with our values."

— George Lakey's co-founding of Training for Change and the Movement for a New Society are highlights in his fifty years of activism.

Del Gandio's powerful and useful book not only teaches us how to communicate more effectively, but offers a framework for re-thinking our strategies by examining activism through the lens of communication. This how-to book is a must for sophisticated radicals, pragmatic dreamers and activists of all persuasions.

— PATRICK REINSBOROUGH, Co-founder
smartMeme Strategy & Training Project

RHETORIC FOR RADICALS

A HANDBOOK FOR
21st CENTURY ACTIVISTS

JASON DEL GANDIO

NEW SOCIETY PUBLISHERS

Cataloging in Publication Data:
A catalog record for this publication is available from
the National Library of Canada.

Cover design by Diane McIntosh.
Talkbubble: iStock/Ryan Burke.

Printed in Canada.
First printing September 2008.

Paperback ISBN: 978-0-86571-628-5

To order directly from the publishers, please call toll-free (North America)
1-800-567-6772, or order online at www.newsociety.com

Any other inquiries can be directed by mail to:
New Society Publishers
P.O. Box 189, Gabriola Island, BC V0R 1X0, Canada
(250) 247-9737

New Society Publishers' mission is to publish books that contribute in fundamental ways to building an ecologically sustainable and just society, and to do so with the least possible impact on the environment, in a manner that models this vision. We are committed to doing this not just through education, but through action. This book is one step toward ending global deforestation and climate change. It is printed on Forest Stewardship Council-certified acid-free paper that is **100% post-consumer recycled** (100% old growth forest-free), processed chlorine free, and printed with vegetable-based, low-VOC inks, with covers produced using FSC-certified stock. Additionally, New Society purchases carbon offsets based on an annual audit, operating with a carbon-neutral footprint. For further information, or to browse our full list of books and purchase securely, visit our website at: www.newsociety.com

New Society Publishers
www.newsociety.com

Recycled
Supporting responsible use of forest resources
FSC
www.fsc.org Cert no. SW-COC-1271
© 1996 Forest Stewardship Council
100%

Contents

Acknowledgments

Many people deserve thanks for helping me along my journey. I thank the folks at New Society Publishers for helping bring this book to print: Christopher and Judith Plant for first offering to publish this work; and Ingrid Witvoet and Murray Reiss for providing many helpful suggestions and ideas. I wholeheartedly thank my family and friends from back home who keep me grounded. They know and understand me in ways that no one else does, and that's a wonderful reminder of my roots. I also thank the Grove family for their unconditional support. I am learning, slowly, how to show that same type of support to others. I must also thank my earlier friends from various subcultures who exposed me to alternative views about the world. My current ideas and actions can be traced to those early days.

I would like to thank my graduate professors from Southern Illinois University, Carbondale, for teaching me how to write, think, and most importantly, how to live. That's especially so for Lenore who was kind and patient enough to mentor me in a million and one ways. Along the same lines, I thank and appreciate my SIU friends who are dispersed across the country. Having such crazy, intelligent and supportive friends is truly a gift! I especially thank Elizabeth and Lea who have been here the whole time — from my first rejection to my acceptance with New Society. And of course, I thank my partner, Amanda, who has read numerous drafts and has seen me tired, frustrated and on the brink of quitting. Through all of this she encourages me to write, live and love with passion, hope and drive. She simultaneously accepts me for who I am and pushes me to be more, and for that, I am forever grateful. Last, I thank all the activists of the world who have taught me how to listen, learn and reflect, and how to fight for social justice. This book is dedicated to all of you. Keep walking toward better realities, and one day we will change the world!

Preface

Streets, Rhetoric and Revolution!

Rhetoric for Radicals is about changing the world. Specifically, it's about changing the world through human communication. This may seem simplistic, but I will argue otherwise. Communication is the basis of the world and the basis of human reality. Subtracting communication from our lives leaves only cold, hard, disconnected things; facts without feeling; a world devoid of human life. But we do have communication and we do have a world — a world worth fighting over and changing for the better. As we change our communication, we change our world. But to do this we need to be smart and strategic; we need to think about our languages, statements, styles, actions, and overall communicative effects. This involves rhetoric. For now, we can define rhetoric as conscientiously crafted communication for the achievement of social and political ends. This may seem basic enough, but it is actually very complex. We often think of communication as a basic exchange of information. Two people talk to one another, exchange information and then go about their business. This common understanding of communication woefully limits our political effectiveness. The *way* we communicate influences and can even determine our thoughts, understanding of and perceptions of the thing we're talking about. This is even truer when talking about — *and actually doing* — politics, social change, resistance and revolution.

Let's consider direct action and civil disobedience. Every action involves multiple modes of communication. All the participants must communicate in order to coordinate the action. The action then communicates outward to whoever will watch and listen. The action could be geared toward a very specific audience or created for the whole world. In either case, there is an intended audience. People have been spending days, weeks, or even months planning the action. They've created or updated websites and blogs; written and designed texts, posters and fliers; reached people through e-mails and cell phones; and contacted particular news media. The purpose, location, message and intended effect have been debated and discussed. Communication is present in every phase of this action.

It's almost inevitable that the participants of the action will eventually stand face-to-face with riot police. This might involve negotiation, argumentation or persuasion; or physical interaction with either silence and limp bodies, or chained arms, lockboxes, shouts, refusals and strained bodies. The police will most likely disrupt and disperse the action. Some activists will get free and others will be arrested. Those who escape will go tell their friends and write up e-mails and online posts while those being arrested are probably being handcuffed and dragged along the pavement.

If you're being arrested, you're probably telling the cops that you're not a criminal but rather a conscientious objector; that you're not breaking the law but rather refusing to comply with unjust laws; that you're doing this not for personal gain but for the improvement of the shared social world. The arresting officer then says that he is just doing his job; that he doesn't care about your motives or reasons; that you are aware of your actions and the consequences; and that you can make your case before an impartial judge. This example obviously involves the exchange of information, but many other things are involved too.

During the interaction, you and the officer try to control the situation by carefully choosing your words. You refer to yourself as an activist, civil disobedient, radical, and even revolutionary while he calls you a criminal. He refers to himself as a server and protector of the law while you call him a Robo Cop or Storm Trooper. He then gets upset and fires back, calling you clueless and ignorant. All of these descriptions are accurate to some degree, and that's due to the nature of language. Words are never neutral arbiters of reality; there's no such thing. Everyone knows this already, at least intuitively. This gives us free license to use language to shape people's understanding. You and the officer thus play rhetorical games by legitimizing your own actions through words and linguistic frames. This example is awfully mild, of course. Real life situations are often intense, chaotic, vicious and even violent. We yell, shout and sling expletives back and forth. We try to get into each others' minds and inflict psychological harm and damage one another's ideologies. These situations aren't pretty, but they commonly occur during mass actions and mobilizations.

At a later point you and the arresting officer might take turns talking and listening to each other. Most likely, you're explaining the importance of radical social change while he nods his head and avoids eye contact. He might even be completely silent, but his silence is *not* non-communicative. In fact, his silence communicates his "professional distance" from the situation, as if his personal feelings are not there. He wants to make the arrest in his professional role instead of as a real person. You, too, might remain silent, but for different reasons. On one level, it's for legal protection, in the sense of having the right to remain silent. But on another level, silence can express your resistance. You're refusing any and all questions and providing no name, address, political affiliation or purpose of your action. You're using your silence to send a small but effective message: you're neither complying with nor obeying the rules of the land. Your silence is suddenly loud, persuasive, strategically powerful and very communicative. In other words, it's rhetorical.

Body language and nonverbal communication are also major factors here. The police officer's upright stance and hyper-confidence clearly mark his arresting intentions. You're also exuding confidence, but differently so. Your legs kick and fight and your heels dig into every little crack or crevice. You're not going down without a fight. This is all great, but it's not your only option for responding. You could go completely limp and lay there utterly uncooperative, forcing them to carry you away. In either case you are communicating refusal. You're obviously being arrested and you've decided to make the cops do all the work. This power reversal is an act of your embodied communication. You're using your body to communicate your resistance.

Other activists, either those from across the street or those still engaged in the action, begin cheering. No actual words are spoken, just many sounds of solidarity. The cheers continue as you're pulled onto the bus which is your makeshift holding cell. Thirty, forty, maybe sixty activists sit there, hands cuffed behind their backs. This isn't fun. Really, it's not. But there's a strange vibe on the bus. You're not entirely sure why, but you know in your heart that you have *communicated* something. You've made it clear that you're not giving up, caving in or bending to the whims of a perverse society. You are free and fighting, even in your precarious state of arrest. There will be other fights and eventually you will win. It's only a matter of time.

This extended example highlights some basic structures of rhetoric. For instance, there is always a communicator, an audience, a message and a surrounding situation. There's also a constant loop of interaction between you and your audience, a desire to accomplish some type of political goal or action, and some medium of expression. Sometimes you are the communicator, other times you are the audience member. Sometimes you send messages, other times you respond to messages. You're constantly living in a situation, but that situation is always shifting, forcing you to adjust and adapt. Your political desires push and pull you towards different goals and actions. And this process unfolds through languages, actions, gestures and even collective vibrations. All of this is the domain of rhetoric.

The example also highlights the interchange between activists and society at large. Activists are full-time communicators standing on public stages and broadcasting messages. Each action contributes to the wider world, and the particular message of each action creates a slightly different effect. You might kick and scream, but you might also walk and sing or talk and negotiate. Each of these choices carries a different message and a different effect. Most activists realize this already, which explains why activists debate the look and feel of direct actions, discuss particular slogans and chants, and choose certain symbols. This is great, but it's not enough. You want to address these things *rhetorically*, which will improve your radicalism. It will help you appeal to wider publics, help you create more effective messages and actions and help you create forms of activism suitable for the twenty-first century. That's what activism, organizing and radicalism are all about: communicating with others in order to create a better world. That's the whole purpose of *Rhetoric for Radicals.*

Overview

This book is written for activists who seek a decentered, anti-authoritarian, radically democratic world. This doesn't mean that you have to be a militant or a direct actionist to appreciate this book. Many radical activists do not consider themselves militants or direct actionists in any way, shape or form. But these activists are willing to walk toward their own visions of a better world and that's what makes them radical. If you're willing to follow your heart and walk toward your own radical desires, then this book is for you.

My own desires are influenced by my activism, which began in the spring of 2000 with the global justice movement. I happened to be watching the evening news and caught the coverage of the World Bank and International Monetary Fund protests in Washington, DC. Something hit me in that moment and I suddenly realized that I needed to be out there in the world, trying to change things for the better. I started doing activist work soon after. Since then I have worked on free trade and fair trade issues, anti-war campaigns, anti-Republican National Convention protests and Latin American solidarity actions. I have organized, facilitated and led various workshops on communication, rhetoric and radical theory at activist conferences, local bookstores and community free spaces. I also traveled with a New York City delegation of activists to observe and report on Venezuela's Bolivarian Revolution. This experience was life changing. Seeing the Bolivarian Revolution in process made me believe that revolution is both possible and necessary. Such experiences, coupled with my academic trainings and teachings in communication studies, have motivated me to write a handbook for radical activists and organizers.

This book is different from other how-to manuals. Plenty of great books already tackle the strategic ins-and-outs of hands-on organizing and activism. To name just a few: Saul Alinsky's *Rules for Radicals* (1971); Kim Bobo, Jacki Kendall and Steve Max's *Organizing for Social Change* (1996); Randy Shaw's *The Activist's Handbook*

(2001); United For a Fair Economy's *The Global Activist's Manual* (2002); Michael Albert's *Trajectory of Change* (2002); and for more directly subversive tactics, CrimethInc.'s *Recipes for Disaster* (2005). But *Rhetoric for Radicals* is different. It approaches activism as a rhetorical issue and argues that effective radicalism must involve sound rhetorical practice. Most if not all of us are aware of this to a certain degree. But this book asks us to go beyond mere awareness and actually approach activism as a *rhetorical labor.*

Rhetoric for Radicals is not completely alone in this call. Some works by George Lakoff — particularly *Don't Think Like an Elephant!* (2004) and *Thinking Points* (2006) — address the intersections of communication and activism. So too does Stephen Duncombe's *Dream: Re-imagining Progressive Politics in the Age of Fantasy* (2007). But there are some key differences. Lakoff is writing for liberal Democrats while I am writing for radicals. And Duncombe outlines reasons why activists should use spectacle-like communication while I provide hands-on instructions for improving activists' communication. To that end, I invite you to become a radical rhetorician capable of manifesting alternative worlds of communicative experience. Here's the underlying logic:

- Change the rhetoric and you change the communication.
- Change the communication and you change the experience.
- Change the experience and you change a person's orientation to the world.
- Change that orientation and you create conditions for profound social change.

This logic is less about what you say and do and more about *rhetorically crafting* what you say and do. I firmly believe that we can say whatever we want. But the trick is finding the right words, the right tone, the right approach, the right rhetoric.

I am not asking you to put up a false front. I would never endorse such a thing. But if we're going to talk about resistance, rebellion and revolution, then we need to talk about them in ways that attract rather than alienate people. There's no honor or glory in bad communication; it simply leaves us alone, isolated and severed from the channels of social change. We obviously want the opposite; improving our rhetorical communication can only help us. And just as our activism changes with the times, so too must our rhetorical considerations and responses. Our post-9/11, globalized and networked era poses unique challenges to social change. *Rhetoric for Radicals* addresses those challenges by providing guidelines, insights, theories, tools, and suggestions for twenty-first century activists.

This brings up an important question. What do I mean by twenty-first century activism? I have two partial answers. The first is historical and the second is intuitive.

Like I said above, the global justice movement was my entry into activism. While I love and appreciate all that I have learned from that movement, its time has passed. Take, for instance, the famous Battle of Seattle. That historical event occurred at the very end of 1999 and marked not the beginning but definitely a flourishing of the global justice movement. That "movement of movements" gathered fierce momentum over the next two years. Mass mobilizations, direct actions, participatory democracies, horizontal communities and feelings of urgency spread like wildfire. Then something happened: September 11, 2001. In the wake of 9/11, our focus shifted away from global capital in general and to the United States' empire in particular. A US anti-war movement soon emerged. That movement has been effective at times. For instance, on February 15, 2003, somewhere between 10 and 30 million people across the world expressed their outrage against a possible invasion of Iraq. And just before the war began hundreds of thousands of people were committing direct actions throughout the US. This was impressive and inspiring, but generally speaking, the anti-war movement has been too concerned with the slow process of lobbying politicians who were responsible for the war. Lobbying is important, but the anti-war movement has rarely addressed the roots of the problem: nationalism, capitalism, empire, a corrupt two-party system and people's acquiescence toward the Iraq war and the Bush Administration's supposed "war on terror." The few months leading up to the actual invasion of Iraq seemed to be riding the wave of the pre-9/11 global justice movement. But that pre-9/11 radicalism waned once the war started.

Looking at the pre- to post-9/11 transition this way is perplexing for one very basic reason: global justice activists are still here; we didn't disappear and we didn't go anywhere else. We're still active, still working and still striving for *global* change. We continue to organize and participate in mass mobilizations, counter summits, no-border camps, world social forums, transnational alliances, cross-cultural solidarities, and all kinds of globally networked actions and movements. But the name, "global justice movement," now seems outdated; it seems marked by the past rather than the edge of the present. Its time, however exciting it was, is gone. We are thus forced to move forward even as we search for new themes, names, identities, slogans, languages and *rhetorics*. This book is written during this impasse. Hence the book's subtitle: *A Handbook for Twenty-first Century Activists*.

I must admit, though, that I am not entirely clear on the meaning of the phrase "twenty-first century activist." I have only a faint feeling, a murky intuition and a cloudy vision. And my vision may be influenced more by a creative imagination than a concrete analysis. But maybe that's not so bad. Imagination helps us surpass moments of impasse and times of indecision. Imagination helps us think beyond the old, stale, crusty thoughts of a decadent society. Imagination helps us dream and desire. My own imagination draws me to the nature of this book: issues of communication and rhetoric. Twenty-first century activists are — or will become — the rhetors of the future. We will translate ideas into actions and communicate visions into realities. We will create worlds so common that we are all included and worlds so unique that we are all inspired. That's activism of the future that must begin today.

We have already glimpsed precedents of the twenty-first century. The Zapatistas are a prime example. Their 1994 uprising was a rhetorical phenomenon. They used the emerging media of the day to create tangible images of their inclusive, non-ideological politics: Zapatismo. The Internet became a revolutionary tool and the word became a weapon. Their stories, poems and communiqués created a political imagination of thought, feeling and action. They created a political perception. Not a fake, phony or erroneous "take on reality," but rather a concrete but open reality of accessibility, solidarity, criticality and self-and-collective determination. The Zapatistas invited us to participate in this ongoing communicative creation and to partake in this rhetorical formation.

While the Zapatistas are a prime predecessor of twenty-first century radicalism, they are not alone. Other groups, movements and actions pave the way for our future politics: Ya Basta! and Disobedianti; Black Blocs, Green Blocs and Pink Blocs; Reclaim the Streets, Critical Mass, Times Up!, and the Clandestine Insurgent Rebel Clown Army; festivals of resistance, parades of life and prefigurative celebrations; anarchists, autonomists, cyber-Marxists and do-it-yourselfers; antiracist workers, militant researchers and activist philosophers; radical cheerleaders, feminist virtuosos, queer knitters and undercover lovers gardening in the dark of night; and of course all the drums, puppets, masquerades, slogans, chants, dances, styles, colors, words, actions and images! Many of us have walked toward this future — a future where we will create unforeseen worlds and materialize uncharted realities. We will achieve the unachievable and we will create the unimaginable. This will become our communication; this will become our rhetoric; this will become our revolutionary change.

Preview

Chapter One takes up this revolutionary call by situating rhetoric as a *communicative labor.* Rhetoric is no doubt an ongoing and ever-present process, but good rhetoric is labor intensive. It takes time, thought and energy. Bypassing this labor has created a *communicative gap* between our actions and the public's reception of those actions. Simply put, our radicalism suffers from a rhetorical crisis. But all is not lost. As this book argues, we can improve our rhetoric and move beyond this crisis. This mending process begins with a conceptual overview of rhetoric for radicals. The chapter provides three different but related definitions of rhetoric, situates rhetoric at the center of social change, connects rhetorical practice to activism and organizing and asks us to approach our activism through the lens of rhetoric. Activism, as the conscious act of changing society, is inherently rhetorical. Political campaigns, social movements, direct actions, demonstrations, rallies and parades of resistance are rhetorical constructions. But Chapter One goes deeper and agues that *all human realities are rhetorically constructed*. Such a framework depicts the world as a pliable process and our activism as a communicative labor for recreating realities. If this is true, then our activism isn't about changing but about creating the world. This insight is foundational to rhetoric for radicals.

Chapter Two is a hands-on chapter, providing plenty of guidelines and suggestions for developing your rhetorical skills. It begins by addressing the two most basic skills: public speaking and writing. These skills, while not what everyone wants or needs, easily transfer to other activist-related issues, e.g., designing websites, running public campaigns, creating T-shirt and poster images, developing visual art, petitioning on street corners and having everyday conversations. In each case we need to develop a clear message that can be effectively communicated to other people. This chapter tackles that concern head-on. The chapter also provides instructions for creating a rhetorical package, which includes a message, audience, strategy, goal and situation. The chapter then addresses different rhetorical approaches, like persuasion, argumentation, storytelling and invitational rhetoric. Understanding how to use these approaches is important, but we must also develop our rhetorical knowledge. This involves using current events, history and self-knowledge to your rhetorical advantage. Chapter Two provides a solid starting point for improving your communication skills, your rhetorical skills and your rhetorical knowledge.

Chapter Three discusses the power of language, particularly how language shapes people's perceptions and understanding. Mainstream media, political strategists and advertising and marketing agencies understand this all too well. Activists need to take heed and consciously consider the wording of every slogan, sentence and demand. Language, thus understood, becomes a tool for radical social change. Deploying the right language can mean the difference between success and failure. This chapter helps you understand how language shapes people's views, how it is used and abused, how it relates to issues of self-identity and propaganda, how to appreciate political correctness without being stifled by it, and how to utilize the rhetorical power of new words and languages. By the end, you'll understand how language not only shapes consciousness, but also, and more profoundly, how it shapes reality. You'll see how changing your language helps change the world.

Chapter Four expands the scope of rhetoric by addressing body rhetoric. At the very least, body rhetoric involves the look, feel and style of your physical gestures, the messages of your nonverbal communication and the meanings and effects of your bodily actions. And just as you can improve your verbal rhetoric, you can also improve your body rhetoric. Since your body is the site of your everyday living, you can cultivate it into a site of radical activity and rhetorical engagement. Chapter Four helps you accomplish that by looking at three things: embodied argumentation, rhetorical style and the human vibe as bodily emanation. The chapter provides examples of and guidelines for improving these forms of rhetoric.

Chapter Five, the last chapter, summarizes and extends the purpose of the entire book: it provides guidelines for building twenty-first century radical rhetoric. The chapter begins with ten observations of contemporary activist rhetoric. Understanding our current actions helps pave the way for future actions. The chapter then discusses "network rhetoric," which is a paradigmatic figure of today's activism. We discuss some examples of network rhetoric and then ways to improve as well as move beyond this rhetorical form. The chapter ends by proposing a new approach to radical thought and action. This approach, called *neo-radicalism,* sets forth a new orientation toward activism that is based on the immaterial and communicative labors of the twenty-first century. Neo-radicalism is a rhetorically-centered activism that encapsulates the nature and purpose of *Rhetoric for Radicals.*

Before closing this preface, I want to lay my motivations on the table. I could easily sit here and write how I am simply trying to make a small contribution, how I am just trying to do my part and how I hope this book will make a tiny ripple in public affairs. All this is true, but only to a degree. Above all, I hope this book starts a revolution. Do I think that will actually happen? Do I think that this book *will* start a revolution? I'm not sure, but my uncertainty doesn't stop me from dreaming and trying. Occupying intersections does not necessarily stop a war. Lying down in front of bulldozers does not necessarily stop apartheid. And shutting down the World Trade Organization does not necessarily stop corporate globalization. But we commit these actions anyway because the uncertainty of their outcomes is better than the certainty of nothing. I am no different. I am trying to change the world and I am doing it through the uncertainties of writing a book. At times I will give suggestions. At times I will make critiques. At times I will say things that you completely disagree with. Okay, fine. Let's talk, debate, discuss, and expand the ideas of this book. Then, together, we can move toward a revolution.

But let's also recognize the gravity of this discussion. We can have provocative debates about changing the system. We can talk about past revolutions and their implications for today. And we can dream and romanticize our radicalism. But some real questions soon slap us in the face. Is revolution actually possible today? Is revolution possible within the United States of America? Is it even sensible to talk about the possibility of revolution? Are we just crazy? Are we out of touch with the times and conditions? The answers to these questions depend on what we mean by revolution. A physical, militant or violent revolution seems foolish. We could not amass enough people with enough violent technology to overthrow the current order. It's simply not possible. The US power structure is armed to the teeth with deadly force. A couple of Apache helicopters could wipe out entire towns within minutes. I don't think this is what we envision or imagine. And I don't think this is a sensible way to a better society or world. We are thus confronted by another impasse, or at least seemingly so. We need a different path to revolution. I believe that rhetorical labor fulfills that need. Rhetoric is not the be-all and end-all for social change and *Rhetoric for Radicals* is not a blueprint for revolution. But rhetoric is a necessary component and this book can help us move in that direction. With that in mind, I say to everyone: *Radical rhetors of the world, unite!*

A Call to Rhetorical Action

Why Rhetoric for Radicals?

Twenty-first century activism advocates for a single world composed of many realities.[1] Different types of organizational structures, communicative approaches and ways of living are explored as we try to change the world without taking power. Swarms of people, identities, orientations, wants and needs are linked by desires for social justice and more meaningful ways of being in the world. Our political actions are grounded in our experiences of hunger, discrimination, unemployment, bombing, occupation, brutality and empire. Diverse movements rise up in opposition to these conditions and we insist that another world is not only possible but absolutely necessary. We improvise, strategize and experiment as we organize local and global resistances, rebellions, revolutions and liberations. Our methodology of revolution is individualist and communal, supportive without suffocating, and expresses a non-reductive and non-universalizing solidarity.[2] Such twenty-first century radicalism is beautiful and handsome, exciting and invigorating. But there is an unintended residual effect: our twenty-first century radicalism suffers from a rhetorical crisis.

We continuously work, act and communicate for better realities, and we undoubtedly succeed in many of our efforts. But the general population lacks a widespread sense of the urgent need for action, which means that our movements lack the critical masses necessary for *profound* social change. This is standard for most radical projects and most sociopolitical eras. We're always working with limited resources and reaching beyond our presumed capacities. But each project is unique and each era is different. We must look at our own situation and evaluate the efficacy of our efforts. For instance, our ideas, words and arguments, while widely circulated among our own communities, are often absent from the wider sphere of public talk. Our activism and organizing, while helpful in altering micro-relations and alleviating immediate situations, seem to fall upon too many deaf ears and too many blind eyes. Our direct actions, while promoting worldwide justice and individual self-empowerment, are easily obscured by the media's decontextualized accounts and easily dismissed by political pundits. And our political philosophies and ideologies, while thought-provoking and heartfelt, struggle for wider exposure, acceptance and mobilizing force. Basically, there is a communicative gap between our efforts and the public's reception of those efforts. This gap is a *rhetorical issue* needing attention and redress. If we are to change the world, we must remedy this situation. That remedy can begin by rigorously attending to the communicative aspects of our twenty-first century radicalism.[3]

Activists traditionally concern themselves with material conditions, seeking to improve their own and others' concrete living situations. To change the world has thus meant to change the conditions in which we live. That's undoubtedly important, but it misses too much. Our world — the very thing we are trying to change — involves more than material conditions, which are only a small part of our project. The world also involves our experience of those conditions. That experience is influenced, if not quasi-determined, by our languages, perceptions, stories, discourses, ideologies, psychologies, social relations and worldviews. In other words, we must consider both the *material conditions* and the *immaterial rhetoric* that surrounds those conditions. Activists always consider rhetoric to some degree. We continually argue over the look and design of demonstrations and direct actions; the wording of manifestos and speeches; and the usefulness of ideologies, philosophies and analyses. But these debates always seem peripheral to our physical actions and material conditions. This is mistaken and debilitating. Undervaluing the rhetoric of our efforts hinders our communication with, and our political efficacy within, the wider public arena. We are due for a paradigmatic shift that equally considers both the material and immaterial.

Let me be as clear as possible here. I am not asking us to reject or ignore our material concerns. We need to eat, be clothed, procure safe and affordable housing, receive quality healthcare, have access to reliable transportation, attain environmental sustainability, etc. We need to fight and overturn dictatorships, military regimes, capitalist infrastructures and gargantuan bureaucratic factories that physically house and produce modern day inequalities. These material concerns correlate with the wants and needs of our living, breathing bodies. However, to do this and to do it right, we need to change people's thoughts, understandings and perceptions. That's an immaterial issue.

Take revolution, for example. A true revolution involves more than replacing governmental, economic, or political systems. That's important, of course; but new systems do not necessarily mean new realities. Socialism within the United States would not necessarily eradicate racism, sexism, anti-Semitism, homophobia, etc. And US Socialism could possibly become a US dictatorship, simply worsening the situation. Changing the system is good, but it does not necessarily mean new and better realities. True revolutions occur when people begin to see and understand themselves, each other and their world in radically different ways. Revolution occurs when people undergo a rhetorical shift that breaks with the past and creates a new framework for different actions, ideas and social relations. Such revolutionary shifts can occur on an individual basis, but are most powerful on a mass level. Hundreds, thousands, and hopefully millions of people undergoing revolutionary shifts in their rhetorical orientations sets the conditions for the possibility of profound and long-lasting social change.

I believe that such shifts are occurring throughout parts of Mexico and Latin America. The Zapatistas in Mexico, the Movement of Landless Workers in Brazil, the protests against water privatization in Bolivia, the Confederation of Indigenous Nationalities in Ecuador and the Piquetero Movement in Argentina are just a few examples. People within these movements have come to see neoliberal economic policies as destructive, oppressive and antidemocratic and are now replacing them with participatory democracies and localized economies that benefit their own communities. These people have come to believe that revolution is not only possible, but necessary and they are actively working toward alternatives to capitalism, representative democracy, governmental regimes, policing and prison systems, etc. They are also creating new languages, discourses, lifestyles, relations and ways of being and acting. That is to say, they are undergoing *rhetorical shifts*. Attending to and facilitating such shifts is the concern of radical rhetoricians and the domain of rhetoric for radicals.

This rhetorical call to action overlaps with some of the popular language coming from contemporary network and affective theorists and activists: We must fashion ourselves into the cognitariats and immaterial laborers of the general intellect. That is, we must become radical rhetoricians who engage and alter the perceptions and languages of contemporary living. In brief, the cognitariat is a combination of cognitive worker and proletariat. An immaterial laborer is one who labors with communicative, emotional, psychological, informational, cultural or knowledge-based resources and/or means. And the general intellect refers to the collective intelligence or social knowledge of a society at a given historical period. These terms emerged over the last twenty to thirty years, beginning with such Italian theorists as Antonio Negri, Paolo Virno, Maurizio Lazzarato, Franco Berardi and others. These ideas have been expanded, migrating throughout a cross-continental vernacular of networks and affectivity.[4] I see at least one major correlation between these ideas and my call to rhetorical action: communication produces our social realities. If this is true, then resolving our rhetorical crisis is absolutely important.

I believe that our rhetorical crisis coexists with, and is unintentionally influenced by, our evolving anti-authoritarianism. This is not to say that all activists, organizers and radicals are self-described anti-authoritarians. The majority are not. Perhaps this occurs because anti-authoritarianism is associated with more direct and militant action and radical critiques of *all* oppressions. People who don't engage in such actions and critiques often reject the anti-authoritarian label. But many contemporary activists do borrow from and are at least sympathetic to anti-authoritarian practices. It is commonly understood that the *way* we change the world influences the type of world we create. Thus, directly democratic procedures like consensus decision making, spokescouncils, affinity groups, direct action and diversity of thought and discussion are commonly practiced. Social forums, conferences, protests, neighborhood assemblies and website clearinghouses often use bottom-up structures allowing individuals, groups and organizations to create large, decentered networks. Rather than leaders and dominating ideologies, we have affinities of people coordinating themselves toward social change. Such anti-authoritarianism is a marker of our twenty-first century activism.

One of the more discussed expressions of this new anti-authoritarianism is provided by Michael Hardt and Antonio Negri. They argue that our radical era now depends upon and encourages decentered, autonomously acting groups, peoples and affiliations linked together by "the common" — land, water and air; information technologies, the Internet and post-Fordist production systems; labor transmigrations, hybrid identities and international communication networks; global discourses, common dreams and world gatherings. The anti-authoritarianism of the common has created conditions for the possibility of a unique revolutionary class. Hardt and Negri refer to this class as "the multitude."[5] The multitude reconceptualizes the more traditional concepts of "the people," "the masses" and the "working class." According to Hardt and Negri, the first totalizes us as a single body of unitary identity, the second reduces us to a uniformity of indifference and the third refers only to specific types of work-related identities, thus ignoring a slew of activities that create power relationships and social realities. The multitude, by contrast, acknowledges our multiplicity of differences, our common struggle for democratic forms of life and the diversity of social actors and actions that create our communicatively created world. For Hardt and Negri, the multitude ushers in the dawn of twenty-first century radicalism.

The multitude's anti-authoritarianism not only changes our understanding of revolutionary identities and movements, but it also changes our understanding of rhetorical communication. Take, for instance, the classic example of Dr. Martin Luther King, Jr. and his charismatic leadership of the civil rights movement. Dr. King's oration and persona helped catalyze and mobilize mid-twentieth century African-Americans and he became the rhetorical face of that movement. He did not single-handedly mobilize the civil rights movement, but he did take on that symbolic force. No single person, face or symbol like that exists today. We are thus perceived as lacking rhetorical leadership. But this is a misunderstanding. Rhetorical leadership still exists, but in a different form: the communicative life force of our radicalism is networked throughout the tiny capillaries of the multitude. Single individuals and/or groups are no longer responsible for mediating between our actions and society at large. That rhetorical responsibility now resides with a plethora of people, ideas and movements. Twenty-first century activism has decentralized our rhetorical leadership. Each of us now assumes the responsibility of rhetorical mediator.

While I believe the above statements to be accurate, I also believe that we have not lived up to our responsibilities. This is evidenced by widespread sentiments that can be found in the mainstream mass media as well as in everyday conversations: "Anti-globalizers: do they really stand for anything?"..."A million messages and no solutions"..."Uninformed activists create havoc, not improvement"... "Local organizers make no sense"..."Plenty of ideas but no substance." Our actions are not solely accountable for such common perceptions — corporate media, conservative commentators and social prejudices play major factors. But we must acknowledge this communicative divide and take responsibility for mending the gap.

I believe that our concern with the anti-authoritarian common has shifted our attention away from the details of how we communicate. This may be an unconscious consequence, but it is a consequence nonetheless. Somewhere along the line we have equated attention to communicative detail with the often arrogant, elitist and power-driven aspirations of fame and fortune. We no longer seek the great speech, the great essay, the great manifesto or the great leader. In one sense, this is fine. But this does not answer commonly asked questions from hostile as well as potentially sympathetic audiences: Who are your great speakers, essayists and novelists? Who among you can sway the masses? Who is the mobilizing face of your movement? Who or where is your leader? What do you actually stand for? What is your issue? What is your cause? Why aren't you more specific and concrete? These questions are an issue of public expectation. The average person expects a certain type of radicalism, one that follows in the tradition of orderly constitutional democracy: a well-defined leader standing upon a single stage advocating for a "sensible" cause. But our radicalism is different. We have many different people utilizing many different stages, advocating for a plethora of interwoven causes. We use our voices, bodies, costumes, masks, pages, stages, streets and various technologies to raise a ruckus of decentered actions and movements.

Some of us may be fine with our communicative divides, dismissing issues of public expectation. That makes sense, but only to a degree. Refusing to respond to those expectations doesn't help our fight for social justice. The public — which includes potential allies and participants — will simply ignore us. And herein lays the root of our crisis. We have come to believe that our actions, and our actions alone, will change the world. That is a mistake. Decentered actions connected through the anti-authoritarian common are great, but they're not enough. Creating networks of world-wide justice must entail *effective rhetorical communication.*

International wars, US imperialism, concentration of global media, hyper-commercialism, compulsive consumerism and an empire of capital demand that we devise smart, intelligent and effective rhetoric. We must continue to say it and say it loud, but we must say it with craft, skill and sensibility. We must become campaign advisors, political strategists, public mediators and political pundits of revolutionary proportions. This characterization may give us pause and force the question: is this really our calling? Given the fact that our world is both material and immaterial, the answer is a resounding yes. Ignoring the communicative labor of our activism is antithetical to social change. We must continue to act in the service of decentered revolutions, global empowerment and the prefigurement of improved social realities. But we must do it through the lens of rhetorical work. And that rhetorical work must be carried out and accomplished *our way* — with openness, honesty and transparency; with reflection, discussion and critical debate; with bottom-up structures of direct democratic procedure; and with the ability to adapt to new situations. Doing this neither undermines nor contradicts our embrace of the common — it in fact strengthens it. Proper rhetorical consideration can deepen and widen the multitude. More of us will come to understand the call of the common, embrace the struggle for local and global equality and participate in twenty-first century activism.

Defining Rhetoric: Everything is Rhetorical!

Activists are full-time communicators constantly working toward sociopolitical achievements. Rhetoric is thus a primary rather than secondary aspect of our work; it is the lifeline of what we do. Marching in the streets, facilitating meetings, listening to others, sending out e-alerts, critiquing the media, posting stories, taking photographs, creating films, swaying officials, arguing with cops, defending ourselves in court, having one-on-one conversations and praising revolutionary victories all involve rhetorical work. We may not consciously think about it, but we *are* rhetoricians. We are thus called to improve our rhetorical communication. Simply put: bad communication leads to bad activism and good communication leads to good activism.

We usually don't talk about "rhetorical work." This is partly due to rhetoric's negative image. Rhetoric is easily coupled with manipulation, dishonesty, deceit and coercion. This is not new; it's been going on for twenty-five hundred years. Plato, an ancient Greek and perhaps the most famous Western philosopher of all time, vilified rhetoric in favor of philosophy. He did distinguish between true and false rhetoric, arguing that the first conveyed true knowledge while the second simply impressed and flattered audiences. True rhetoric expressed the insights of philosophy while false rhetoric deceived and tricked people. For Plato, rhetoric and even true rhetoric didn't really deserve serious consideration. Many Western thinkers followed Plato's lead. People like René Descartes, John Locke, Ludwig Wittgenstein (in his early work), and many other big-time intellectuals, argued that knowledge, insight and understanding come from philosophy, science, math and logic. Rhetoric, these thinkers argued, simply conveys knowledge. These thinkers reduced rhetoric to the communication of ideas. They never thought of rhetoric as actually *creating* ideas.

This same type of thinking plagues our activism. We assume, for instance, that concrete political change happens distinctly and separately from how we communicate our messages about that change. We place our activism on one side and our rhetoric on the other. We do this because we associate rhetoric with dishonesty, distortion, fabrication and exaggeration. There is good reason for this. We are simply tired of all the political hot air. We are fed up with the *shallow rhetoric,* the *rhetorical tricks* and the people who are *all rhetoric and no action.* We're simply tired of rhetoric, period. This perception of rhetoric is understandable but also problematic. We are conflating the rhetoric of particular people with rhetoric in general. This is wrong. Rhetorical abuse by some does not destroy the general power of rhetoric. We can and should use rhetoric for our own purposes. We don't have to be dishonest or corrupt; we can be ourselves — upfront, honest and radical.

The formal study of Western rhetoric first began in ancient Greek society. The Sophists are often credited as being the first rhetoricians. They were contemporaries of Plato who migrated from other cities and countries to Athens. In some ways they challenged the Athenian status quo, arguing against Plato's notions of absolute truth, transcendent realities and a world untouched by language and symbolic construction. The Sophists were in some ways nomadic, traveling from place to place, searching for audiences and students. They claimed the ability to improve the oratorical and argumentative skills of anyone, thus challenging the popular myth that only particular people were suited for public affairs. But Sophists charged students for instruction and earned their living through rhetorical teachings, creating a classist distribution of rhetorical powers. By attending to the rich and ignoring the poor, they perpetuated the aristocratic divide of ancient Athens. The already well-to-do could receive instruction on public speaking, memorization, debate, persuasion, craft and social, cultural and political grooming. This divide is much like our own era's: we, too, have a maldistribution of rhetorical powers, with political dynasties, social elites and the world's wealthiest receiving instruction on media relations, public personae and political grooming. Our supposed "marketplace of ideas" boils down to money. Those with money and power are trained for public exposure while the majority of us are ignored. This lack of rhetorical training hinders our ability to communicate with the public.

Socrates was another Greek philosopher and Plato's mentor. He was also at odds with the Sophists. Socrates believed that wisdom was the highest human pursuit, akin to spiritual enlightenment. A person of wisdom not only understood but lived out truth, virtue and justice. A person of wisdom could also teach others to understand and practice such worldly knowledge, and should do so for free. Socrates publicly challenged the Sophists on multiple issues and strongly argued against their monetary pursuits. He would start free conversations with random people on the streets by asking them, "Are you living justly?" His hope was that he and his conversational partner would both reach a higher state of earthly existence. Conversation was, for Socrates, a method of self-improvement; he believed that dialogue could awaken people to truth and self-knowledge. Socrates, though far from perfect, did live his words. He was a staunch advocate of critical reflection and believed it was his duty to freely mentor the people of Athens. But Athens' city council viewed it differently. They charged Socrates with corrupting the youth of Athens and sentenced him to death. Socrates' trial testimony has been studied for more than two thousand years and it demonstrates his dedication to wisdom and righteousness. As he stated before his death:

> You would have liked to hear me weep and wail, doing and saying all sorts of things which I regard as unworthy

> of myself, but which you are used to hearing from other people. But I did not think then that I ought to stoop to servility because I was in danger, and I do not regret now the way in which I pleaded my case. I would much rather die as the result of this defense than live as the result of the other sort. In a court of law...neither I nor any other ought to use his wits to escape death by any means.[6]

Both Socrates and the Sophists, despite their differences, have contributed to rhetoric for radicals. They challenged various aspects of their society, studied multiple topics and issues, touched the minds and hearts of many, engaged in public affairs, perfected their argumentative and conversational skills and understood the importance of communication. These characteristics reflect the wants and needs of today's activists.

My own understanding of rhetoric is more nuanced than either Sophistry or Socratic wisdom. My approach is influenced by such twentieth-century thinkers as Friedrich Nietzsche, Edmund Husserl, Antonio Gramsci, Jean-Paul Sartre, Simone de Beauvoir, Kenneth Burke, Louis Althusser, Michel Foucault, Jacques Derrida, Judith Butler and many others. Many of these names are obviously deceased white guys. This is not necessarily a conscious choice but rather a result of an education steeped in European and North American biases. In time my knowledge will expand, and so too will my list of influences.

This list also seems to privilege "intellectuals" over "hands-on radicals." But this isn't true. Emma Goldman, Gandhi, Malcolm X, Dr. King, Abbie Hoffman, Che Guevara, Subcomandante Marcos, Hugo Chavez and the CrimethInc. Collective are just a few of the names that also influence my understanding and approach to radical rhetoric. Then of course there are folks like Noam Chomsky, Howard Zinn, Cornel West and bell hooks who are intellectuals and activists. All these people have their own strengths and weaknesses and each influences me in a different way. The important thing to realize is that all these people are practicing rhetoricians. This should tell us something: our most beloved radicals are often the greatest communicators.

Through my studies and travels I have come to believe that rhetoric is an ever-present aspect of radical work. Rhetoric is not simply the art of speaking persuasively and it is not reducible to the hollow promises of false leaders. Rhetoric is all pervasive; everything we say, do, think and feel is rhetorical. Our rhetoric implicates others and the rhetoric of others implicates us. We influence and are influenced by the conscious and unconscious communication of others. We speak and are spoken to, even when we don't realize it. We teach and are taught on a continual basis and we construct and are constructed in ways beyond our immediate control. We are continually thinking, rehearsing, crafting and adapting ourselves to every situation. This view of rhetoric — and of human existence — re-shapes how we understand politics, the public mind and radicalism. Our lives suddenly appear as rhetorical processes that drive social change. Properly understanding this approach to rhetoric necessitates some explanation. In what follows, I provide three definitions of rhetoric: (1) rhetoric is persuasive, (2) rhetoric is discursive and analytical, and (3) rhetoric is the creation of reality.

Rhetoric is Persuasive

We can define rhetoric as *the study and practice of persuasion and its ways and means*. Rhetoric studies and also creates tactics for persuasion. For instance, how can a logical argument help you win a debate about healthcare? How do emotional stories help mobilize anti-war movements? How does credibility help you persuade an audience? What are some techniques for pumping up crowds at large rallies? How can you establish common ground with oppositional groups? How can we better motivate and inspire people? What can we say or do to create revolutionary fervor? These questions deal with persuasion, and persuasion is part of rhetoric.

Aristotle, another ancient Greek philosopher and a student of Plato, is often considered the first person to systematically study rhetoric.[7] He's the first Western theorist to approach rhetoric as a field of study. Aristotle defined rhetoric as *the ability to recognize in any given situation the available means of persuasion*. This definition emphasizes the *ability* to persuade anyone, anywhere, about anything. This may sound cheap and deceptive, but it's not. Persuasion and deception are not the same and such a conflation misses the point of Aristotle's definition. Aristotle is talking about the ability to adapt and craft your message to the wants and needs of your audience in order to achieve maximum effectiveness. We do this all the time.

Let's assume, for instance, that we're at a spokescouncil and we're debating the next direct action. Everyone is putting forth ideas, suggestions, arguments and assertions. We're all listening, hearing each other out and rearranging our stances to better fit the rhetorical demands of the conversation. Some of us use logic and hard facts about the city's layout. Others of us are using emotional stories about being arrested. A few more argue that they are the most experienced and should have the last word. A final choice is made after several go-arounds. We eventually agree on what angle to take. There is nothing deceptive or dishonest about this tactical debate. Instead, it demonstrates the process of persuasion and our daily applications of Aristotle's definition. We continually analyze every situation in order to put forth our best ideas, hoping to bring about a favorable outcome. Almost every imaginable situation relates to Aristotle's definition of rhetoric. Persuasion is simply part of the activist livelihood.

Rhetoric is Discursive and Analytical

We can also understand rhetoric as *the science of discourse*. In other words, rhetoric studies what people say, how they say it and the effects thereof. This definition includes but also goes beyond persuasion. For instance, how does the phrase "collateral damage" affect the public mindset? Why are certain labels and words offensive to some cultural groups but not others? Why has the radical imagination been captured by the language and metaphors of the Zapatistas? Why do so many people see direct action as violent but see capitalism and war as altruistic? How should we adjust our language, voice inflections and nonverbal communication to different audiences? Why might an author use particular words to describe particular groups, movements or experiences? These questions highlight different aspects of human communication and seek to understand what works and what doesn't and why.

Let's consider, for instance, the rhetorical styles of Malcolm X and Dr. Martin Luther King, Jr. Malcolm used quick-witted, wise-talking, urban street smarts of controlled and justified fury. Dr. King used an uplifting, soulful baritone of southern Baptist oration. The "ballot or the bullet" exemplifies Malcolm, while "I have a dream" exemplifies Dr. King. Both speakers exemplify different but equally important aspects of mid-twentieth century civil rights and Black struggles. Consider, also, the different writing styles of Howard Zinn and Noam Chomsky. Zinn uses a personal and story-like voice that is influenced by a Marxist predisposition. Chomsky uses hardcore analysis and detached observation and he favors a quasi-anarchist critique of the political economy. Zinn and Chomsky have their own unique styles that are noticeable and undoubtedly radical.

These examples underscore the discursive and analytical focus of rhetoric. Every rhetorical choice affects our minds, emotions and responses. We can investigate these choices and understand why different people, messages and approaches create different effects. Such investigations often but not always focus on language, oral and written articulation and the use of rhetorical tactics. We can also analyze our own rhetoric. This helps us make better rhetorical choices, improving our ability to create social change.

Rhetoric is the Creation of Reality

We can also understand rhetoric as *the practice and study of how people create their realities*. This definition obviously relates to the idea that everything is rhetorical. If rhetoric is the study of reality and if reality is all-encompassing, then just about everything can be understood as rhetoric. This approach helps us understand how human beings materialize their realities through immaterial means. In other words, how do our languages, thoughts, signs, symbols, narratives, perceptions and actions materialize our realities? Here, we are no longer concerned with persuasion only, and we move beyond basic analyses of language. We are now approaching rhetoric as an immaterial labor and we are seeking to understand how human environments are created, maintained, altered, dissolved and recreated.

Subcomandante Marcos of the Zapatistas understands that

rhetoric is the creation of reality. Since their 1994 public uprising, the Zapatistas have consciously sought to disseminate and create a Zapatista reality applicable to our globalized world. They have organized international conferences, assemblies and delegations, and have released press packets, communiqués, photographs, stories, poems, books and websites. They have also disseminated a well-crafted image: black-masked indigenous revolutionaries declaring "all for everyone, nothing for ourselves!" But this image is not just an image. Instead, the Zapatistas have created a Zapatista reality that is tangible to themselves and onlookers. This is not surprising since, to the best of my knowledge, Marcos was a professor of philosophy and communication — both of which are foundational aspects of rhetoric.[8] In the words of Marcos:

> Zapatismo is not an ideology, it is not a bought and paid for doctrine. It is...an intuition. Something so open and flexible that it really occurs in all places. Zapatismo poses the question: "What is it that has excluded me?" "What is it that has isolated me?"...In each place the response is different. Zapatismo simply states the question and stipulates that the response is plural, that the response is inclusive...[9]

Zapatismo, then, is something we embody. It is a set of values, outlooks and beginning points. It is a way of seeing and living. Zapatismo is not reducible to an ideology or a ten-point program. It lives within us as we live it, and is passed on through our languages, utterances and actions. It is passed on through our communication. Zapatismo is an active and participatory creation of a twenty-first century revolutionary reality.

Understanding rhetoric as the creation of reality is difficult. This is because we commonly equate reality with the things of the world and we assume that those things are separate from human experience. We assume that we are here and the things of the world are over there. This is true, but only partially so. The world does have a concrete existence of its own. I can bend down and touch the earth, verifying that it is distinct and separate from me. The earth does exist by itself, and so do I. This is true for all the things of the world. But we and the world are also mutually constitutive. We and the world are of each other. We create one another. We and the world stand before one another, giving rise to our existences. Furthermore, how I see the world influences my experience of the world. We can use a very basic example and ask, what is a rock, really? Is a rock a composite of minerals bound together by heat, compression and gravitational force? Is a rock dead material available for my stepping and sitting comfort, to be used at my own free will? Is a rock part of Mother Earth, to be respected as its own unique existence? Is a rock the face of God, to be revered and harmoniously lived with? Each of these questions implies a particular answer, and each of those answers is a very legitimate understanding of a rock. In other words, each of those answers are a different way of experiencing the "reality" of a rock.

Rhetoric as the creation of reality is even more applicable to social and political issues. For instance: Is war good or bad? Was the US invasion of Iraq justified? Does the mass media do its job? Does free trade help or hurt the poor? Is same-sex marriage constitutional or unconstitutional? Are migrant day laborers illegal aliens or undocumented workers? Is pacifism a viable solution to the world's problems? Does direct action help or hurt the radical cause? Are the Zapatistas terrorists or postmodern revolutionaries? The examples could go on all day long, but the point is made. Our responses to these questions are part and parcel of our lived-through realities. And that's why it is so difficult to sway folks one way or another. Our realities, even small parts of them, do not shift and change quickly and smoothly. It's a long and complicated process.

This explanation should give us pause and help us realize that appealing to "objective facts" does not always change people's minds. We often present hard facts and then get upset when people are not swayed. "How can they not see the truth of the situation! They must be lying to themselves! They're ignoring the facts!" The facts are always important, but our lives are not based on facts. Instead, our lives are based on values, beliefs, perceptions, thoughts and ideas. Objective facts are merely the raw materials of our realities; they are not the realities themselves. We have facts, and then we have our interpretations of those facts. This explains our need for rhetorical labor.

If we're going to change the world, then we need to change people's rhetorical constructions of the world.

Abbie Hoffman, a cultural revolutionary of the 1960s, understood the relationship between rhetoric and reality. Hoffman's famous courtroom testimony during the trial of the Chicago Seven touches upon many of the issues we're discussing. While on the stand, Hoffman testified that the hippies constituted a unique culture held hostage within American society. Hippies did not necessarily constitute a physical or geographical entity with national standing and binding legislations, he argued. Instead, hippies constituted a way of life that existed within their minds, hearts and bodies. They carried around this way of life wherever they went and in whatever they did. This hippie reality was not something false, phony or made up. It was not a figment of imagination. Instead, it was a concrete, viable and tangible reality. It was a rhetorically constructed world.

Abbie, during the trial, was asked for his place of residence. He replied with, "Woodstock Nation." He was then asked to explain.

> It is a nation of alienated young people. We carry it around with us as a state of mind in the same way the Sioux Indians carried the Sioux Nation around with them. It is a nation dedicated to cooperation versus competition, to the idea that people should have better means of exchange than property or money, that there should be some other basis for human interaction. It is a *nation*...[10]

Abbie may not have realized it, but his testimony articulated relationships among facts, interpretations, realities and rhetoric. And he was doing this as a hands-on radical, not as a detached theorist. Hoffman's statement basically says that, yes, there is a nation called America. But it is not beautiful, bountiful and benevolent to *everyone*. Yes, there is a system called capitalism, but it neither includes nor benefits *all* of our wants, needs and desires. And yes, you, Mr. United States of America, must recognize that we will not hide, suppress or give up our reality in favor of your reality. Abbie was arguing that the hippies have a right to fight for and defend their reality just like everyone else. With this in mind, we can understand that the

Chicago Seven trial was not simply a political trial, but a trial over reality.

Explaining the Creation of Reality: A Five-Step Process

Hoffman's testimony, despite its brilliant ingenuity, misses a key distinction. Abbie was fond of saying, "reality is in your head," meaning that we can create any reality we want. This is both true and false. We *can* create any reality we want, but only to a limit and only in conjunction with other human beings. Creating a reality is not an anything goes process. I cannot just make up any interpretation and call it a reality. This not only invites ridicule from others, but it isolates me from the collective community. We must first realize that there *are* concrete facts. But those facts need interpretation, articulation and symbolic understanding — they need rhetoric. We must also realize that our realities are communal phenomena. No person is an island; we create our realities in conjunction with other people. To better understand how this works, I have broken down the process into the following five categories: interaction, time and patterns, social norms, standpoints and forgetfulness.

Interaction

Everything starts with human interaction. We are born into the world from two biological parents. Those biological parents had to interact at some point and in some way. Interaction occurred even if it was just the sperm and egg. Once those two things mix, an embryo is formed. That embryo then interacts with the mother's body, maturing until birth. After it is born, the child must be looked after and cared for. This must occur for at least a few years. The child will die if that doesn't happen. As the child is cared for it begins to adopt the ways of its society and culture. The child must learn those ways or perish. It will defecate itself if it does not learn the proper toiletries. It remains speechless until it adopts the rules of the surrounding speech community. Every human being is born into a world of interaction and we must all learn how to interact or die. Interaction is foundational to our existence.

Our interaction with the world is obviously influenced by all those that surround us. Caretakers, relatives, teachers, friends, neighbors, etc. We live not in a vacuum but in conjunction with others. We are taught from the time we are born how to walk, talk, gesture, laugh, love, tie our shoes and brush our teeth. We learn other things, too, like the meaning of life, the purpose of human existence and the design of the cosmos. But there's a catch. We also teach others. We are influenced by others, but we also influence them. It's an ongoing, symbiotic process. As we begin to learn the details of our society, we can and do add our own twists. We are active participants in, rather than passive receivers of, our social and cultural realities. It all begins with our everyday, mundane interaction.

Time and Patterns

Our interaction also involves time and patterns. In other words, our interaction occurs over time — yesterday, today, tomorrow, next week, next year, and so on. As this time unfolds, patterns will emerge. For instance, we do something once. Then we do it again, and then again and again. Soon we have a pattern of interaction. We can see these patterns occur on the individual level as well as the social level.

First, think of you and your best friend. The two of you share certain ways of talking and gesturing that only you two understand. Those gestures and those meanings didn't fall from the sky. Instead, they emerged over a period of time. You two met, became friends, started hanging out more and more, and then developed patterns of interaction. Those patterns are now recognizable to both of you, allowing you two to be best friends. Take away those patterns and the "relationship" no longer exists.

Now, envision this same process occurring on a large social scale — people interacting across an entire society or culture. Over time, these interactions give rise to patterns of actions, behaviors, ideas, words, sayings, beliefs and values. This is the process by which societies and cultures turn into societies and cultures. A few people interact, then a few more and then a few more. We soon have large numbers of people interacting. As this process unfolds, new behaviors and ideas emerge and some of them get repeated over and over. Those repetitions give us patterns of interaction. Some of the patterns remain with us for centuries while others fall to the wayside after a few years.

We can use gender relations as an example. It used to be a common American belief that women shouldn't be able to vote. That cultural belief was a pattern of thought and practice. But that pattern was eventually challenged and replaced by a different pattern: women should and now do have the right to vote. This is a positive, progressive change, but we still have many other sexist and misogynist patterns. For instance, women are still seen as birth-givers, as caretakers, as dainty and feminine sexual objects and as less valuable workers. These patterns are often challenged, but many discriminatory patterns remain. It is our job to change these patterns and to create new ones. We must keep in mind, though, that this process (unfortunately) takes time.

Social Norms

Our patterns of interaction eventually become social norms. Every norm begins as a pattern. The pattern then gets repeated so often that it becomes second nature to us; it's as if that pattern was always there. When that happens, the pattern becomes a taken for granted social assumption. We assume that we and others should and must follow this pattern. At that point we have a social norm. Social norms are not inherently bad, but they can become suffocating and limiting. That's because social norms often set limits for "acceptable" behavior, action and thought and most people fail to realize that these norms are socially constructed rather than inherently given. So, following our above example, it is now normal for women to pursue education, careers and their own personal and political lives. That's all good, but our society still carries historical baggage. Society assumes that women should pursue their own endeavors as long as those endeavors don't interfere with the "female responsibility" to bear children and create a home. Although it is "normal" for women to pursue personal endeavors, it's even "more normal" for women to be caretakers and home makers. This is a sexist social norm that restricts women's life choices. Such norms should be challenged and overturned. We should realize, though, that erasing all norms is not possible. Social norms are natural outgrowths of human interaction. It's not about erasing all norms but about keeping the norms in check. We must continually check our norms and abolish all discriminatory, oppressive, harmful or unfair norms. On the flipside, we must work toward norms that are socially just and personally empowering. If we can do that then we will have created a truly just society.

Standpoints

The idea of an absolute social norm as *the* absolutely correct way to live, act and think is a myth that needs to be challenged. There is no single, absolute norm that we all can follow. This is because each person occupies and composes a different *standpoint.* A standpoint is your place in the world. We all have standpoints that emerge from our personal, familial, educational, spiritual, racial, sexual and class experiences. These standpoints do not determine, but they do affect and influence, our views and orientations. The important thing to realize is that our standpoints are forever diversified. No two people are exactly alike. We all occupy and see through different standpoints.

Our diverse standpoints complicate our social norms. We are all different; therefore, we all relate to the social norms differently. While those in power may prescribe a single, monolithic social norm there is no way that everyone can follow their norm. It's just not possible. Our approaches to and applications of the social norms differ. Going back to the example of gender relations and sexism, it's a social norm for women to be caretakers and homemakers (even while pursuing careers and public lives). But each woman does this differently. Some women are stern and tough-loving while others are unconditionally supportive. Some women do all the household chores while others ask that all family members contribute. Some women balance their careers and caretaking expectations while others put their careers on hold. And of course some women adamantly and rightfully reject this gendered expectation. These examples highlight the fact that no norm is executed exactly the same. There are no absolute social norms; we all enact these norms differently.

This realization is obviously important, but it does not safeguard us from oppressive social norms. Those who believe in monolithic norms persecute those who break or challenge them. If you don't enact the norm correctly, you are marginalized, berated and even physically assaulted and abused. We must educate people on the nature of standpoints and social norms. But we must do other things, too, like demand the acceptance and inclusion of *all* standpoints. We must fight for a world that includes and appreciates our diversity. Only then will we have the type of world we are looking for — radical, diverse and mutually appreciative.

Forgetfulness

Much of this social persecution stems from our forgetfulness. That is, we commonly forget that we ourselves create our realities. This forgetfulness directly contributes to social oppression, marginalization and the pressure to conform. But let's be clear here. It's not that we once knew and then literally forgot that we socially create norms and standpoints. That's not it. Instead, most people just don't consider how the process works. We do not sufficiently think through the situation. Most people just accept and never question their culture and society. This is partially due to mental laziness. But it mostly occurs because the creative/rhetorical process hides itself. Once a social norm has been created, it appears as if it's always been there. A new norm may be created in our lifetime, but the following generation doesn't see that creative process; they don't witness the norm's creation. That generation assumes that the social norms are natural and unalterable. It is our job as radical rhetoricians to point out the creative process. We must get people to understand that all norms are socially created.

This explanation of rhetoric as the construction of social reality, while complicated and heady, benefits us in at least three ways. First, this conceptual framework makes us more conscious of how social relations, social systems and our shared realities are actually created. We can now argue with confidence that no particular social system is inherently necessary — some systems may be better than others, but none are essential. If this is true, then reality is up for grabs. We are free to create a reality that *we* feel is ethical and socially just. Second, we can see how our own embodied, lived-through realities are radically different from those of the wider society. There is the reality of mainstream society and then there is the reality of our radical lives and movements. The trick is to close that gap and then turn mainstream society into a radical society. That's the point of revolution — to create radical change on a massive scale. And third, this rhetorical framework actually challenges our own radical endeavors. If we're going to change society, then we must learn to *articulate* our realities. We must find ways to voice not only our wants and demands, but also our visions, dreams, desires, experiences and realities. If we can't do that, then we're not going to get very far. Others will not simply bow down and accept our calls to social justice. It is our responsibility to communicate the benefits of an alternative world; it's our responsibility to explain why it's worth all the trouble. That is our rhetorical burden and that's the whole point of rhetoric for radicals.

Responding to this rhetorical burden necessitates the use and application of all three definitions of rhetoric proposed in this section. We must study the available means of persuasion and perfect our abilities to use them. We must be able to analyze what people say, how they say it and the effects thereof. And we must learn to materialize our realities through immaterial means. Achieving these tasks involves overcoming some myths about rhetoric, which is the focus of the next section.

Radicals and Rhetoric: Debunking Some Myths

Our activism and organizing efforts often reflect our society's general distaste for rhetoric. We sometimes assume, for instance, that worn out slogans, simple strategies, and rehashed ideas don't really matter. We often appeal to "the facts" as proof of our righteousness. We sometimes assume that information alone will take care of itself. And many of us fall victim to various radical myths about rhetorical practice. These myths affect our activism and our ability to change society. Here are ten frequently repeated myths:

- A big heart alone can change the world.
- Actions speak louder than words.
- Real radicals don't need to rehearse or craft their communication.

- Rehearsal and craft make our communication less authentic.
- Adapting my message makes me a sellout.
- Yelling and screaming are true expressions of radical change.
- Anger is always good.
- Outrageousness equals radicalism.
- Structure and organization are inherently oppressive.
- Leadership inherently excludes multiple voices.

These myths, like all myths, have a grain of truth. Leadership, for instance, can be oppressive. But it does not have to be, and that's the key issue. Oppressive leadership is a result of a particular type of leadership. Leadership itself is not oppressive. Such misguided perceptions permeate our activism. The following comments seek to unpack and overturn these myths.

1. *A big heart alone can change the world.*

A big heart *can* change the world. But hearts don't speak, people do. The heart, if it is to be intelligible to others, needs to be verbalized or at least symbolized. We should thus seek to cultivate our voices, articulations, verbalizations and narrations to the best of our abilities. The title of the widely read Zapatista book says it all: *Our Word is Our Weapon.*[11] It is their language, words, signs, symbols and overall communicative intelligence that allow Zapatismo to be so powerful and effective. We must take that cue and run with it.

2. *Actions speak louder than words.*

Actions *do* speak louder than words — they speak volumes, in fact. Sit-ins, die-ins, hunger strikes, banner droppings and civil disobedience can shake the core of society. But this usually occurs after we have exhausted all other possibilities. We talk, debate, argue and then, after all else fails, we take to the streets. But words *are* actions, and they're usually the first actions we take. Words set commands and demands, and can elevate, lift, love, change, challenge and revolutionize societies. The actions of our words are the backbone of our activism and organizing. Developing our verbal capacities is similar to learning intellectual combat — every word counts and making a wrong move could jeopardize our goals. We need to approach words *as* actions.

3. Real radicals don't need to rehearse or craft their communication.

It is somewhat true that real radicals don't need to rehearse or craft their communication. But it's true only if they have been doing it for twenty years and can act and speak without thinking. Folks like Noam Chomsky, bell hooks and Cornel West do not rehearse before every speaking engagement. Why? Because they've been speaking almost every day for years, even for decades. If they still need to rehearse, then they've been doing something wrong. And let's not forget that someone like Chomsky, despite our love and admiration for his analyses, is not known for his dynamic speaking. His contribution is analytical genius, not master oration. Even Chomsky could benefit from a little rehearsal and crafting.

4. Rehearsal and craft make our communication less authentic.

It is also true that too much rehearsal can make your presentations flat, mechanical and less lively. But the failure here is too much, or the wrong kind of, rehearsal. Musicians continually rehearse over and over, perfecting their songs. Visual artists spend years practicing their craft. And theatrical performers work on their lines and gestures hundreds if not thousands of times. All this time and effort allows them to enter the zone of their particular artistry and create amazing works. Activists can and should strive for similar results. We are performers, orators, poets and essayists. We are artists of social change and harbingers of revolution. The trick is to rehearse, rehearse, rehearse...and then rehearse some more. We must then let go and allow the moment to take us wherever we must go. Such an approach to radicalism is based on practice, but it also leaves room for chance, experimentation and growth. Balancing the poles of rehearsal and improvisation is the key to rhetorical effectiveness.

5. Adapting my message makes me a sellout.

Adapting a message to an audience can make you a sellout, but only if you lose sight of your wants, needs and desires. Adaptation does not inherently jeopardize your integrity. Human beings continually adapt to every situation; we are adaptive creatures. If this were not true, then we would still be freezing and burning with each weather change. Adaptation should be the norm rather than the exception to rhetorical practice. We'll discuss this further in later chapters, but in general it is not simply what you say, but how you say it. And how you say it is relative to your audience. Ignoring this distinction may save your "integrity," but it also jeopardizes your organizing accomplishments. Most of us will agree that accomplishing our goals is the most important thing.

6. Yelling and screaming are true expressions of radical rhetoric.

Yelling and screaming often characterize radicalism. But such forms of expression do not speak to or for *all* radicalism. The more you think about it, the more you'll realize that yelling and screaming are really baseline expressions. Newborn babies yell and scream because they have not yet developed the capacity for sophisticated articulation. Yelling and screaming can be used as possible tactics, and when done right, can be beautiful, moving, chilling and enthralling. But there's no need to scream when you can be heard when you talk. The overall goal is to articulate your thoughts and feelings with a clarity and passion that is equivalent to, but more sophisticated and more inviting than, a scream.

7. Anger is always good.

Anger is good because it expresses your deepest cares and concerns. And as an emotion, it should never be bottled or ignored. But it must be expressed, controlled and channeled in positive ways, giving you unbounded energy, resilience and confidence. Although anger can lead to great things, it can also destroy meetings, projects, campaigns, friendships, societies and movements. This is antithetical to social change. Anger, like yelling and screaming, can and should be used when appropriate. But your array of emotions should not be reduced to the single emotion of anger. You should try to feel and understand your anger and then find positive ways to express it.

8. Outrageousness equals radicalism.

Outrageousness and radicalism are often equated with one another. This makes sense since each challenges society and sits at the margins of acceptance. But radicals come in many shapes and sizes and sometimes our radical ideas look best in common, everyday clothes. Such ordinariness may appear boring and unattractive. But it can actually have the opposite effect. Ordinariness can sometimes appeal to a wider audience, thus attracting more people to your cause. The trick is to find a balance between radical outrageousness and the moderation of mainstream consciousness. This approach compels onlookers and passersby to stop, look and listen, giving you a better chance of soliciting their interest and involvement. I'm not saying that we should give up who we are. If you're outrageous, then great; be as outrageous as you want. But be smart about it. Don't sacrifice rhetorical effectiveness for outrageousness. The two are *not* the same.

9. Structure and organization are inherently oppressive.

Particular forms of structure and organization can be very oppressive. A single person running a meeting and dictating orders to everyone is oppressive. Being forced to conform to specific social standards is oppressive. And following strict guidelines on when to talk and how to talk is oppressive. But structure and organization are not inherently oppressive. Our lives are always structured and organized to some degree. A completely unstructured and disorganized life would be chaotic and most likely unpleasant. The same is true for our communication. Our communication always follows some organized format. Resisting or ignoring such structure leads to incomprehensible gibberish. No one would be able to understand what you are saying. That's bad rhetoric and thus bad activism. You want people to understand you. This involves organizing your thoughts so you can effectively communicate with others. Rather than rejecting structure and organization altogether, we must devise forms that suit our goals and maximize our efforts. We'll talk more about this in the following chapters. But for now, just realize that structure and organization are not bad but rather part of the communication process. The trick is to create structures and organizations that fit the ideals of a decentered, participatory democracy.

10. Leadership inherently excludes multiple voices.

Leaders who exclude voices have not learned much from our radical histories. Such leaders do exist and will continue to exist. But this doesn't mean that *you* have to be exclusive and it doesn't mean that leadership is inherently bad. Every activist is already a leader. You have taken it upon yourself to change the world. This will involve giving speeches, writing articles, sending out e-mails, creating websites, talking to people, listening to people, challenging society, lying down in the streets and basically putting yourself out there for the world to see. This is leadership and there's nothing wrong with that. What we need to avoid is arrogance, egotistical power trips and the feeling that we are better than everyone else. Those things *are* bad and they should be avoided. This is unfortunately difficult for some of us, largely due to our social conditioning. We are born into a society that longs for the rewards of wealth and fame. When people get a little taste of this, even at the grassroots level, it can go to their heads. They finally feel important and needed, and that turns into a power trip. This is a common scenario and is actually more saddening than upsetting. We as individuals need to resist this and our surrounding communities need to find supportive ways to cope with those who fall victim. Leadership is here to stay; it's part of activism and good communication. We don't have to forego leadership altogether. Instead, we need to devise leadership styles that are suitable for twenty-first century radicalism.

These ten myths reveal an underside to our activism: we often lack rhetorical sensitivity. We need to do our activism differently and become hypersensitive to the rhetorical demands of every situation and find ways to effectively respond. Radical social change is built upon rhetorical choices. Making the correct choices moves us forward and making the wrong choices moves us backward. We need to develop sophisticated ways of articulating well-crafted, meaningful messages. Our speeches, conversations, essays, articles, books, blogs, websites, videos, personalities, personas, actions and lives should engage the public mind and encourage folks to adopt more radical if not revolutionary ways of being. We need to appeal to the widest audience possible while maintaining our revolutionary stance. This double-edged sword is the lifeline of our radicalism.

Some Rhetorical Challenges of Our Times

Debunking our myths is important, but we must also take note of our contemporary challenges. By challenges, I mean those obstacles we must deal with in order to create twenty-first century change. We want to analyze the situation, figure out what new developments are affecting our radicalism and then use that knowledge to create new forms of activism. This first chapter thus ends by looking at some key issues currently facing radical activists and organizers. We will look at five challenges: creating decentered movements, developing new forms of leadership, learning to communicate across contexts, building transnational alliances and dealing with the media juggernaut. Please realize that this list is not exhaustive and we are focusing on the rhetorical and communicative aspects of these challenges.

Creating Decentered Movements

A push toward decentered movements has been developing for some time now. Rather than having one single, solitary movement, we have many interconnected movements. For this movement of movements to succeed we need to improve our ability to explain and justify such a movement to others. The inability to explain ourselves exposes us to common critiques: we have no leadership, we lack a coherent political agenda, we are a loose collection of confused people, we provide long laundry lists but no clear messages, our movements contradict one another, etc. We know in our hearts that these critiques are misguided and ill-informed. But knowing that is not enough. We must do a better job of explaining *why* these perceptions are misguided and ill-informed. We can't assume that others will simply get it. That's not how it works; our movements and actions are not self-explanatory. We are thus called to task: we must explain and justify why we do what we do and the way we do it. This entire book addresses this issue. But for now, we will cover only one suggestion: developing a new vocabulary.

We need to develop a new vocabulary that properly depicts our twenty-first century radicalism. This vocabulary should involve words, terms, phrases, definitions and meanings that help explain our actions. This vocabulary can take many different forms — it could be philosophical and theoretical, poetic and lyrical, provocative and shocking or average and mundane. Whichever form it takes, it must do two things. First, it must explain what we're doing and why. This helps people understand the nature and purpose of our actions. And second, it must capture the public imagination. That will attract people to our movements and create an air of interest and excitement.

Developing New Forms of Leadership

Decentered movements must involve new forms of leadership. Specifically, we need a form of "leaderless leadership." Each person must become a leader, ending the duality of leaders and followers. This only works when each person respects the wants, needs and choices of everyone else. Then, together, we form a non-hierarchical collective of leaderless leaders. This form of leadership differentiates us from the previous century in which social movements were led by vanguard parties. Vanguard parties are small, dedicated groups that initiate and lead movements or revolutions. This form of organizing has been critiqued in recent decades, and for good reason. Vanguard parties understand themselves as *the* leadership. They organize and train communities and then expect those communities to follow them. This structure perpetuates a hierarchical divide between those who give the orders and those who follow them. Many contemporary activists are skeptical of that divide, fearing that the new world will be tainted by the structures of the old world.

Vanguardism has been modified over the years and has taken on different forms. For instance, a vanguard party might provide initial command and organizational effort, but individual cells then develop and act on their own. This type of structure can break off in different ways, too. The original vanguard party might retain decision-making power and disseminate orders to the cells or it might dissolve altogether, giving rise to individual cells without central command. This last structure closely resembles decentered, anti-authoritarian activism, which is the predominant paradigm of contemporary activism.

The success of anti-authoritarianism depends upon personal responsibility — each activist must become personally responsible for communicating with the public. We don't have and we don't want "rhetorical leaders." We don't want others to speak for us; we want to speak for ourselves. This is great, but it only works when each one of us becomes a rhetorical leader. This will be further discussed in the final chapter. For now, just realize that leaderless leadership involves everyone making concerted efforts to improve their own communication. This dissolves the need for rhetorical leaders and creates decentered communities of rhetorical laborers.

Learning to Communicate Across Contexts

Today's activists increasingly organize across social, cultural, economic, political and personal differences. Different people of different backgrounds and ideologies commonly work together for collective gain. Because of that, we must increase our sensitivity to the wants and needs of different people, communities and movements and then find ways to adapt our communication. We cannot be everything to everyone, and we're not looking to pander to each group. But we can and should become educated about how different people live, talk, gesture and communicate. This makes us more amenable and inviting and easier to work with. This isn't about being fake or phony, and it doesn't entitle us to participate in each and every community. Instead, it's about finding ways to build human connections across different realms of experience. The most effective activists can adapt to and communicate across diverse situations. Many sections of this book deal with this issue. But for now, here are a few steps that can help you communicate across contexts.

- Read the surrounding context.
- Figure out how and why people are communicating in the manner that they are.
- Try to adjust to their communicative traits and norms.

- If possible and if you feel comfortable, adopt some of their traits.
- Be sincere in your attempt; any sign of entitlement or falsity will be met with suspicion.
- Realize that you are trying to connect with these people, which is different than trying to become someone you are not.
- These steps improve your ability to communicate with different people of different backgrounds, which makes you a better activist.

Understanding Cultural Differences

We are living in an era of transnational alliances. We build connections with people from all over the world and we act in solidarity with people from different regions and nations. These transnational alliances raise issues of intercultural awareness and intercultural sensitivity. We must become more sensitive to the communication of other cultures. Most of us are already aware of this and consciously work toward sensitivity. That's great, but such sensitivity must become a primary aspect of our organizing. We can do this by conducting more workshops and teach-ins on the following issues: intercultural exchanges, intercultural communication, culture-specific rhetorics, translation issues and creating transnational rhetorics.

- Intercultural Exchanges: Invite activists from different cultural backgrounds to share their histories, cultural traditions and forms of resistance. This broadens our horizons and allows us to understand how different people live, love and struggle.
- Intercultural Communication: Hold workshops on communicating across cultural differences — how certain words, languages, actions and gestures mean different things for different cultures. This increases our cultural sensitivity and helps us work past cultural tensions, confusions and barriers.
- Culture-Specific Rhetorics: Ask activists from different countries to share and explain their culturally-specific rhetorical tactics. This helps us understand what other activists are doing and gives us some ideas for creating our own culturally-specific rhetorical tactics.
- Translation Issues: Teach one another the proper etiquette of

translation. This involves at least two sides. First, teach one another how to translate from one language to another. It's one thing to speak two languages, but it's another thing to be able to translate between two languages. We thus need more instruction on how to translate. And second, we need to teach one another how to speak in the presence of a translator. People often speak too fast for the translator to follow. Much of the translation is then lost. Becoming more sensitive to the translator helps build cross-cultural alliances.

- Creating Transnational Rhetorics: We can consciously work together to create transnational rhetorics. This already occurs in many ways. Internationalism has been an ongoing theme for well over a century and it has been revised in recent times with the rise of economic globalization. We want to continue to update this tradition to meet the challenges of the twenty-first century. Specifically, we need to balance the autonomy and the interconnections of our different movements. We want to emphasize both the uniqueness and similarities of each movement. This is not simply a political issue, but also a rhetorical issue. We want to create messages, slogans and languages that maintain, express and create that balance between autonomy and connection. We can use the Latin American concept of *specifismo* as an example. *Specifismo* denotes the relationship between diversity and unity, between autonomy and solidarity. Basically, each movement is autonomous, but each movement also works with other movements. Together, all the movements work for collective gain. Creating more of these concepts helps us better frame and explain our movements, actions and politics.

Dealing with the Media Juggernaut

Approximately one hundred corporations own the majority of the world's media. This includes television, film, radio, print and Internet service.[12] These media corporations are not on our side, which forces us to work against this media juggernaut. The fact that the media ignore or misrepresent our movements and actions is not really new; radical voices have always fought this battle. But the media's reach and pervasiveness is new. There's no escaping the media landscape. It's everywhere, all the time: billboards, jingles, iPods, texts, pop-ups, logos, car radios, flashing signs, running scrolls, overhead announcements and all kinds of insidious and invisible messages affecting our minds and perceptions. So how do we break past this media juggernaut? There is no overwhelming, sure-shot answer. Instead, there are various moves we can make, helping us deal with the media one step at a time.

We can begin by creating our own media, which we are already doing. Take Indymedia, for example. These autonomously run websites exist all over the world, allowing activists to communicate in noncorporate environments. But activists and organizers have utilized different forms of mass communication long before the Internet age. Newspapers, fliers, stickers, pamphlets, pirate radio stations, occasional television programs and even graffiti have been used. The Internet is obviously the mainstay nowadays. This includes basic e-mails, websites and blogs, and participatory and social networking sites like Wiki sites, YouTube, Facebook, and MySpace are also used. Other modes and channels will arise in the future. The trick is to utilize — and preferably create — the newest forms of mass communication. This lessens our reliance upon mainstream mass media.

Creating our own media is great, but it's not always the best option. At some point you will want to use mainstream media. This is tough because the media can easily distort your actions and messages. The trick is to adapt to the media landscape — create actions and messages that are difficult for the media to misrepresent. That's difficult and often frustrating, and many activists are skeptical of such media relations. But I believe that we must deal with the power of the media rather than ignore it. This isn't about selling out to the media. Instead, it's about adjusting to the media's ability to negatively frame our actions and movements. Here are three steps to help you cope with media distortions:

- First, *analyze* the political and media landscape. Figure out what's going on and take note of how the issues are being framed and discussed. Pay attention to the rhetorical packaging of the news and literally analyze the media and politics.

- Second, *anticipate* the media's misrepresentations. If you do X, then the media will call it Y. You need to anticipate this cat and mouse game and create messages and actions that either avoid or directly challenge the media's misrepresentations. You want to predict and outsmart the media. This gives you an upper hand and keeps you ahead of the game.
- And third, *engage* in disaster control. Be able to respond to and reframe the media's misrepresentations. Ideally you would be able to speak for yourself on the major news networks. If given that chance, make the best of it. Be prepared and figure out ways to reframe the media's distortions. Of course, very few of us ever have that chance. But we can use our own media outlets to respond to the mainstream media — Indymedia, Democracy Now!, Pacifica Radio, Infoshops, weekly and monthly newspapers, etc. Use these outlets to recoup your own meanings, images, explanations and justifications. That's the whole purpose of liberation and self-determination. And given the nature of the twenty-first century, that liberation and determination must involve mass mediation.

Improving your communication skills is probably the best way to deal with the media juggernaut. Good speakers and good writers are more likely to be discussed in the media. Realize that newspapers, magazines, journals and radio and television shows prefer articulate, charismatic activists who speak and write well. This is because good communicators are able to clearly explain the purposes and motivations of their politics and actions. This ability not only increases your chances of media exposure, but also complicates the media's ability to misrepresent your actions and messages. Good communicators provide definitive, clear-cut responses that are difficult to misconstrue. Improving your communication allows you to become your own media center — you become your own spokesperson, your own writer and your own message board. This self-empowerment can help you change the world.

Labors of the Multitude

This chapter covers some basic skills, strategies and approaches of rhetoric. We begin with overviews of public speaking and writing. Here, you will learn how to speak and write for public audiences, learn a few tricks of the trade and develop your understanding of how these are helpful mediums for activists. We then focus on creating rhetorical packages. A rhetorical package includes your message, audience, rhetorical strategy, goal and situation. Accounting for each of these aspects can help you create better campaigns, teach-ins, workshops, rallies, etc. Next, we turn to four different approaches to rhetoric: persuasion, argumentation, storytelling and invitational rhetoric. You probably use these more than you think, and this section will teach you how and when to apply these different approaches. The chapter ends with a discussion of current events, history and self-knowledge. The purpose is to use these to enhance your knowledge, credibility and overall rhetorical effectiveness.

Please realize that this chapter covers a lot of ground. Trying to memorize or master all the guidelines in a single sitting will be very difficult. I suggest reading through the chapter once and then going back to specific sections when needed. Next time you're preparing a speech, article, argument, teach-in or action, come back to this chapter and use whatever seems helpful and appropriate.

Public Speaking

Public speaking begins with courage. That's because speakers expose themselves to the whims of the audience and the possibility of failure. You may falter, fumble, stutter and forget your words. You may be booed, laughed at and judged harshly. You may be boring and inarticulate and you may be a bad speaker, period. Despite these anxieties, you step to the podium (or soapbox, or street corner or whatever) and you *speak*. That's it; you just crossed the threshold and you're in the moment. You now stand there naked before the crowd crying, laughing, screaming, demanding and doing whatever is necessary. You use language in ways you never thought possible. You call out the social ills, denounce the power structures, condemn the oppressors and tear down social apathies. You tell it like it is and it feels good. But who do you think you are, saying all of this? The answer is no one, and that's the point. Public speaking doesn't belong to any one person; it is free to all and it has been occurring forever. Public speaking is part of the radical tradition and you are now carrying that tradition into the twenty-first century.

Public speaking also involves immediacy. You and the audience are there, together, in some kind of unified moment. Body language, eye contact, voice inflections, rates of speech, hand gestures, head nods, pauses, silences and even distant coughs and fidgety fingers help create the moment. This occurs on both sides: you, the speaker, can feel it, and so too can the audience. This collective experience you share with the audience creates a person-to-person connection. Che Guevara, referring to Fidel Castro, captures the moment:

> In the big public speaking meetings one can observe something like the dialogue of two tuning forks whose vibrations summon forth new vibrations each in the other. Fidel and the mass begin to vibrate in a dialogue of growing intensity which reaches its culminating point in an abrupt ending crowned by our victorious battle cry.[1]

This quote evokes the heart of the situation: good speakers, the very best speakers, defy gravity and lift the audience above the fray of global oppressions, iron cages, social prisons and one-dimensionality.

These speakers raise our passions, alter our perceptions, and create communal vibes of togetherness. We can't all be great speakers, but everyone can become a better speaker. It's about doing your best and reaching your full speaking potential. If you're willing to do that, then there's no telling what you might accomplish. But reaching that potential begins with the basics of public speaking, which includes: content, organization, delivery, rehearsal, memorization and speaking style and dealing with speech anxiety.

Content

Speaking starts with content. This involves information, instructions, suggestions, ideas, thoughts, feelings, emotions and visions. Speaking and writing are different; developing content for one is not the same as developing content for the other. For instance, *reading* facts and statistics is fairly easy. We can sit there and read the numbers over and over until they make sense. But *listening* to facts and statistics is very difficult. These numbers pass by our ears with only a moment's notice. We usually forget the statistics even before we've heard them. Thus, good speaking content is low on numbers, facts, figures, etc. We can and should use numbers when necessary. For example: nearly three billion people live on less than two dollars a day; hundreds of billions of dollars have been spent on the war in Iraq; more than one billion people lack clean drinking water. These examples are easy to remember in isolation. But lists upon lists don't cut it for public speaking. People tune out and don't listen. If you are forced to use a lot of numbers or lists for your speech, go slow. Again: *go slow.* This gives the audience enough time to absorb the information.

You also want to avoid an excessive amount of points or ideas. Too many points will muddle the speech and confuse the audience. Develop *one main point* and then figure out how to flesh it out. Restricting your points is also an issue of time. You don't have all day to make your point. You usually have somewhere between one and twenty minutes. One minute is very brief; it is basically a single comment. Twenty minutes is much longer, giving you more speaking leeway. But no audience wants to listen to twenty points in twenty minutes. That's simply too much. Develop your content with a specific time in mind. That allows you to maximize the audience's attention span. Here's a rough correlation between length and time.

- One minute equals one brief paragraph of information. That's somewhere between 150 and 180 words.
- Five minutes equals one and one-half single-spaced, typed pages. That's between 750 and 900 words.
- Ten minutes equals three single-spaced, typed pages. That's between 1,500 and 1,800 words.

Much more could be said about speech content, but we will cover many of the same issues in the "Writing" section below. Here's the bottom line on speech content: Develop your content for the ear, not the eye. Realize that your audience is listening rather than reading. You are communicating orally and you are constrained by three things: the time length, the audience's inability to stop you and ask for clarification and the audience's capacity to absorb information during a live presentation. You want to make it quick, precise and to the point without sacrificing substance. This is tough to do, but sticking to one main point allows you to balance these constraints.

Organization

The point of public speaking is to facilitate an understanding between the speaker and audience. That cannot happen if the speech is poorly organized. It is the speaker's responsibility to organize the content and overall communication. The audience does play a role and it has its own responsibility to listen and process the speech. But it is the speaker's job to organize the speech in a way that allows the audience to understand and follow along. The most basic organizing format involves three steps: an introduction, a body with the main content and a conclusion. Again, we will discuss this format in more detail later when we cover messages and rhetorical packages. But for now, realize that this format is very logical — it has a beginning point that introduces the speech, a main section that discusses the content and an ending point that wraps it all up. There's nothing fancy going on with this structure, but it does allow you to communicate your thoughts and feelings in a precise, systematic manner.

Also realize that different communities and cultures follow different formats. That's fine. You cannot be familiar with the organizing formats of every community and culture. That's not possible. But the introduction-body-conclusion format provides you with a starting point.

There are some basic things to consider when organizing your speech. For example, avoid jumping around from one point to another. Think of one point you want to make, and then find ways to flesh it out. Also make sure that each supporting idea ties back to your main point. This provides cohesiveness to the overall speech. Also think about how you will start and end the speech. What is the first thing you will say? What is the last thing you will say? Now what are you going to say in the middle? All of this work should be done *before* you begin speaking. Once you start, it's too late; you're in the moment and the audience is expecting you to carry on. Sometimes you will not have enough preparation time. You might even have zero preparation time. That can happen with off-the-cuff remarks. Someone leans over and asks you to say a few words. That is not the best situation to be in, but at least be aware of your organization *while* you are speaking. Take a pause before you begin. Go slower than normal. Think on your feet and adjust when you need to. And realize that others are listening and they are trying to follow along. That's the key. Such awareness will guide your public communication, allowing you to organize your thoughts as you move forward. That's good communication.

Delivery

Delivery is the visual component of speaking. The speaker's body is on display and the audience watches and responds to that display. Good speakers are in control of their bodies, not letting nervous habits (like bouncing knees or fidgety fingers) distract the audience. But good speakers go a step further and seem to speak effortlessly. They're comfortable, in control, and their bodies appear natural, as if they have done this a million times. Some people *have* spoken a million times. But most of us have spoken only a few times, if at all. Despite these experiential differences, we can all look natural. That's the key to good delivery — look like you're comfortable and natural. Here are some basic guidelines.

- **Volume.** Speak loudly enough so that everyone can hear you. Pretend that you are throwing your voice into the back row. This is easy for some speakers, but it can be very difficult for others. Some people simply have soft voices. In either case, you're trying to project your voice up and out of your body. This is done by speaking from your diaphragm rather than your throat. Your diaphragm is a little muscle that sits just above your actual stomach and just below your ribcage. Your diaphragm pushes air up, through and out, giving you more sound, volume and resonance. Try to visualize this process and try to speak from your "heart" rather than your throat or voice box.
- **Articulation.** Speak as clearly as possible. Mumbling, speaking under your breath, trailing off at the end of sentences and under-pronouncing words impedes the audience's ability to hear and follow along. Also realize that a lack of articulation is perceived as a lack of intelligence. While this is a misperception, it is still read that way, hindering your interaction with the audience. Take your time and try to articulate each syllable, each word and each sentence. This helps you be more precise and helps control your rate of speech. Some of us talk too fast while others talk too slow. Both have their drawbacks and of course all of this is relative to your cultural and regional background. In either case, try to find a rate that is balanced and easy to follow. Also pay attention to your pauses. A slight pause between each thought and idea is good. This creates a dramatic effect. But too many pauses or unintended pauses negatively affect your delivery — you appear uncertain and unprepared.
- **Facial Expressions.** Your face is the most visible part of your body. Most of your body is covered with clothing and is often behind a desk, podium, lectern or crowds of people. But your face is almost always exposed. Your eyes, mouth, forehead, cheeks and ears all express something. Emotions are expressed through these facial muscles. We smile, frown, laugh and show grief, surprise and anger through our faces. Keep this in mind

while speaking and try to match your facial expressions with the emotions of the speech. In other words, use your facial expressions to enhance and further communicate your message.

- **Eye Contact.** Western cultures appreciate and respect eye contact. It communicates confidence, poise, control and sincerity. Looking up at the ceiling, down at the floor or to the side communicates the opposite. Eye contact is usually tough for beginning speakers. It can throw you off if you're not prepared for it. But eye contact becomes easier with experience, no different than having a one-on-one conversation. It can actually be easier than a conversation because as the speaker you are in control of the situation. You are expected to make and maintain eye contact, and the audience likes that. But realize that this is a cultural bias. Many Asian cultures, for instance, read eye contact as disrespectful. It is more respectful to bow one's head, which shows deference to the other person. There's no way to know the rules of every culture. Simply read the surrounding culture and adjust to the best of your ability. Most audiences will appreciate the attempt.
- **Upper-body movement.** Your entire upper body should be used to communicate your message. Your posture, shoulders, hand gestures, fingers and the sway of your torso are all part of the delivery. People see and respond to these things. Try to use your upper body as a way to enhance or complement your speech. For instance, throw your hands in the air when you're excited. Lower your shoulders during disappointment. Raise your fist for power. Throw your shoulders back for anger. And so on. These gestures and movements enliven your speech, making it three-dimensional and real. But at the same time, don't act out these gestures. Forced or over-dramatic gestures are interpreted as fake and phony. Try to be natural and in the moment.
- **Lower-body movement.** The same goes for the lower body, although less so. The lower body does not carry as much communicative weight as the upper body. But it's still important — your overall stance, the placement and movement of your legs, the style of your walk, etc. Many beginning speakers ignore their

lower bodies, as if their bodies ended at the waist. The audience then sees these speakers tapping or twisting their feet and bouncing their knees. These nervous habits are distracting and are read as a lack of confidence. Just remember that your whole body is on stage — every gesture matters. Despite all of this, you want to remain loose. Don't over-think the exact detail of your foot placement or knee movement. Such miniscule control actually flattens your delivery.

- **Overall Attitude.** Be aware of your overall attitude and orientation to the audience. Your confidence, poise, composure, emotional state, personality, liveliness, spontaneity, engagement and overall vibe are part of the speaking experience. Audiences are affected by these things. Try to be aware of — and if need be adjust — your presentational attitude. If you come out and the audience is flat, then you need to increase your own energy levels. If they are angry then you need to lighten the mood. If they are too rambunctious then you need to calm them down. These adjustments are done through your own presentational attitude. Also realize that a good presentational attitude goes a long way. You may not have the loudest voice or best articulation. But people will like you if you're sincere, endearing and passionate. Most audiences appreciate those traits.

Rehearsal

Too many activists think rehearsal is unnecessary. That's a huge mistake. Rehearsal helps you improve your delivery as well as your content and organization. Standing up and putting the speech on its feet allows you to see the positives and the negatives. You can then highlight the good and avoid the bad. That's the whole point of rehearsal — to get better. Rehearsing often feels awkward. You feel weird standing in front of a mirror or in an empty room. This usually happens because you're so apprehensive about giving the speech that you want to avoid the experience altogether. Get over this and simply practice. Everyone needs to rehearse.

The amount of time spent rehearsing is really up to you. It's a personal judgment call that only you can make. Some people need to practice over and over again. Others need to go through it only once or twice. And still others only need to sit down, visualize the event and mentally rehearse. This is relative to the demands of the situation and to your own level of speaking experience.

There are different ways to rehearse. Creating small rehearsal groups is probably best. Get some friends together and create a small public speaking group. This helps because everyone in the group has to practice their speeches in front of everyone else. This gives you a live audience and you get immediate feedback. When giving feedback, try to give specific suggestions on how to improve. Don't point out every little detail. Instead, pick one or two things that the speaker can work on. Then, during the next rehearsal, point to a few other things. This allows the speaker to improve little by little. Also remember to be gentle. Most people are already worried about speaking in public. Harsh criticism makes that even worse. The rehearsal group can avoid this by taking inventory at the very beginning. Go around the room and allow everyone to explain what they are looking for and what they are hoping to improve. Then, during the feedback, the group can focus on each person's desired goals.

Rehearsal groups are not always possible. If that's the case, you can record your speeches or practice sessions on video. This allows you to see for yourself what needs changing. Sit down with your video and go through each aspect of the speech. Think about what's working and what's not. Then find ways to improve. Most people despise this process. Seeing yourself on video makes you cringe; you feel like you're the worst speaker in the world. This is very common. But try to work past that. Seeing your own speech gives you a better idea of how you move and how you sound. In the end, you'll be a better speaker.

You won't always have time for groups or video recordings. Usually, you're working on your speech alone the night before an event. Okay, fine. Get on your feet, stand in an empty room and go through the speech over and over until you get it right. Make the necessary corrections, find the right words and feel the speech in your body. You'll know when it's done because it will feel right. You'll be hitting the right moments, getting the right lines and doing it with smoothness and style. At that point put it away, relax and get ready for the big day.

Memorization and Speaking Style

Memorizing a speech is not always necessary, but it is something to consider. If you do want to memorize it, then you must figure out how much time and effort is needed. How long does it take you to memorize a two-page speech? A five-page speech? Can you memorize it in one night or will it take you five days? Do you need to memorize the whole speech word-for-word? Can you simply memorize the main ideas and improvise the rest? Speakers must answer these questions for themselves while considering the nature and demands of the speaking situation.

Try to avoid over-memorizing. This can lead to a stale and boring delivery. But a boring delivery is not really about memorization itself. Instead, it's about the speaker's dynamism and spontaneity. I've seen speakers do a wonderful job of reading from the page. Although they are reading, they are still in the moment, connecting with the audience. I've also seen memorized speeches that were absolutely horrible — the speaker is totally disconnected from the audience. The trick in either case is to connect with the audience. Speakers want to be in the moment and engage the audience. This can be done with or without memorization.

In general, memorizing your speech gives you a better chance of engaging the audience. That's because you're not looking down at the page, worried about losing your place. A memorized speech allows you to look up and out into the crowd; it allows you to loosen up and maintain your eye contact. All this makes for a more engaging speech. But some speakers are hindered by their memorization; they become stiff and disconnected. This happens because they speak directly from their memories. Such speakers look like they're reading from invisible teleprompters. Their eyes roll up into their eyelids, they speak too quickly and their bodies stiffen up. This is no better than reading from a page. You want to memorize your speech to the point where you are at ease with the text and its organization. But you also need space to maneuver, adapt and be in the moment. Basically, you want to achieve an *extemporaneous effect.* You want to prepare and rehearse as much as possible, but you also want to appear as though you are speaking from your heart. That's good speaking.

The extemporaneous effect can be achieved in different ways. You can use note cards to keep your place. Here, you use the cards as a place holder in case you forget something. You're not reading the tiny print word-for-word. Instead, the cards are there as a comfort zone. If you forget something, you simply glance down and remember your place. You could also achieve the extemporaneous effect by reading from a manuscript. This is tougher and technically it's not considered extemporaneous. But it can still be engaging. Realize that you're giving a speech, not reading to yourself. You must still consider everything we've discussed — rate of speech, eye contact, gestures, etc. Spend some time going over the text, thinking about the words, language and punctuation. Highlight the key words to emphasize and accentuate, noting places for voice inflection and dramatic pause, trying to anticipate audience reactions, etc. These cues make for a better speech. Regardless of your approach, you are striving for a thoughtful, exciting and passionate speech. You want to be alive and in full effect. That's a good speech.

Speech Anxiety

Speech anxiety is a major concern for most of us. We get nervous and can feel our knees buckle, lips quiver, hands shake and voices crack. There are two reasons for speech anxiety: physiological and psychological. In terms of the physiological, the body actually senses the situation as stressful or a threat and enters a fight or flight syndrome. Your body prepares itself for the speaking experience. Blood circulation moves away from the limbs and toward the heart, lungs and voice box. This explains cold feet and clammy hands. The heart pumps out extra blood and the lungs seek extra oxygen. This explains your thumping chest and accelerated breathing. Your body pushes air through your vocal chords at a more rapid pace to produce greater sound. This explains your squeaking and cracking voice. The biggest thing to realize is that all of this is natural — your body gets nervous on its own.

There are some basic ways to deal with these physiological responses. First, feel what your body is doing and then accept it. Allow it to happen. Understand that it's your body's way of dealing with the experience. Second, try to use this energy to your advantage. Allow your body to channel its anxiety into greater voice projection and more animated gestures. Third, use breathing techniques to calm everything down. Try to focus on your breathing *before* you stand to speak. This gets oxygen into your lungs and helps pace your inhalation and exhalation. This is similar to meditation — relax your body, clear your mind and be at peace with the experience. And fourth, use proper breathing *during* the actual speech. Try to breathe normally and in a controlled manner. This slows down your thoughts and speaking rate and increases your speaking volume.

Speech anxiety is also a psychological issue. It is based on your perception of the situation. Self-doubt, fear of failure and the weight of the moment make you more nervous. This psychological anxiety exasperates your physical anxiety, creating a cycle of nervousness. But if this is true, then you can use your psyche to calm yourself down. This begins with positive visualization. Envision yourself doing well; think about moving the crowd and changing the world. Such positive self-affirmation helps you do a better job. Also realize that a single speech, however important it may seem, is simply one fleeting moment. You won't be condemned for missing a word or forgetting a thought. Just do your best and strive for continual (rather than final) improvement. When you're done with the speech, sit down and assess your positives and negatives. Then use that knowledge and experience for the next time. Proper preparation and rehearsal also help your self-confidence. You always know if you've put in enough time and effort. And last, realize that everyone gets nervous; that's part of the game. Activism and public speaking often make us nervous. That's just the way it is. If it's not making you nervous then it's probably not worth doing. Anyone can sit on the couch and watch television. But that's not the life you've chosen. Learn to enjoy rather than fear the anxiety. Let the nervousness run through you, allowing it to propel rather than hinder your speaking.

Writing

Libraries, bookstores, infoshops and websites are filled with books, essays, articles, pamphlets, fliers, zines, manifestos, novels, poems, theories, biographies, reviews, analyses and reports. And nowadays we can add e-mails and blogs. Each kind of writing is obviously structured by different rules. Personal and public e-mails are not the same, and neither are investigative reports and editorial commentaries, or manifestos and biographies. But these writings are united by common purposes of social justice. The trick is to turn your radical expressions into well-written public texts. The following sections help you do that by discussing four things: some basic characteristics of writing, seven steps of the writing progression, three ways to improve your writing, and one example of good writing.

Basic Characteristics of Writing

The following sections discuss the differences between writing and speaking, the distant, solitary and intimate nature of writing, and the laborious nature of reading. Understanding these characteristics helps you translate your thoughts and ideas to the written page.

Writing is different than speaking. To begin with, realize that writing and speaking are two different forms of communication and should be approached as such. Lots of good writing has an oral tone to it. The Beatniks were great at this. The coffeehouse performances of Allen Ginsberg and Jack Kerouac transfer well to the written page. But it's still writing, and the Beats recognized that. They're known as writers, not speakers. Slam poetry provides a different example. Slam poetry is written to be spoken. It has an urban, gritty, fast-paced style that's driven by live performance. Take away that live performance and it doesn't "read" the same. It's meant to be heard, not read. There are exceptions, of course. Some slam poetry is enjoyable to read. But usually, slam is an oral mode of communication. Most good writing is the opposite — it's made to be read silently and not spoken aloud to others. Understanding this distinction can help enhance the effectiveness of your writings. If it's intended to be read, then you need to craft it for the eye. If it's intended to be heard, then you need to craft it for the ear. And if it's intended to be both read and heard, then you have a double duty. Any of these intentions are fine, but be sure that the intention is clear to you and to your listeners or readers.

Writing is distant, solitary and intimate. The writing process is also distant, solitary, and intimate. It's distant because there's no immediate audience giving you constant feedback; you and your readers are separated by time and space. It's solitary because you're usually writing alone in the privacy of your own home. You sit there by yourself and write to an imaginary audience. These conditions may seem lonely, but they allow you to stop, repeat, stutter, erase and rewrite over and over. Audiences then see a well-crafted, final piece. Hopefully that final cut allows readers to feel as though it was written for their eyes only. This invites readers into your private world and lets them personally experience your words, thoughts and emotions. This doesn't apply to all writing, but it's a good guideline, even for theory, analysis and reporting.

Reading is labor intensive. Also realize the effort involved in reading. Reading takes more time and effort than listening; it asks the audience to do more. This feeling of effort is partly due to our sound-bite culture. Our newspapers, e-mails, text messages and online postings have conditioned us for brief messages. We usually need a good reason to read past a few pages. That reason can take different forms, but it boils down to an interesting idea and good writing. People want to be captured by both the content and the form. They want new and refreshing ideas and an enjoyable read. Well-written ideas attract people to your politics. They'll think, "Hey, that's interesting; that's some good writing. What's this person all about?" But poor writing and unexciting ideas, even if people agree with your politics, turns them away.

The Writing Progression

Every good writer begins with the basics. That includes selecting your issue, finding your hook, creating a thesis, writing a rough draft, editing and proofreading, getting feedback, and finalizing your piece.

Select your issue. Every writer needs an issue to write about. That issue could be very personal or very general. In either case, your issue should be personally inspiring. Don't pick any old issue; pick something that you want to spend hours, days, or even years writing about. There's a whole world out there. What moves *you* to action?

Using my own work as an example, I have spent about three years on this current book. That's a long time, but the relationship between communication and activism is part of my everyday life. It is an issue that I am *capable* of writing about and that I *want* to write about.

Find your hook. A "hook" is an original angle or perspective on the issue. There are millions of activists with millions of ideas. But what's *your* angle? With this book I created a hook by bringing together rhetoric and radicalism. Surprisingly, not many activists have done that before, making for a unique angle. Finding such an angle is tough, especially for people who are just beginning. You need to spend time in the world of activism — and the world of writing — before you can develop new ideas. Realize that radicalism is a historical conversation that has been going on long before you were born and will continue long after you're gone. Finding ways to participate in that conversation takes time. But the world is always changing and new perspectives are always welcomed. Choose an issue and then think of a unique angle on that issue. This is your hook, and that hook should be inspiring, exciting, and worth your effort.

Create a thesis. Craft your hook into a clearly articulated thesis. Realize the difference here: a hook is a general perspective on the issue, while a thesis is a single statement or idea that is teased out and supported. For example, "rhetoric for radicals" is my hook, while "communication helps us change the world" is my thesis. The hook pulls people in and the thesis carries people from chapter to chapter. You can begin by stating the thesis in one complete sentence. This will be your guide as you expand it and write more. This process doesn't work for everyone. In fact, it is not how I write. Instead, I start with some faint idea and my thesis emerges after a considerable amount of writing, deleting and re-writing. But a thesis emerges nonetheless. After I find that thesis, I flesh it out as an essay, article or book. You need to discover your own writing process. But almost every writer develops and then follows through with a thesis. The thesis is the main point that drives the piece; it is the reason why you are writing and others are reading.

Write a rough draft. Working out your ideas involves a rough draft. Notice the phrase *rough draft*. This is important; too many people bypass this step, wanting to jump from a hook to a final draft. Some of us can do that, but most of us cannot. A single draft will look like just that — a hastily written piece devoid of effort and artistry. You don't always have time to write a beautifully crafted essay. Deadlines and due dates are real. An article due next month gives you plenty of time to mull over your ideas and craft your writing. An article due tomorrow doesn't grant that luxury. But any good writer reads through a piece at least a few times, making corrections here and there. That's a rough draft.

Edit and proofread. Editing and proofreading are essential. We all make mistakes, and that's fine. But those mistakes shouldn't be presented to the world. Rhetoric is about maximizing your communicative effectiveness. Mistakes are not effective. People read your misspellings, grammatical errors or ideas that make no sense and they walk away uninspired and unmoved. They also judge your mistakes. This may seem unfair and it might even be bourgeois bias but it doesn't stop people from rejecting your writing — and your political views. If you are going to write, then edit. The two go hand in hand. You can never catch all your mistakes. Even the best writers miss commas here and there. But writing is a direct interface with the public. You want to put forth your best effort. This involves reading, re-reading, and re-re-reading until you get it right. Here are some basic things to look for as you edit and proofread: spelling, grammar, organizational structure, flow of thoughts, accessibility for your audience, narrative voice, overall style and emotional and intellectual attraction. The last one is about *rhetorical force:* Is the writing compelling? Does it hook people in? Does it sustain the reader's attention? Rhetorical force is not the goal of all writing, but it should be the norm rather than the exception.

Get feedback. Feedback can be extremely helpful. It helps with editing and proofreading, but more importantly, it provides an audience prior to public exposure. Getting feedback is not always easy. The large majority of us do not have personal editors. That's a luxury saved for a lucky few. But there are some ways to generate feedback: ask a willing friend for advice; partner up with someone and agree to read each other's work; start or join a writing group; or put your work online and invite comments. With the last one, blogging works well. People visit your site, read your work and then leave comments. This does not always produce commentary on the writing itself, but it is still helpful. Generally speaking, the best feedback is concrete and specific. It points to some problem with the writing and then gives suggestions for improvement. You can solicit this kind of feedback by explaining to people what you are looking for and asking for specific things. Should the person look for basic grammar? The way the idea unfolds? The rhetorical force? The hook? The organization? After you get the feedback, seriously consider the comments. Having someone judge your work can be tough, but take it in stride and be willing to rework your piece.

Final cut. This is what you've been waiting for: sending your piece out into the world. This means different things to different people — an official publication, your own website, a zine or a flier, etc. Whatever it means to you, realize that you are interacting with the public mind. You have labored over this writing and you are now placing it into the world. Maybe it will change the world and maybe it won't. Either way you have attempted to communicate with the public. That's what counts — taking the risk and putting it out there. Now it's time to start the whole process again. What are you thinking about right now? Okay, go find your hook and starting writing!

Improving your Writing

This next section offers three guidelines for improving your writing: reading as much as possible, writing as often as possible and continuously thinking about your own writing.

Read as much as possible. It may sound like a cliché, but reading is one of the best ways to improve your writing. Reading exposes you to different ideas, arguments, styles, uses of grammatical rules and rhetorical approaches. The more you read the more options you have to choose from. Reading is probably common for most of us as we try to stay abreast of public affairs. But as you read, consider the details of the writing itself. Pay attention to the choices each writer makes. Listen to the voice you hear when reading. Watch for the hook. And ask yourself some questions: Why does the author write like *that?* Could I write the same way? Do I want to write like that? How does my writing compare with that writing? What are the pros and cons of this type of rhetorical approach? How does this hook differ from other hooks? Do I like this writing? If so, then why and if not, why not? These questions attune you to the writing itself. From there you can pick and pull from different authors, helping you develop your own writing. And don't be afraid to read up on your favorite writers. If you enjoyed a particular book, then go out and read everything written by that author. That's a great way to develop your writing: allowing yourself to be influenced by your favorite writers. Beginners sometimes ignore this advice because they want to develop their own style. That's a great goal, but we're all influenced by others. We must begin by picking and pulling from other writers. Over time you can develop your own writing style.

Write as often as possible. Everything takes practice, and writing is no different. You have to write more in order to write better. Try to consciously improve with each piece of writing. Don't be satisfied with the previous article or essay. Push yourself to get better. Don't overdo it and beat yourself up; that's cruel and unjust. But strive for your maximum potential. Experimenting with different genres can help. Straightforward political analysis is different than creative nonfiction, which is different than autobiography, and that's different than poetry, etc. Each genre has its own rules. Experimenting with different genres helps you perfect your writing. This is not always easy and it's sometimes impossible. We usually find one genre we like and we stick with it. That's fine. But beginning writers, and writers who are looking to expand, should experiment with different genres. In time you'll find what you like and what you're good at. In the end, the more you write, the better.

Think about your writing. Thinking about your writing keeps you in the writing groove even when you are not physically doing it. Some of the greatest thoughts occur while sitting on the train, walking the streets or staring out the window. Sometimes you'll have an idea about the writing itself. Other times it's a great line that you might use. Other times it's an insight to a social problem. All these little thoughts should be captured and written down if possible. It helps to carry a pen or pencil and a notepad or Post-it packet. Have a thought? Okay, jot it down. Once it's in your pad, you can look at it later. If it's on a Post-it or scrap paper, then place it in a drawer or folder. You can go back to these in the future. Some of them will lead to extended ideas and insights. Many of them won't. Either way you're thinking about your writing. This can lessen the pressure to write at a specific time and location. Some people are forced to write in the morning before work. Other people write at night after the kids are asleep. Maybe you write on your lunch break. Designating times to write can be tricky. It can be helpful because you are dedicating parts of the day to focus on your writing. But this can be a drain for some people; it starts to look too much like actual work. That's why you should strive to be a fulltime rhetorician. Staying in a rhetorical state of mind allows your writing to become natural; it becomes part of your orientation to the world. From there you begin to develop a rhetorical sensibility. The whole world then becomes a rhetorical construction and your writing becomes part of that creative process. That's a good place to be; it means that your rhetorical labors are indecipherable from your everyday labors. You are now a radical rhetorician rewriting the world.

An Example of Good Writing

Below is an example of what I believe to be good writing. The example, excerpted from a piece entitled "Anarchists Can Fly" by Sophia Delaney, captures the drama and excitement of street actions. This is not the only possible example of good writing; millions exist. But this passage seems appropriate given the nature of this book. A breakdown of the writing is just below.

"The Flying Anarchist"

> He was surrounded by angry patriots with pepper spray and batons at the ready. To hop down would be to take a beating and maybe a felony charge, so he did the only thing he could: he breathed deep, lifted his arms, and flung himself straight out over the cops and the crowd, stage-diver style. The crowd let out a collective frightened grasp. It was the shocked response of people watching something so daring it looked, at first glance, suicidal.... My heart stopped too in that moment. It seemed both lightening quick and eternal, that one second when the flying anarchist hovered horizontally in the air. When he fell to earth, landing in the arms of his comrades and escaping the police, everything felt different, like we were living in the pages of history, as though in that moment there was a crystal clear delineation of past and future. Something had just Happened... the problems in the world had looked impossible before.... In that incredibly bold leap over the heads of the riot police, the option of saving the world from the jaws of destructive, violent capitalism seemed possible somehow. One quick, bold move — it made other acts of amazing audacity seem possible...if that flying anarchist taught me nothing else, it was that when shit looks absolutely impossible, don't worry. Don't stop to analyze too much. Be courageous. Do what they don't expect. Take a leap. Anything is possible.[2]

This passage is descriptive, concise, dramatic, layered, bold and courageous, and it captures the tension, emotion and excitement of street action and social justice. It balances description and concision, taking its time with the details without being melodramatic. It also uses descriptors that speak to the radical imagination — words like collective, flying anarchist, horizontally, eternal, earth and collective, reflect contemporary activism. A flying anarchist leaping into the unknown pretty much nails it on the head. Such writing invites others to identify and connect with the piece. Most importantly, though, is the mythological quality: Yes, anything really *is* possible.

Skeptical readers might pose some critical questions. Isn't this too romanticized? Is the author exaggerating? How do we know this really happened? These questions are legitimate but out of place. The writing is a bit romanticized, but that's because of the experience itself. It's triumphant and the story accentuates that triumph. The result is a great piece of writing that cuts to the heart of rhetoric: the ability to stir our imaginations and create worlds of personal and collective experience. As far as it being truthful, I have no reason not to believe that something like this happened. The details may not be absolutely perfect, but that's not the intention. The writing tries to capture the personal experience of the moment. The author accomplishes that, making it a very enjoyable read.

Creating a Rhetorical Package

This section helps you create a rhetorical package, which includes your message, an audience, a rhetorical strategy, a goal and the situation. These aspects can be formulated into questions, helping you create your package.

- What is my message?
- Who is my audience?
- What is my rhetorical strategy?
- What is my goal?
- What's the situation?

Here's an example of how this might work:

- Message: Wal-Mart destroys small-town rural communities.
- Audience: Average middle-Americans from the suburbs.
- Rhetorical Strategy: To use personal narratives of small-town

business owners in order to evoke emotional sentiments from my audience.

- Goal: Motivate my audience to take action against Wal-Mart.
- Situation: A teach-in at a local suburban library.

This rhetorical package outlines your approach and gives you a strategic plan of action. Starting in reverse, you can see that you will be conducting a teach-in. Most likely, you will have anywhere from one to three hours. You can probably count on an interactive atmosphere, which is common for teach-ins. These two things should be specified *before* the actual teach-in. Your goal is also specified — to motivate the audience to action. This goal is different than simply informing the audience. You're trying to get them to actually do something. You thus need a strategy that facilitates action. You're trying to accomplish this by telling real life stories of people who have been hurt by Wal-Mart. Within this strategy, you can do a variety of things: show video clips, invite people from rural communities to speak, ask audience members to role-play narratives, etc. You should specify this too before the teach-in. Also realize your persuasive approach: you're evoking the audience's emotions. Emotions are powerful and can often motivate people to action. By the end, the audience should realize that Wal-Mart is destroying rural communities and that action must be taken, *now*. It's best to provide very specific actions they can take — petitions, phone numbers, congressional letters, names of activist organizations and even ideas for direct actions.

These five guidelines help structure your rhetorical engagements, giving you strategic plans that can be easily executed. They are discussed in more detail below. Much of the information below also relates to the previous sections about speaking and writing. Drawing out those connections for yourself will further improve your speaking and writing; that's especially true for the sections on message and audience.

What is my Message?

A rhetorical package begins with a message that will be communicated to other people. People cannot be moved if they cannot understand that message. I do realize that communication is not always about sending specific messages or about moving people to action but both are common goals for activists and organizers. We can improve our messages with five steps: clarity, organization, outlining, length and refinement.

Clarity. Your message should be as clear as possible. This means being clear in your own mind, first. If you're confused about your own message, then others will be even more confused. We've all experienced that confusion. As audience members listening to a speech, we'll turn to a friend and ask, "What was the point of that speech?" As speakers, we'll sometimes think, "I didn't get my point across." As readers, we'll wonder, "Why am I reading this?" During organizational meetings, we'll sit there and wonder, "What is that person trying to say?" These examples highlight the difficulty of constructing clear messages. The following questions help you focus so that others can understand and respond.

- What am I trying to say?
- What is the main point of my message?
- Am I clear about my own message?
- Do I think my message will be clear to my audience?
- Am I staying on point as I speak, act, write, converse or facilitate?

Organization. A three-pronged format is commonly used for organizing messages: an introduction, a body and a conclusion. This format was originally introduced when we discussed organizing speeches, but it is fleshed out here in more detail. The introduction gets us ready and prepares the audience for the forthcoming material. The body is the major content and it outlines your argument, story, main point, plan of action, etc. And the conclusion wraps it all up, giving the audience a last chance to reflect and be inspired.

Introductions can take many forms. Oral presentations — whether they be speeches, teach-ins, workshops or whatever — usually begin with basic salutations. Say hello and thank the audience and the organizers. With written pieces, it is common to start off with some type of leading statement, "The following essay is about..." Or you might begin with describing the scene or action that anchors the writing. Regardless of whether the message is spoken or written, try to capture attention quickly — pull the audience in and get them situated. This can be done with descriptive language, strong images, astonishing facts, personal stories and even well-known song lyrics. So, for example, you might say or write: "As Emma Goldman once said, 'If I can't dance to it, then it's not a revolution for me!'" This quote is intriguing, humorous and well-known. It grabs attention and compels people to read or listen. You can also use rhetorical questions, which are questions that do not need an actual response. For instance: "Does social change really happen by itself, or does it happen through hard work, sweat and effort?" You and your audience already know the answer; the question is not intended to elicit actual discussion. It simply sets the stage for the overall message. Whatever strategies you choose, do not spend too much time on the introduction. Save your time and energy for the body.

The body is the heart and soul of your message. So get to your main issue and give us what you've got. What's on your mind and why are we listening or reading? Be concise and to the point, but avoid the sound-bite syndrome; take your necessary time. Clearly demarcate your main message from the introduction and conclusion. All three sections should simultaneously stand alone *and* connect to the others; this gives a sense of coherence and enables others to follow along. Much of the discussion above on clarity relates to the body of your message.

The conclusion parallels the introduction — it should be short, concise and thought-provoking. You may want to repeat your main message before closing. But don't overdo it. Respect people's ability to understand your message. The best conclusions include a dual sense of closure and longing. People should know that you're finished and they should feel a sense of finality. But if they liked it, then they will want more. That's a good thing; they want more of your knowledge, ideas, suggestions, etc. Also realize that the conclusion is the final aspect of your message, so give people something to chew on for future thought. Use the last few words to encourage and inspire. And with a formal speech, do not end it with "that's all" or "I'm done." That's fine for teach-ins and workshops, but not for speeches. Your voice intonation, body language and final words should be conclusive. A brief "thank you for your time" can easily mark the end.

Outlining. Think of all the confusing e-mails you have read, all the disjointed speeches you have listened to and all the disorganized workshops, panels and teach-ins you have attended. These are neither fun nor effective. Outlining helps avoid these problems by structuring your thoughts before you speak, write, teach or facilitate. Outlining is tedious, but we do it more than we think. We sit down and plan our direct actions, marches, rallies and demonstrations. If that's true, then why not do it for our communication?

Your outline does not have to follow any strict format. Roman numerals, upper and lower case letters, and "proper" indentions are unnecessary. Just do a basic outline — a few notes jotted down on paper or typed up on a computer. This directs your thoughts before their full development. It also saves you time and energy on revising, backtracking and second-guessing. In many ways, the five guidelines for a rhetorical package can serve as your outline. Just go through the steps and answer each question before you actually begin to communicate.

You can also approach it differently by beginning with one basic question: what's my main message? Answer that in one complete sentence. Now find ways to support and substantiate that message. Think of good quotes, astonishing statistics or compelling stories. Jot those down or type them into your Word document. Now figure out where these quotes and statistics should be placed. At the beginning, at the end or somewhere in the middle? Then decide how you're going to begin and end. In other words, create your introduction and conclusion. Make sure these beginnings and endings are effective, attention grabbing and inspirational. These basic steps have just outlined your message.

Length. Always consider the length of your presentation, regardless of whether it is spoken or written. Should it be one minute, five minutes or twenty minutes? One sentence, one paragraph, or one page? Be concise and to the point; realize that less is more. Also think about how much space or time you have. You cannot cover the history of radicalism in a single-page essay or an hour-long teach-in. You would need an eight hundred-page book and a three-day workshop. Such goals are too broad. Go back to your rhetorical package and think of a more manageable message or goal. And that's a key to proper length: manageability. What can you and your audience handle? A three-hour talk is tiresome for both you and your audience. Well-seasoned speakers could do it, but beginners will find it very difficult. Similar issues apply to written messages. Good writers can write pages upon pages without missing a beat. But less experienced writers fair better with shorter pieces. This allows for greater rhetorical impact. As you gain more experience, then you can writer longer works while maintaining your rhetorical effectiveness.

Length is also an issue of respect. Communication always involves an audience. That audience is giving you their time and attention. Speaking too long chews up that time and signifies disrespect. And readers may never finish your long, drawn-out essay or book. The trick is to find the right balance: what do you want to say and how much time will others grant you? This balance allows you to create a rhetorical package that maintains the interest of your audience or readers.

Refinement. The last step is about refining your message — slimming it down, making it more precise and tweaking it to the best of your ability. Here's a four-step process:

- First, articulate your message into one clear sentence.
- Second, explain your message in one solid paragraph.
- Third, be prepared for extended conversation.
- Fourth, turn your message into a catchy sound-bite.

These steps prepare you for multiple lengths. Sometimes you only have time for a single line. Other times you'll need something a little longer and still other times you'll need a full explanation. Sound-bites are almost always helpful, but make sure that the sound-bite comes last. This ensures that you truly understand your own message before you condense it into a couple of words. Doing this first may actually hinder your own clarity. These four steps also formalize your message, allowing you to be ready for multiple situations and audiences. You can now take your message out into the world and be ready for anything.

Who is my Audience?

Your message should always be constructed for a specific audience. You may have a general message that is adapted for different audiences and situations. That's fine. But whatever you do, make sure you're thinking about an audience. A message without an audience lacks direction and focus. It's as if you're communicating with an amorphous mass. You want to do the opposite and specify your audience. This involves three things: identifying your audience, analyzing it and adapting to each and every one.

Identify the audience. Identifying your audience allows you to shape your communication. Realize that different messages are more or less suitable for different audiences. Grade-school children differ from teenagers, who differ from college seniors, who differ from senior citizens. Moderates differ from liberals, and liberals differ from radicals. Each audience is unique, and the first step of all rhetoric is to identify your audience. You cannot have a rhetorical package without an audience. It just doesn't work. Ask yourself: who am I communicating with?

Analyze the audience. Start with audience demographics. Figure out the basics — political affiliations, gender, race, sexual orientation, economic status, cultural background, education level, regional background, etc. You don't have to go crazy, but realize that the details do matter. Knowing the demographics helps you communicate with the audience. Without those details, you've got nothing to go on; you're simply communicating into a black hole. But knowing the details allows you to communicate with specific people.

Adapt to the audience. Once you've identified and analyzed the audience, you must create a message that fits that audience. Here are some things to consider.

- *Choose a target audience.* You can't reach everyone, so choose a specific audience that has the most potential to be affected by your message.
- *Decide upon the audience's level of knowledge.* If they are very informed, then you want to advance their knowledge. If they know very little, then you want to start with the basics. If the audience is mixed, then you need to navigate both terrains.
- *Personalize the issue for the audience.* Make sure the audience feels personally connected to your message. Figure out the audience's wants and needs and apply your message to their everyday, personal lives. This pulls them in and inspires action and dedication.
- *Adjust your level of radicalism.* Being too radical pushes people away. Not being radical enough loses their interest. You need to negotiate this tension and find effective ways to address issues from a radical viewpoint.
- *Always build common ground with the audience.* This is established when you and your audience identify with each other and you can relate to each other's sphere of experience. "Common ground" is a collection of traits, characteristics, views and values that you and your audience share together. You cannot communicate with others if they do not identify with you. Building common ground is the first step to all effective communication.

Saul Alinsky, the famous labor organizer from Chicago, understood the importance of common ground. In *Rules for Radicals* he talks about "getting in another's experience." As he states:

> Communication with others takes place when they understand what you're trying to get across to them. If they don't understand, then you are not communicating regardless of words, pictures, or anything else. People only understand things in terms of their experience, which means that you

> must get within their experience. Further, communication is a two-way process. If you try to get your ideas across to others without paying attention to what they have to say to you, you can forget about the whole thing.[3]

Alinsky is right. Moving people to action begins with common ground. This is true regardless of any differences between you and your audience. Yes, we are all different and some of us are extremely different from one another. But everyone can find something in common. You need to find that commonality and use it as a bridge. This helps your audience identify with you, which gets them listening and responding to your message.

What is My Strategic Goal?

Think about the goal that you are trying to achieve. What are you trying to accomplish, exactly? What's the purpose of your action, speech, teach-in, meeting, rally or protest? Specify that goal in relationship to your message, strategy, audience and situation. In other words, match your goal with the other elements of your rhetorical package. For instance, trying to educate the general public on military spending can be accomplished with a workshop or teach-in at the local library. But you need to rethink those elements if you're trying to persuade the American population to overthrow the government. Likewise, getting people to sign a petition is not the same as getting them to join your organization. And getting them to march around the White House is not the same as getting them to shut down Washington, DC. These different goals need different rhetorical packages. Goals can also change over time, and that's fine. This happens with long, drawn-out campaigns and movements. You might start off wanting to end a war, but after a few years your campaign expands to impeaching the president. That's fine as along as you adjust your rhetoric to the new goal. Here are four guidelines for creating goal-oriented rhetoric:

- Specify your goal in one clear sentence.
- Think about your goal in relationship to your message, audience, strategy and situation.

- Make sure these other elements help you achieve your goal.
- After completing your task, judge whether or not your rhetoric helped you achieve your goal. Use that knowledge in the future.

What are My Rhetorical Tactics?

You must make tactical choices that help you effectively communicate. There are millions of tactics to choose from. Below are a few of them. We will cover other rhetorical tactics in different sections of this book. For now we will simply touch upon a few basic ones.

- Provide straightforward, logical arguments.
- Tell emotional stories.
- Use scientific facts to prove your point.
- Show personal video footage of actual events.
- Juxtapose shocking images.
- Recite poetry.
- Use thought-provoking analogies and metaphors.
- Use official government reports.
- Highlight hypocrisies, biases and inconsistencies.
- Use language that evokes community, togetherness and collective sensibility.
- Draw upon collective identities like class, race, sexuality, gender and religion.
- Connect radical ideas to traditionally accepted ideas of free speech, equality and self-determination.
- Provide long, detailed lists of corruptions and abuses.
- Invite audience participation, even role playing.
- Repeat your message over and over regardless of what the other person says or does.
- Communicate with passion and urgency.
- Speak to people's desires and imaginations.
- Get people to envision a better world.

We often use these tactics without ever thinking of them as such. But you want to stop, think and consciously choose your tactics so you can better adjust to the audience and situation. Let's assume, for instance, that you're walking into a room with the intent of persuading people about the benefits of affordable housing. Five minutes into the meeting you realize that your plan isn't working. What do you do? If you're unaware of your rhetorical strategy then you may be at a loss for words. But if you are aware of your rhetorical plan, then you can realize that it's not working and that new tactics are needed. This kind of strategic and tactical awareness helps you maneuver and adjust.

You can develop systematic approaches by following the steps below. These steps help you understand your intentions and prepare you for unforeseen circumstances.

- Choose a strategy.
- Critically think through that strategy while considering your message, audience, goal and situation.
- Anticipate any drawbacks or blind spots.
- Use and apply your strategy.
- Be willing to adjust in the moment.
- Reflect on the successes and failures and use that knowledge for the future.

What is the Situation?

The surrounding situation affects your rhetorical choices. This is because each situation creates different constraints. For instance, teach-ins usually involve intimate atmospheres of group participation and group learning. But teach-ins don't provide space for in-your-face revolutionary fervor. Such rhetoric is more common at large demonstrations. But at the same time, large demonstrations don't involve group discussion and intimacy. Developing your ability to recognize the different situational demands helps you create appropriate rhetorical packages. So, for instance, think of the different demands of the following situations: soliciting donations on a street corner; protesting on the steps of city hall; giving a speech to a five hundred-person crowd; giving a multimedia presentation in a small classroom; conducting an interactive workshop on street theater; conducting a workshop inside a hot, humid, overcrowded room; facilitating a fifty-person spokescouncil; writing a three-page journalistic report; writing a three hundred-page autobiography; sending out a blast e-mail; organizing an emergency protest that will occur in three hours. Each of these situations is different and each demands its own rhetorical package. In many ways, the same steps are involved for approaching the situation as the audience: identifying the situation, analyzing the situation and then adapting to the situation.

- Identify the situation and outline its concrete parameters. Specify whether it's a teach-in, rally, spokescouncil, formal speech, group presentation or something else. This should be the first step, with everything else following from here.
- Analyze the situation and identify and prepare for the audience's expectations. Audience members expect something specific, and you want to match those expectations. Those expectations *can* be broken, but you need to prepare for and be able to explain why you've broken them.
- Adapt your rhetoric to the demands of the situation. This involves adapting your message, strategy and goals to each and every situation. Just as you adapt to the audience, you must also adapt to the situation. That's part of your rhetorical package.

Rhetorical Approaches: Persuasion, Argumentation, Storytelling and Invitation

This section covers four approaches to rhetoric: persuasion, argumentation, storytelling and invitation. Sometimes your rhetoric uses straightforward persuasion. If that's the case, then you might use logic, emotion, values or credibility. Other times you might argue with someone. That involves making a claim, backing it up with evidence and providing an overall rationale. Sometimes you use stories to communicate your message. That's done by narrating political action through characters, a scene, a conflict and resolution and a plot. And other times you might provide a rhetorical invitation. That's done by offering up your worldview and inviting others to learn from your experience.

Persuasion

Activists are in the business of persuasion. We may not want to admit this, but it's true. We are constantly trying to persuade people about all kinds of things. But contrary to popular belief, persuasion is not always about changing someone's views. It involves at least three approaches:

- Persuasion can *change* someone's views.
- Persuasion can *shape* someone's views.
- Persuasion can *sustain* someone's views.

Shaping and sustaining someone's views may seem counterintuitive to the idea of persuasion, but we do it all the time. Speakers at an anti-war rally try to sustain the protesters' anti-war stance. There's no point in changing those views. These same speakers might be speaking to a different audience, one that is undecided about the war. The speakers then seek to shape the audience's views, trying to sway these undecided individuals to the anti-war side. The speakers would, of course, seek to change the views of a pro-war audience. In each case the speakers are engaged in some form of persuasion. Here's the breakdown:

- Audience disagrees with you — change their views.
- Audience agrees with you — sustain their views.
- Audience is undecided about the issue — shape their views (in your favor).

Some activists may feel that "persuasion" is manipulative or unethical. That's not true. Persuasion occurs all the time in a million different ways. The manipulative or unethical qualities are relative to what you're actually doing. Lying to persuade is wrong. So, too, is omitting or falsifying information. But there's nothing wrong with open and honest communication that changes, sustains or shapes someone's views. Besides, you have every right to fight for the world you desire, and persuasion is a major part of that fight.

You can improve your persuasive skills by understanding the four basic approaches to persuasion: logic, emotion, values and credibility.

Logic

Logical persuasion involves rational thought that proceeds systematically from one point to the next. At the end you draw a justified conclusion that others can agree with. Logical persuasion can take different forms — it could be an argument, a story or even a basic description. But it must involve a systematic progression of ideas that moves toward an assertion and conclusion. Logical persuasion allows you to speak to people's rational minds. Logic allows others to say: "Yes, I see your point. That does make sense!"

Logic is persuasive because people see it as truthful. But we should realize that this is not always the case. Consider the following statements:

All activists are human beings.
I am an activist.
Therefore, I am a human being.

This statement contains two premises and a conclusion, and it is known as a syllogism. This syllogism is interesting because it is absolutely true. If we agree with the first and second premise, then we *must* agree with the conclusion. And barring the far-out possibility of extra-terrestrial activists, this argument is absolutely true. It really can't be wrong, ever. But slight changes can affect its truthfulness.

All activists are violent.
He is an activist.
Therefore, he is violent.

This statement follows a logical (and syllogistic) structure, but empirical evidence disproves it. There are many activists who are not violent. But that fact doesn't always matter within the public mind. Many people hear this statement and shake their heads in agreement: Yes, activists *are* violent! The "evidence" for their agreement comes from their prior "knowledge" of activists, which comes from popular portrayals of decontextualized street altercations between activists and police.

This example highlights the underbelly of logic: people's perception of a logical statement is influenced by their personal and cultural experience. People perceive a statement as logical if it aligns with their personal experience; they perceive it as illogical if it contradicts their personal experience. Some logical statements are absolutely true, period. But such statements are rare. The believability of most logical statements is tenuous and debatable. This is why persuasion is so difficult: there is no sure-shot way to persuade someone. Almost all logic and reason are relative to the situation, the issue, the audience, etc. Generally speaking, successful logic depends upon the details. Each word matters. A slight change can alter the audience's perception of the argument. Pick through your own and others' statements with a fine comb, spotting faulty details, hidden meanings, confusing language, decontextualizations, insufficient evidence, illogical leaps, rational holes, hasty generalizations, totalizing claims, etc. Use logic that avoids these pitfalls, and pinpoint these pitfalls in the logic of others. This makes you a more persuasive activist.

Emotion

Emotions are awfully persuasive and can be manipulated to sway people against their conscious judgment. That's obviously unethical and should be avoided. But emotions can be used for socially just purposes. This is usually done by evoking emotions through images, stories, poems, biographical accounts or brief anecdotes of personal experience. Here are a few common examples:

- Narrate the brutal conditions of a young sweatshop worker.
- Provide the gruesome details of unjustified mass bombings.
- Use an eyewitness account of the US military's torture techniques.
- Show images of famine-ridden populations.
- Highlight the personal and social effects of gross economic disparity.
- Create a documentary about children dying from preventable diseases.

These accounts provoke profound empathy and compel people to stand and act. That's the power of emotional persuasion. This does border on emotional manipulation, but there's a fine line between revealing the unsavory facts of human cruelty and manipulating someone's emotions. That line can be easily blurred, and I believe that outright manipulation is wrong and unethical regardless of any self-righteous, radical politics. But in many ways we are obligated to reveal these heart-wrenching images and stories. If we don't, who will? The mass media does not do its job and the public is woefully undereducated about world atrocities. These images and stories are "shocking" because people are not used to them. But be cautious with that shock value; always be respectful when using emotionally shocking stories and images. You must be respectful of the people who are enduring that harm. And you must be respectful of your audience by not over-shocking them with emotion. Disrespecting and over-shocking the audience is alienating and thus unpersuasive.

We've been discussing the dark side of emotional persuasion, but there's also an uplifting, inspirational side. Emotions can be used for love, honor, encouragement, excitement, humor, and respect. Here are some basic examples:

- Upload videos of people successfully turning away rightwing paramilitaries.
- Use images of activists escaping the clutches of riot police.
- Write biographies of people who have dedicated their lives to social justice.
- Tell stories of people overcoming decades of unjustified political incarceration.
- Document the triumph of historically oppressed people.
- Create humorous street antics that poke fun of political leaders.
- Make a film about revolutionary heroes.
- Create a story about making love in a post-revolutionary society.

These accounts allow people to identify with the positive and uplifting emotions. That identification process then inspires people to take similar actions. In other words, some human emotions can motivate people to join movements, become activists and to change the world.

Values

Values are beliefs that guide our daily decisions and actions. Values are often used as persuasive tools, and this is usually done by using values to either unite or divide people. For instance, we tend to listen to, trust and affiliate with people who share our values. Likewise, we usually ignore, distrust and dissociate from people whose values differ from our own. Your values can also increase or decrease your credibility with an audience. We'll discuss credibility in more detail below, but just realize that an audience will deem you as credible or non-credible depending on whether or not they respect your values. Values are also an issue of common ground. Highlighting shared values helps you build common ground with people. If no values are shared, then establishing common ground is nearly impossible.

An inability or unwillingness to explain and justify your values will cause many problems. People want to know why you do what you do. Usually, that comes down to values. Valuing cooperation over competition might motivate anti-capitalist sentiments. Valuing personal integrity over material success might motivate non-profit activity. And valuing equality among species might motivate vegetarianism and veganism. These correlations probably make sense to many of us and seem to need little explanation. But that's not true; they need lots of explanation. Other people cannot be swayed toward your radical perspectives if they cannot understand — and then accept and adopt — your values. Explaining and justifying your values can be difficult, but three basic steps can help: use first-person pronouns to diffuse any possible tensions, highlight the personal and social benefits of your values and provide concrete examples of how your values can be applied.

- To begin, use a first-person statement like "I believe in peace rather than war." The use of "I believe" expresses your perspective rather than challenging the other person to an argument. This lessens the tension and creates a more open atmosphere for talk and discussion.
- You also want to highlight the personal and social benefits of your values. There's no point in valuing something if it has no benefits. So, for instance, you might say, "Peaceful individuals are psychologically and emotionally relaxed and peaceful societies, such as Sweden and Switzerland, avoid wars, take care of their citizens and encourage creativity and self-expression."
- You should also provide concrete examples of how your values can be applied. So you might say, "Peace can be practiced

> through small acts of giving, kindness, and generosity. These acts may not change the world but they are a lot better than murder, war and killing.

Explanation and justification do not always sway people toward your radical values, but you'll earn their respect. That's rhetorically helpful and can even lead to longer term persuasion. Your audience could eventually realize the utility of your values and adopt those beliefs as their own.

Credibility

Credibility alone does not persuade people. Instead, credibility aids in the persuasive process. People are more likely to listen to you and trust you if they see you as credible. And that's the key — credibility exists in the eyes of the audience. It's not whether or not you are actually credible; it's about whether or not your audience perceives you as credible. Credibility is a perceptual game and you need to learn how to play that game if you want to become a good persuader. You may not like this, but it's true — establishing your credibility is essential to the persuasive process.

Credibility is not about selling out or fakery. You're trying to balance your personality with the wants, needs and expectations of the audience. I believe that Cornel West, a famous public intellectual, serves as a great example. Cornel West is a bold and defiant Ivy League professor who highlights his African heritage while embracing the best of his American heritage. He wears an Afro and very thick, dark-rimmed bohemian-type glasses while also wearing a suit and tie. He addresses issues of race, class, religion and American imperialism with a combination of eloquence and coolness. His success and notoriety grant him significant influence upon the public mind. You may not always agree with Cornel West, but you have to respect him. He's earned his credibility while maintaining his personal integrity. Cornel West is obviously a unique example since very few of us have his Ivy League credentials. But he serves as an example of how you can balance your own personality with the demands of each situation. Be yourself, but be credible.

You should also realize that activists, organizers and radicals also respond to credibility. For instance, you probably accept Noam Chomsky's analyses of the corporate media. Why? Because you believe that Chomsky's analyses of how corporate media favor big business interests at the expense of accurate and informative news are well-substantiated and can be verified through independent research. In your eyes, Chomsky is credible while corporate media are not. There is an obvious danger here — you, too, could fall victim to the dogma of an ideologue. But you will continue to assign Chomsky his credibility until someone proves otherwise. This proves that we all appreciate and respond to credibility to one degree or another. It's inherent to rhetoric and communication.

Credibility generally hinges on three key characteristics: likeability, trustworthiness and knowledgeableness. Establishing these three characteristics in the eyes of the audience almost guarantees your credibility. However, it does not guarantee that the audience will agree with you. That's something different. The audience could perceive you as credible and still disagree with your ideas. That happens. But establishing these characteristics encourages the audience to at least consider your ideas. That's all you can really ask for.

There are no sure-shot ways to establish these key characteristics. Instead, it comes down to your own personality in relationship to each particular audience and situation. You can begin with your own favorite activists, organizers and radicals. Analyze how they establish their credibility. What do they do to evoke likeability, trustworthiness and knowledgeableness? Try to apply those traits to yourself. You don't want to mimic these other people, but you do want to learn and then use their strategies for your own purposes. Here are a few guidelines:

- Be open, loose and accepting of each audience and situation.
- Be yourself in every instance.
- Find points of connection between yourself and others.
- Always be as honest as possible.
- Avoid defensiveness — it turns people off.
- Avoid a condescending tone — nobody likes that.
- Stylistic flare is helpful, but avoid arrogance.

- Sincerity and endearment can go a long way.
- Be informed about the issues, know the facts and be as articulate as possible.
- If you don't know the answer, try to find a sophisticated way of saying so—for instance, saying, "I am not familiar with that particular issue" is more sophisticated than saying, "I don't know."
- Always do an audience analysis, which sets up your ability to establish credibility.
- Last, realize that everything you say, do, write and express is being analyzed by others. You're perpetually in the process of establishing and maintaining your credibility.

Argumentation

Taking a stand on an issue and asserting your opinion is the basis of argumentation. We do this all the time; it's a mainstay of activism. For instance, critiquing and then providing alternatives to social problems is argumentative. So, too, is confronting oppression and speaking truth to power. This section helps you improve these skills by discussing three things: how to create arguments, how to practice arguments and how to improve your arguments.

How to Create Arguments

A basic argument consists of three things: making a claim, providing evidence, and using reason to tie it all together.

A **claim** is an opinion, idea, or assertion. Here are three different claims: "I think we should have universal health care." "I believe the government is corrupt." "We need a revolution." These claims make sense, but they need to be teased out and backed up with evidence and reasoning.

Evidence involves facts, conditions, statements, beliefs or views that others can observe and potentially verify. Common forms of evidence include the following: statistics, empirical facts, graphs, charts, photographs, videos, personal experience, testimonies, eyewitness accounts, brief anecdotes, narratives and stories, etc. Your evidence must be observable and verifiable. Those two things allow others to be persuaded and convinced.

Reasoning is the overall rational link between your claim and your evidence. Your reasoning is the glue that holds it all together. Sometimes the reasoning is part of the claim and evidence. Other times you will need to explain the claim and evidence. That explanation is the "reasoning" of your argument.

Here's an example:

> **Claim:** Iraq has weapons of mass destruction that pose a threat to American security.
> **Evidence:** Colin Powell's UN speech on February 5, 2003, that outlined the Iraqi threat.
> **Reason:** US intelligence reports state that Saddam Hussein did not fully disarm after the 1991 Persian Gulf War and, given his track record, he is likely to use WMDs and/or provide them to our enemies. Iraq is thus a threat.

This barebones argument highlights the persuasiveness *and* fallibility of this kind of basic argument. It is persuasive because it makes sense; all the necessary ingredients are present to make a case for invading Iraq. Many people read this argument and then nod their heads in agreement, "Yes, Iraq *is* a threat!" But this argument is also fallible because it is false or at least inaccurate. Iraq, at the time of the 2003 US invasion, did *not* pose a threat because Saddam Hussein did *not* possess WMDs. Let's try another example.

> **Claim:** George W. Bush misled America into an unjustified war.
> **Evidence:** It is clear that Saddam Hussein possessed no WMDs and had no connections to Osama bin Laden or the al Qaeda network.
> **Reason:** Bush's original reasons for going to war have turned out to be false and it is obvious that Iraq posed no threat to America. The US military has been in Iraq for five years and has discovered no weapons and no link was ever established between Saddam and bin Laden. It is safe to conclude that Bush fabricated the threat in order to go to war.

Many of us agree with this argument, but we should realize that the evidence and rationale are not fully supported. The evidence is true — Iraq did not have any WMDs. But that by itself does not really prove anything. Did the Bush Administration actually know this? That's the key point. For instance, at some point Saddam Hussein did possess weapons of mass destruction. That's a known fact backed up by official reports and US intelligence. But we must uncover the date of Saddam's disarmament and, most importantly, the date when President Bush learned of that disarmament. Those dates are the key evidence for proving the above argument.

Although evidence is important, it's not the final say to an argument. That's because evidence alone does not sway people; you need to rhetorically craft the evidence. Let's assume that we have an official White House document addressed to the president. It states the date of Saddam's disarmament, clearly marking that the Bush Administration knew that Saddam disarmed prior to the US invasion. Such foolproof evidence seems to completely implicate the Bush Administration. But naysayers could claim Bush's ignorance with something like, "No president is responsible for reading every White House document," or "Bush and his top aides were not privy to that memo." These reactions are bogus to us, but not to everyone. One little crack and the argument is over; a reasonable doubt has been created. This highlights the need for rhetorical awareness: even foolproof evidence needs rhetorical packaging — you must consider your credibility, emotional approach, language, ability to write or speak well, etc. A good argument involves good rhetoric. It's a package deal.

How to Practice your Arguments

You can practice your argumentation skills by sitting down and writing out different issues in terms of a claim, some evidence and overall reasoning. Below are three examples. Each example makes a different type of claim and uses different types of evidence and reasoning. Those differences are explained beneath each argument.

> **Claim:** We need direct democracy rather than representational democracy.

Evidence: Under representational democracy, most people don't vote, the representatives don't respond and the system favors the rich and powerful.
Reason: Representational democracy creates an essential rift between the people and their elected representatives, leaving most wants and needs unmet. In contrast, direct democracy enables people to govern themselves, which is the expressed purpose of true democracy.

This argument is based on the ability to define different types of democracy and prove that direct democracy is true democracy. The argument's push for direct democracy is based on common sense aspects of American society — people don't vote, representatives don't respond, etc. Such evidence is self-evident to most people, thus making the argument more persuasive. The overall reasoning blends and slightly extends the claim and evidence. It also implies a culturally accepted, constitutional sentiment — "for the people, by the people, of the people." That allows the argument to appear self-justifying.

Claim: The scientific community agrees that global warming is due to human activity.
Evidence: Professor Naomi Oreskes, a specialist in the history of scientific development, conducted a study of 928 peer-reviewed scientific journal abstracts from 1993–2003. All major scientific organizations — specifically those specializing in global climate change — agreed that global warming is a human-caused problem.[4]
Reason: With such consensus, it is hard to believe that global warming is not caused by human activity. This hypothesis could of course be mistaken, as could all hypotheses. But at the current time, this hypothesis is agreed upon by all major scientific organizations.

This argument is persuasive because it deals with science and uses an empirical investigation. We can actually conduct this study ourselves and see if it is true. Also, the author cited has credibility — she's a professor working within her specialty. And the reason acknowledges its own fallibility, but still stands by the evidence and argument.

Claim: The US should adopt a universal healthcare system.

Evidence:

- 46 million Americans are uninsured.
- Other countries successfully use universal systems.
- Individual healthcare is too expensive.
- More money in each person's pocket improves the overall economy.

Reason: Universal healthcare improves both the physical and economic well-being of average Americans and improves America's status and reputation among other industrialized, democratic nations. The more humanitarian our society becomes, the more we will be respected and appreciated.

This argument is written for average US citizens rather than activists or radicals. The evidence is written out in easy to read bullet point format and is self-justifying — people's own experience and knowledge verifies it. The evidence and reasoning both highlight the individual and collective benefits. As society benefits, so too does the individual, and vice versa.

This type of exercise is helpful for sharpening your skills. You may not wish to explain each detail as I have done above, but the barebones exercise is still beneficial. It can help you outline your essays and speeches, prepare for interviews, create sound-bites, and crystallize your messages, slogans and mission statements. It can also be used for small group exercises at teach-ins and workshops. Regardless of how you use it, it provides a solid starting point for articulating ideas.

How to Improve your Arguments

First, make people accountable to their arguments. Learn to decipher the claim, evidence and reasoning of arguments and call people out when they are missing something. This isn't easy to do because conversations, debates, editorials and street corner arguments rarely follow the three-step model. But learning to decipher those steps helps you win and critique arguments.

Second, familiarize yourself with prevailing arguments and counterarguments of the day. Keep a mental note of popular arguments and then prepare to use or argue against them. This keeps you abreast of the public mind and prepares you for conversation and debate.

Third, strive for new and unique arguments. Repeating an old argument has its place and some arguments can stand the test of time. But redundancy is ineffective. New arguments are often intriguing and convincing.

Fourth, your delivery is just as important as the argument itself. People are turned off by arrogance and cockiness. The most effective arguments are often delivered with humility, sincerity and honesty. That establishes your credibility and motivates people to at least consider the argument.

And fifth, continuously think through and fine-tune your arguments. Try to argue with and against everything you see, hear and encounter. This isn't about antagonism. Instead, you're engaging the arguments that surround you on a daily basis. This helps you sharpen your argumentative skills.

Storytelling

We tell stories in order to evoke the meaning and importance of events, issues, struggles, and experiences. Good stories are based on human identification: we identify with the story, allowing us to see the world through that narrative frame. We then envision ourselves as the characters living out that story. That human identification shifts people's perceptions and understandings of the world. They now see the world through other people's eyes.

There are all kinds of stories — long and short, mythological and mundane, fictional and nonfictional, linear and convoluted, character-based and plot-driven, etc. We cannot cover all the genres here. We will only cover the stories that we commonly encounter, which are brief stories that emphasize our activist work and/or political issues. We'll begin with an overview of the most basic parts of a story: characters, action, scene, conflict and resolution and plot. We then cover some guidelines for storytelling and then end with one concrete example.

Basic Parts of a Story

Characters. These are the people in the story. It could be you. It could be you and other people. It could be people you have never met. It could be fictional people. It could even be non-human characters, like corporations or political parties. Whoever your characters are, be sure to clarify them. Think about their names, their personal histories, their likes and dislikes, their desires, their political goals, etc. These background characteristics may not make it into the actual story, but they help flesh out your characters. Human beings are multidimensional and your characters should be too. Good characters show different emotions, live through various trials and tribulations, have moments of self-doubt and struggle with personal and political choices. These traits make for intriguing and well-rounded characters.

Action. This is what the characters actually do — fight city hall, lead a revolution, struggle to get by, mourn the loss of loved ones, get shafted by an unjust and uncaring system and, of course, beat that system. Whatever they are doing, try to *show rather than tell the action.* In other words, don't give us a laundry list of actions: I did this, then that and then that again, etc. That's boring and flat. Instead, tie the actions together through a plot that has conflict and resolution. This enlivens the action.

Scene. This is the place where the action unfolds. It can be more or less detailed depending on how much time you have and the importance of the scene itself. A specific story about buying locally-produced food probably needs a lot of scene. People will want to understand the local town and its culture. So, for instance, the local farmers have for years sustained the surrounding towns with nutritious and affordable food. Shopping at the weekly farmer's market enabled people to talk, gossip and keep tabs on one another, creating a strong sense of community. But corporate globalization eradicated that tradition, leaving your people with over-priced, genetically modified food imported from halfway around the world. The food is tasteless, less nutritious, ecologically unsustainable and it ruins local camaraderie. Your neighborhood is now sterilized by strip malls, convenience stores and corporate-produced culture. In other words, the *scene* has been changed.

Conflict and Resolution. This is what keeps us interested in the story. The characters face a major problem and must find ways to overcome it. How will the characters deal with the insurmountable obstacle? How will they save the day? How will they work past that problem? Most activist stories inherently involve conflict, but you want to highlight that conflict — bring it to life through your storytelling. You also need resolution — you need to narrate your struggle into victory. Struggle is part of life, but struggle alone is drudgery. Your story needs struggle *plus* resolution. That provides the story with meaning, purpose, and most of all, hope. Audiences like that; it gives them a reason to act, live and be idealistic about the future. For example, you might tell a story about stopping the war: "We stopped the war by taking to the streets! It was a long haul that took many years. But in the end, our so-called leaders were forced to listen to the voice of the people: "End the war now!" And that's just what they did. The power of the people trumped their imperialist greed. They realized that we're in charge, not them!" The conflict and resolution are established in a few lines. The conflict: how to end the war? The resolution: people in the streets pressured the government to end the war. Realize, though, that not all stories have clear-cut resolutions. While some political battles are won and clearly resolved, others are lost and some just fizzle away. Regardless of the actual outcome, your story still needs a well-rounded conclusion. You may not have concrete resolutions like ending wars or winning campaigns, but you can always use ones like moral victories, personal insights, knowledge gained by the experience, etc. These, too, are resolutions, and they satisfy the audience's desire for meaning, purpose and hope.

Plot. The plot is the sequence and structure of events and action. The characters engage in specific actions, but the plot ties those actions together, giving the story cohesiveness. As the storyteller, you must make decisions. Which events are included and excluded from the story? Which actions come first, in the middle and at the end of the story? How can the actions be narrated for suspense and intrigue? Answering these questions helps create the plot. Without plot, you have only discrete and loosely connected actions. But with plot, you get a meaningful and purposeful story. This allows the audience to follow along and make sense of the story; it allows the audience to understand the story's message. That message is structured around the ups and downs of the characters, through the defeats and victories of their actions, and through the dramatic tensions of the plot. A good plot builds throughout the story until the message is finally revealed. The audience then sighs in relief and says, "Yes, I got it!"

Guidelines for Good Storytelling

More could be said about each of these components. But for the sake of brevity, realize that many of the issues of storytelling relate back to issues of speaking, writing, message construction, organization, etc. For example: make sure you have a beginning, middle, and end; be clear on the point (the thesis) of the story; practice your storytelling techniques; think about your audience when working on your story; and adjust and adapt when needed. Here are a few more things to keep in mind when working on your activist stories.

- Be dramatic and aesthetic. Storytelling involves theatrics and performance. This can be tough for beginning storytellers, and it can be intimidating. But your audience will appreciate it, and that's the point.
- Stories should be even more well-crafted than your average writings and speeches. A disorganized message is tough to follow, but a disorganized story is painful. If you're not going to craft it, then simply give a bullet point presentation.
- Don't be afraid to be emotional and passionate. Place your story on the table and let us feel what you're saying. A straight-

forward analysis is cold and detached, but a story is warm and passionate.

- Use vivid and descriptive language. You don't have to be a poet, but you should strive for poetic descriptions. This pulls in the audience and evokes the lived experience of the story.
- Along the same lines, write for the senses — sight, sound, smell, taste and touch. This helps the audience experience the story. Don't tell us about revolution; show us the revolution. What does revolution look like, feel like, smell like and sound like?
- Create little "wow moments" throughout the story. Use moments that make the audience gasp, choke and clutch up. This gets the audience emotionally and personally involved.
- As always, think about your time and length. Good stories usually take a while to unfold, but you don't always have that time. If you're speaking at a rally or demonstration, you might have one to three minutes to tell your story. In written form, that translates into one half to one full single-spaced, typed page. If you are presented with this kind of time constraint, then you need to shorten your story as much as possible. For your activist purposes, this usually means less character development and more emphasis on the conflict and resolution. This is a good centerpiece for a political story: what are you fighting for and how will you win the fight?
- And last, stay focused; avoid unneeded or tangential details. The audience does not need *every* detail. They only need the juiciest, most exciting details that advance the story. Always ask yourself: does this detail move the story forward? If so, keep it. If not, then cut it. This produces a more refined and focused story.

One Example: The Healthy Healthcare Story

This section closes with a hypothetical example that you might use for publicizing a rally or demonstration. It's short, to the point and festive. It could be used for a website, flier, radio announcement or newspaper advertisement. Basically, it is a small political blurb put into storytelling format. As you read through it, see if you can spot the characters, action, scene, conflict and resolution, plot and the overall rhetorical effect. Does it work? How could it be improved? Who is the intended audience? Does it have rhetorical zip? Is it too brief, too long or just right?

Next Saturday at the White House:
The Healthy Healthcare Rally!

The world is overtaken by evil corporations and their money-hungry political minions. Stuck in the middle are average citizens who are struggling…struggling to pay their medical bills! But fear not, for all is not lost. Justice-loving healthcare activists are making a house call! Yes, the **Healthy Healthcare Coalition** has been working behind the scenes for the past five years, organizing grassroots coalitions across the country. We are now going public and taking our healthcare demands to the top. We want universal healthcare and we want it now! Stacks and stacks of healthcare research have been complied. Doctors, nurses and patients have been interviewed. And Canada, Cuba, Britain and all the other fully-covered countries have been analyzed. Do you know what we've found? Common sense! Yes, the richest, most powerful country on earth can and should provide full coverage for all citizens! That's our proposal. That's our demand. It's now on the table. We've made our move and now it's time for the corporate shakers and political bakers to make theirs. And remember, "no" is *not* an option and compromise is *not* an answer. Full coverage or bust! Let's see what happens. Join us next Saturday for our house call. The Healthy Healthcare Coalition is on the move!

(For more information, visit www.healthyhealthcare.org)

Invitation

So far rhetoric has been discussed in terms of persuasion. This is true for the argumentation and storytelling sections as well as the persuasion section. But rhetoric is not reducible to persuasion. Think of the consensus models used at spokescouncils and organizational meetings. Those models aren't always about persuasion. Often, they are about facilitating the best idea or plan of action that we can all agree upon. Yes, persuasion is used to a degree. People will voice arguments and tell stories to make a case. But the process is about consensus rather than persuasion. This non-persuasive consensus model is still a form of rhetorical communication, but it's based on respect, trust, openness, common agendas and a desire for communal rather than individual outcomes. This is known as "invitational rhetoric," and it has been developed by two feminist scholars of rhetoric.

Sonja K. Foss and Cindy L. Griffin, in "Beyond Persuasion: A Proposal for Invitational Rhetoric,"[5] argue that Western rhetoric is dominated by a masculine paradigm. That paradigm privileges persuasion, competition, individualism and a win/lose mentality. Both rhetoric and political efficacy are mistakenly reduced to a domination/submission dichotomy. Someone wins and someone loses. Someone is correct and someone is wrong. The loser is a failure and the winner is a success. This masculine paradigm obviously perpetuates many of the social ills that we fight against. We are thus called to reflection: is there another way to approach rhetorical communication? Yes, and it's called *invitational rhetoric.*

Invitational rhetoric proposes a feminist approach to rhetoric. Rather than asserting the correctness of your views, you can invite others to see the world through your eyes. As other people accept your invitation, you allow them to access your views as they wish. Rhetoric is no longer about me versus you, but rather about "us" searching for different ways to understand the world. This approach *offers* rather than *asserts;* it *asks* rather than *attacks;* it *invites* rather than *demands;* it *proposes* rather than *exclaims.*

Invitational rhetoric does not inherently preclude argumentation or demands. Sometimes a masculine approach to rhetoric is best, other times a feminine approach is best. For instance, demanding that pharmaceutical companies lower drug prices is a masculine approach. We are undoubtedly making a demand and we are doing everything in our power to persuade these evil companies to change their ways. But this cannot and should not work in, say, our organizational meetings where we're *asking* for everyone's input. How should we take down the pharmaceutical industry? What should we do? What does each person think? Is everyone comfortable with this action? Are there any concerns? We are still striving for clear, audience-centered communication. But we are not looking to persuade anyone. Instead, we are offering and exploring different ideas. It's a group effort; there are no insiders and outsiders, no winners or losers.

Persuasive rhetoric and invitational rhetoric are not diametrically opposed. Different situations call for different approaches. Confronting corporate power might involve invitational rhetoric and organizational meetings might involve persuasion. It all depends on the situation. Invitational rhetoric actually allows for and encourages multiple approaches. Sometimes persuasion is best, sometimes invitation is best and sometimes we need something entirely different.

Invitational rhetoric should not be seen as passive, either. Instead, it's a different way to be active. Gandhi and Dr. King, two of the most famous invitational rhetors of all time, would be the first to say this. Rather than forcing or cajoling consent, you invite exploration and discussion. The participants converse and communicate in order to move further and deeper into a better understanding of one another's standpoints. There is no final arrival point, but only further and further progress. Such conversations often end for pragmatic purposes; we cannot go on forever. But no person is silenced, cut off or left out. All people (or groups or parties) walk away pondering their changed perspectives.

There is no single way to do invitational rhetoric. At the most basic level, it is simply open and honest communication. But given the nature of this instructional manual, some helpful guidelines seem pertinent.

- Invitational rhetoric can be used in all forms of communication — conversations, small group discussions, speeches and even essays and books. Each situation is different, and each will allow for more or less dialogue. Writing, for instance, isn't really dialogical. But the author can write in a dialogical and invitational manner.
- Invitational rhetoric should be used honestly. Don't use an invitation in order to persuade someone. That defeats the whole

purpose. Your invitation to dialogue should be sincere and genuine, not manipulative.

- Clarify your intentions at the start of the communication. Announce what you are doing: "I am not trying to persuade you. Instead, I am offering up my perspective on the issue." This frames the situation and allows others to understand the parameters of the communication.
- After making your initial statements, ask for others to respond. This isn't really possible with a written format unless you're using e-mails or blogs. But you can (and for good rhetoric, you should) anticipate hypothetical responses. You can then incorporate those possible responses into the body of your writing or you can write up a separate section entitled, "Conversing with the Responses."
- Genuinely listen to the responses. Avoid interrupting or defending your previously stated views. Just listen.
- Now respond to the responses. Realize that you are seeking greater understanding among everyone involved. This is not about defending a position, but about exploring all positions. You might ask for clarification or further elaboration. Others may ask the same of you.
- After sufficient time passes, ask for everyone's input: What stands out for people? What was most striking or most interesting? Have your initial views changed? If so, how and why? These last questions advance discussion and dialogue.
- Now ask people to articulate their new understandings. What have people learned? Do they have any new ideas or appreciations? If so, why? If not, why not?
- Now try to re-articulate your own initial statement/proposal/offering. Take into consideration all the comments you've heard. This can easily occur in a traditional speech setting where you have the floor. As you stand there, seriously think about the positions in the room and see if your views have been changed. If so, then talk about those changes. If your views have not changed, then talk about that. Either way you are processing and progressing toward a deeper understanding.

- Last, realize that invitational rhetoric does not always run so smoothly. Sometimes we are too different or too antagonistic with one another. Sometimes we get too defensive. And sometimes we simply don't have enough time to let it play out. Despite these obstacles, invitational rhetoric is still a good guide for exploring ideas and feelings. It's a different approach to rhetoric that opens space beyond the competitiveness of persuasion and argumentation.

Building Rhetorical Knowledge

Rhetorical knowledge is any type of knowledge that improves your rhetorical practice. For example, you've just finished a speech at a local town meeting and people are interested in your issue and start asking questions. You're responding, keeping in line with your presentation. But then someone asks about the connections between your proposal and the town's political history. You have no idea what to say. Some audience members shrug it off, not thinking too much about your lack of knowledge. But others read this as a sign of ignorance, even disrespect. They no longer see you as credible and they start second-guessing your presentation. The local news reporter even uses it against you, writing in the next day's newspaper, "Local Activist Stumped on Local History." This is an example of rhetorical knowledge: activists working on local issues need to know the history of local struggles. You don't have to know all the history of all issues and places. That's unrealistic for anyone. But you are responsible for knowing some history about the issues you are working on.

There are many different types of rhetorical knowledge. The following sections cover three of those types: current events, history and self-knowledge.

Current Events

Activists are supposed to know about current events, right? Yes and no. You obviously need to know the major events of the day, the general policies of current politicians, the important players in domestic and international affairs, etc. Then, of course, there are the major breaking stories, the latest controversies and so on. This is all important. But these current events can be approached from a rhetorical perspective. What events affect your campaign? How do certain events relate to the issues you are working on? How might you incorporate certain events into your speech or essay? What are the connections between this event and that issue? How does your audience see those connections? Will they see any connections at all, or will you have to tease them out? Basically, how do current events affect the rhetorical packaging of your issue or topic?

Let's say you're a universal healthcare activist and Michael Moore's movie about US healthcare, "Sicko," comes out. That movie increases the national dialogue about universal healthcare and you must prepare for that dialogue. Do you agree with Michael Moore? Does he get all the facts straight? Why do some people disagree with the movie? Are they wrong? Do you support Moore's depiction? On top of all this, you should be using that movie as a springboard for your own cause. That can be done by either affiliating yourself with or distancing yourself from the movie. Either way, you need to rhetorically package your cause in relationship to Michael Moore's movie. That's a good use of current events.

As another example, you might be preparing a teach-in on the debate between militancy and pacifism. You're going to need a concrete example that gets at both sides. You decide to use the Israeli-Palestinian situation, looking at different forms of Palestinian resistance. Palestinian militancy is widely discussed and documented while Palestinian pacifism is not. This is a good choice on your part because it is more pertinent and up to date than, say, the Civil Rights era of Malcolm X and Dr. King. That Civil Rights debate could be touched on during the teaching, but it's outdated and overdone. The militancy of Malcolm X is not the same as suicide bombers' and the pacifism of Dr. King is not the same as stopping bulldozers. Your teach-in will be more intriguing and relevant if you can use current, twenty-first century realities.

You must also be respectful of the Israeli-Palestinian situation and brush up on your knowledge of the conflict. You don't need to know everything about that situation, but you do need to know enough to have a conversation, answer some basic questions, etc.

That entails knowing some of its intricacies, but not the entire history. Your obligation changes, though, if you're doing a teach-in on Israel and Palestine specifically. Your teach-in now depends upon your in-depth knowledge of important facts, debates, issues, histories, statistics, etc. In this case, you need to know as much as possible about the current state and history of the Israeli-Palestinian conflict.

The level of knowledge you need depends on your project. That's a sound guideline that fights off overload and burnout. Trying to stay abreast of every story every day is exhausting. You can be selective — but you need to be smart about your selection. Ask yourself:

- What are the latest developments on the issue that I am currently working on?
- What other stories and events affect what I am doing and how can I use that knowledge to my rhetorical advantage?

It's also helpful to think about the public's reception of current events.

- How does the general public understand and orient itself to the events of the day?
- How are people interpreting the news and reading the headlines?
- How are they talking and thinking?
- How does the overall public mindset affect my rhetorical approach to my issue, topic, or message?

Answering this second set of questions does three things. First, it helps you understand how the public is processing and making sense of current events. This helps you create more effective messages. Second, it attunes you to your own radical perspective. Every perspective and standpoint is limited and biased, and you are no different. Tracking the public mindset in relation to your own mindset keeps you self-aware and helps you create audience-centered rhetoric. And third, it helps you trace the flow of mainstream responses of today back to last year, the last election, the last debate, the last decade, etc. Keeping a record of current and previous responses lets you see the social and political patterns. You can then predict how people will respond to certain ideas, debates, images, speeches, etc. This is an imperfect science, of course, but it's better than nothing. In general, you should know how others think, how you think and how mainstream responses change. This helps you choose better topics, content, angles, approaches, hooks, slogans and actions.

History

In general, historical knowledge helps you understand who you are, where you come from, how you got here and how to move forward. As the saying goes, those who don't know history are condemned to repeat it. But that goes the other way, too. While you want to avoid past ills, you also want to repeat past successes. Studying previous movements and the lives and times of past activists and organizers helps you do that. The history of labor struggles can inform your current push for sweatshop abolition. The history of church-state relationships can inform your current push for same-sex marriage laws. And the history of Roman, French and British empires can inform your current fight against the American empire. Such histories are not dead but alive. You can use those histories for contemporary purposes. Below are five specific ways that you can use historical knowledge.

First, history can be used as raw material for organizing and activism. Any good organizer knows some history of the issues being worked on. If you're organizing around free trade agreements, for instance, then you need to know something about the North American Free Trade Agreement, the General Agreement on Tariffs and Trade, and the president's fast track authority. You should also know how certain people and communities have been affected by these agreements and policies; how free trade has perpetuated economic inequality, worker abuse and corporate rule. You may not know these histories when you first begin organizing; that knowledge often comes from your interactions with people at meetings, teach-ins, rallies, etc. But once you have that knowledge, it can be used to further your activism. You can use it to stir emotions, make compelling arguments, create stories, devise slogans, lobby officials, rally people and fight unjust policies. Then, as you share your knowledge, others start to understand the problem and start organizing for themselves.

Second, history can be used to enhance your credibility. Knowing facts, figures, famous names, dates and court cases lets people know that you've done your homework. People associate that historical knowledge with knowledge in general. They are then more inclined to listen to you, wanting to know more of what you know. Historical knowledge grants you legitimacy and respect, which helps you communicate with wider, more diverse communities.

Third, history can be used as evidence and justification for your arguments. For example, arguing that current free trade agreements hurt the poor can easily be justified by the history of NAFTA. Canadian, US and Mexican workers have suffered, and that can be statistically proven by the history of wages and living standards. Those statistics justify a slogan like "Fair Trade, Not Free Trade!" Many other examples exist: Black reparations are justified by the historical inequalities resulting from slavery; anti-capitalism is justified by histories of gross economic disparities; free speech movements are justified by the histories of silence and repression; LGBT liberation is justified by histories of same-sex relations and the oppressions thereof; indigenous resistance is justified by histories of imperialism; and revolutionary hopes are justified by histories of revolutionary victories. Every issue, movement and community has its own history and knowing that history helps justify your arguments, actions and rhetoric.

Fourth, history can be used to inform your cultural identity. Past struggles, movements and activists have created the paths that you now walk. You are enveloped in an ongoing lineage of liberatory practices, problems and personalities. That history provides you with a sense of hope, belonging and community. Howard Zinn's *A People's History of the United States* is a great example. It speaks from the dark side of American history, highlighting the numerous struggles that have taken place within the US. Learning those histories helps you feel connected to something larger than yourself and inspires a fuller, more self-aware life. Your actions suddenly mean something more and you realize that you are not alone. You are neither the first nor the last but rather an important contributor to the ongoing struggle of human liberation.

And fifth, history can be used for strategic purposes in each of the above scenarios. You can and should use historical knowledge for organizing purposes, credibility enhancement, argumentation and cultural identity. History should not be obscured for deceitful purposes, regardless of how righteous and benevolent we think we are. But we don't have to. History is there, waiting to be investigated. Different people will say different things about it. There's nothing wrong with that. Put forth your own interpretation, justify yourself as you go along, explain why and how you came to that perspective and allow people to debate your vision. Elevating this process to a strategic level enhances the depth, richness and effectiveness of your rhetoric. History *is* rhetorical, and it can be used for radical, contemporary purposes.

Self-Knowledge

Self-knowledge is about understanding who you are and recognizing your strengths and weaknesses. No one is good at everything, but everyone is good at something. You want to know what you're good at and then develop skills that maximize your full potential. But realize that self-knowledge is about continual growth rather than a final destination. Your self-knowledge expands with every experience. Rhetoric and activism actually facilitate that process. You place yourself in challenging situations and are forced to analyze and respond to diverse communities and audiences. You must meet deadlines and goals, read the public mind and create thought-provoking slogans and deal with defeats and victories. During all this you stand on the frontlines and directly confront the powers and oppressions of society. These experiences don't simply uncover but actually produce your self-knowledge. You create yourself through your rhetoric and activism. The trick is to understand who you are, where you come from and where you want to go. That self-knowledge can then be used for choosing rhetorical tasks, contributing to collective efforts and sharing your skills with others.

Choosing your Tasks. Use your self-knowledge to choose your rhetorical tasks. Know who you are and what you're good at and then use that to your advantage. Some people might excel at live, public debate. The audience, energy and immediate challenge are invigorating to certain types of people. But this isn't true for everyone. Others may absolutely hate such situations. These folks might excel at less publicly oriented tasks like theoretical reflection, written analysis or web and poster design. That's totally fine. No task is necessarily better or worse than another. Instead, different tasks are more suited for different types of people. That's simply part of being human.

Contributing to the Collective. Use your self-knowledge to contribute to collective efforts. Just as you choose your own personal tasks, you must also choose tasks when collaborating with others. Good speakers should volunteer for the speech. Good writers should volunteer for the flier. Good listeners should volunteer for the spokescouncil. And good facilitators should volunteer for leading group discussion. Knowing your strengths and weaknesses helps you accomplish these tasks with effectiveness and efficiency, and that contributes to collective success. But this use of self-knowledge must be reflective and self-critical. You don't want to choose the same task over and over, and you don't want to forbid people from trying out new tasks. That's bad for everyone. Doing the same task again and again leads to burnout and mimics the drudgery of the social workforce. Punching in and punching out everyday, forever, deadens the soul. So, too, does leading every workshop, or giving every speech, or researching every new project. Tasks should be rotated on some type of regular basis. It doesn't have to be every day or even every week or with every project. But tasks and responsibilities should be switched at different points in time. This allows people to experience and practice different skills. This rotating process only works, though, when everyone is willing to share their knowledge.

Sharing your Skills. Use your self-knowledge to help others acquire new skills. Teach one another how to speak in public, how to write newsletters, how to lead discussions, how to solicit donations and signatures, how to argue with angry audience members, etc. This can be done through informal conversations among group members, through question-and-answer sessions at meetings or through structured skills sharing. For the last one, set aside specific meetings in which group members share their experiences with different skills, tasks and talents. These structured conversations advance everyone's knowledge and help ease people's anxieties about taking on new roles and tasks.

Conclusion

This chapter has covered *a lot* of ground. Each major section could be turned into a chapter, and the chapter itself could easily be a book. But like I said at the beginning, there's no need to memorize this whole chapter in a single sitting. Now that you've read through it, take what you need and then come back to particular sections later on. Also realize that things don't always go as smoothly as outlined here. Real-life situations are filled with uncertainties and you never know how your rhetoric will play out. But hopefully this chapter has laid some groundwork for real-life application.

The Power of Language

Language is a social force that can be used as a revolutionary weapon. This may seem like an overstatement. Can language really be used as a weapon? Can it really change the world? Yes and no. Language alone doesn't do much. But language used as a political tactic for changing public consciousness suddenly becomes a tool for radical social change. Human beings think in language and if you change the language, then you change how people think. That's the power of language. P. M. Bergman, writing in the preface to the 1970s *Anarchist Cookbook*, speaks to the revolutionary power of language:

> Calling a policeman a "pig" seems silly and must antagonize the very people the revolutionaries want to win over or to neutralize. But the actual relationships of power are such that name-calling is the only weapon available at the moment. Besides, name-calling is an emotional outlet (and revolutionaries also have emotions). "Pig" is an assault, no doubt — an assault against the whole power structure. It is an assault — and a crime punishable by law. Here is the strong policeman, heavily armed, with the entire physical and ideological power of the state behind him, and he is attacked by a word — by a word only, but it is still an attack.[1]

As this passage indicates, name-calling is effective for several reasons. First, it is a mode of self-defense. As you are attacked and stripped of all other weapons, language, something seemingly so bland and humdrum, becomes an emotional and psychological protection against brutality. The attackers suddenly realize that you are not a passive object but rather a human being refusing handcuffs and billy clubs. No matter how hard they try, they cannot break your revolutionary spirit and mentality. Second, it is a mode of aggression. Name-calling does not smash windows or buildings, but it does smash ideologies, discourses and power differentials. The word "pig," for instance, violated and subverted socially sanctioned police authority. Radicals, especially Black radicals, were suddenly in a position of power and the police were the ones being violated. This did not completely reverse the power relationship, but it did play an important role. Third, name calling is an act of freedom, helping you assert your independence in the face of oppression. During the 1969 trial of the Chicago Seven, Bobby Seale, a leader of the Black Panther Party, was beaten, gagged and strapped to a chair. The court restrained his physical action through chains, handcuffs and mouth gags. Despite all this, he screamed, shouted and uttered his convictions. His words, some of which involved name-calling, expressed Seale's freedom. That *linguistic action* actually got Seale removed from the trial. The original Chicago Eight became the Chicago Seven. This testifies to the power of language. And fourth, name-calling builds community. People using the same word or phrase share certain symbolic understandings, which create communal relations. The shared use, intent and meaning of a word or phrase bonds them together; they now see each other as a group, collective or community. This was the case in the 1960s with people becoming indoctrinated into the world of radicalism through their shared use of the word "pig."

This example of "pig" highlights both the power and danger of language. Most activists are probably sympathetic to this name-calling. But we should be self-reflective about that sympathy. Does every police officer warrant the subhuman label, "pig"? Under particular conditions and during particular times, yes, some if not all police officers could act as pigs. In such instances, the verbal assault of "pig" is warranted and perhaps necessary. But it is difficult to believe that every police officer in every instance deserves this. But such was the cut and dried logic of the 1960s and 70s. Our own times are not so easily understood.

We want to maintain our radicalism while critiquing this either/or logic. Perhaps this is why "RoboCop" and "Storm Trooper" are used rather than "pig." The word pig essentializes police officers, turning them into pigs regardless of their actions. But "RoboCop" and "Storm Trooper" acknowledge the complexity of social roles. People are RoboCops and Storm Troopers when they wear certain uniforms and engage in certain actions. Stepping out of those roles allows them to reclaim different identities.

Not everyone will agree with this analysis, but it's obvious that times have changed and radicals see with decentered, kaleidoscopic eyes. This is not an impasse but rather a rhetorical challenge that must be addressed and surpassed. Contemporary radicals must find ways to invent twenty-first century languages. Understanding the matters of language, and how language matters within our radicalism, can help us with this task.

This chapter discusses six aspects of language. First, we discuss the nature of language and how language constitutes consciousness. Second, we discuss some basic steps for analyzing the political implications of language. Third, we focus on the relationships between language and the self-identities of cultural heritage, race, gender and sexuality. Fourth, we analyze the relationship between language and propaganda. Fifth, we discuss the pros and cons of political correctness and some ways to negotiate this slippery terrain. And sixth, we explore ways to create new radical words. Hopefully by the end of this chapter you'll be able to harness the power of language and use it for your own socially just purposes.

The Nature of Language

Language is often reduced to a tool that enables conversation or talk. This is because we use language to talk about objects, places, people, experiences, etc. There is an object and then there is a word that refers to that object. That word allows us to talk about that object. We must realize, though, that language involves more than referential communication. Language actually *creates* thoughts, perceptions, experiences and realities. That creativity is the power of language.

Language as a reality-creating process is a fairly new idea. For centuries people have understood language as simply corresponding to objects. This began to change a few hundred years ago when people began arguing that language actually shapes our understanding of the world. This idea eventually became a mainstay of twentieth-century thinking. Now, we can talk about language as actually creating reality.[2] In the following sections I explain how activists can approach language as a reality-creating tool. My explanation is divided into six sections: the definition of language, how language constitutes consciousness, how language frames issues, how language is contextual, how language, thought and activism relate to one another and how to use communication-friendly language.

Defining Language

Language is defined as an organized system of signs and symbols. Within that system, all the signs and symbols are linked together, formulating an interlocking whole. Each language thus forms a grid, a worldview, and/or an outlook. Looking through a language is like looking through a prism, and if you change the system then you change the outlook. This explains why different languages (English, German, Japanese, etc.) have different worldviews. But language systems are never foreclosed but rather they are open-ended. Languages change over time, with new words coming into vogue and old words acquiring different meanings. Think of the English alphabet with its twenty-six letters. Those twenty-six letters produce thousands upon thousands of words. This occurs because we are able to arrange and rearrange the letters and create and recreate the meanings. As activists, this means that we can create new words and languages in order to create new perceptions and understandings. The possibilities are endless.

Language Constitutes Consciousness

Language shapes how you understand, perceive and thus orient to the world. In other words, *language constitutes consciousness.* Use different language and you deploy a different perception or conception of the world. Or, to be more dramatic, different languages create different realities. For instance: Are dead Afghani children collateral damage or murdered victims? Are migrant workers illegal aliens or undocumented workers? Do free trade agreements liberate or exploit workers? The language of these questions evokes different understandings. Those understandings are not simply "word games." There's no absolute reality that sits behind the language. Yes, something concrete does exist. But we are never outside our language and we can never understand, discuss or debate without a language. Using language inherently shapes our perception and understanding of whatever we're discussing. There's no way out of it. Each use of language creates a specific outlook that motivates political choices, emotional responses and social behavior.

This insight should not be taken lightly. Simply put, language messes with people's minds. Because of that, your strategic use of language should be guided by some ethics: being honest; avoiding language that lies, distorts, confuses or fabricates; and using language that is accurate, fair and balanced. No language is absolutely correct, but some language is more accurate than others. Here are five questions that can guide your strategic and ethical use of language.

- What perception or understanding is created by your language?
- Is that perception or understanding accurate and fair?
- Why are you using this language? What are your intentions?
- Would other people use the same type of language? If not, why?
- Can you justify and explain your choice of language?

Language Frames the Issue

Framing is another way to understand the relationship between language and consciousness. All issues are inherently framed by some language and that language frames our consciousness. That linguistic frame creates a particular window of understanding; it creates a lens by which we see and understand the issue. Think of a pair of eyeglasses. Each pair of eyeglasses focuses your vision on particular aspects of the world; specific things come into relief while others fade away. Some eyeglasses actually blur your vision because your eyes are not used to those glasses. In other words, your eyes are not used to looking through that language. It does not allow you to see the world the way you normally do. You thus reject that linguistic lens and opt for something more suitable, helpful or customary. This is how language and framing work. Each use of language alters your perception of the issue. Such framing is a major theme of this entire book — good rhetoricians successfully frame the world according to their views and beliefs.

There are two aspects to framing. First, always analyze the linguistic frame that others are using. And second, use linguistic frames that benefit your own political agenda. Both are accomplished by attuning yourself to the framing aspect of language. Many arguments, debates and conversations actually revolve around the framing itself. For example, you say "undocumented worker" while someone else says "illegal immigrant." You say "same-sex marriage" while someone else says "gay marriage." You say "regime" while someone else says "administration." Each example points to linguistic framing and how different people seek to use different frames. Always analyze the frames and then use frames that help you bring about your desired social changes.

Language is Contextual

All language is contextual— it takes place within a certain context. "Context" refers to the place or space in which the communication occurs. A context could be a one-on-one conversation between two friends. It could be a group discussion, a public speech or an extended essay. It could be a spokescouncil or a workshop. It could be a small rally on the steps of City Hall or a day of international protest. Contexts can be small or large, personal or impersonal, formal or informal. Regardless of the actual setting, there is always a context. And most importantly, your linguistic effectiveness depends upon your awareness of and adaptability to the communicative context. Previous discussions about audience analysis, rhetorical situations, etc., led to similar insights. The audience, situation and context are all very similar. Just as you read and respond to the audience and the situation, you must read and respond to the surrounding context. This rhetorical awareness allows you to use the most appropriate language.

The context also allows you to interpret other people's language. Just as others are trying to understand your language, you are also trying to understand theirs. This isn't always easy. I'm sure we've all asked the following questions: "What is she talking about?" "I don't understand." "Why did he say that?" "What's going on?" "I don't get it." Contextual awareness helps you avoid these confusions. When in doubt, ask yourself the following questions: Where am I, who am I with, what is occurring and what was just said? Answering these contextual questions helps you clarify the language and move past miscommunications.

Language, Thought and Activism

Language creates thought. There is no human thought without language. There may be alternative forms of *knowing,* like embodied knowing or spiritual knowing. But there is no *thinking* without language. Take a moment and try to think without using language. You may be able to summon up images, emotions or experiences. But you cannot think about those things — identify, comprehend or understand them — without language. Perhaps you are able to clear your mind of everything and tap into some type of intuitive knowing or understanding. That's fine, but that knowing or understanding is devoid of thought without language. Thus, to think is to think in language. If this is true, then changing our language changes our thinking. That's a key insight for activism. You want to change the language that people use in order to change their thinking. This allows you to engage social change at the level of human thought: Change the world by changing how people think about the world. The following four-point progression breaks this down.

- Change their language and you change how people think.

- Change their thinking and you change their orientation to the world.
- Change their orientation and you change their beliefs, values, behaviors and actions.
- Change all of this and you change the direction of society.

This kind of progression is already common to activism. Feminists try to change how people think about gender relations. Anticapitalists try to change how people think about the work and profit system. And environmentalists try to change how people think about the relationship between nature and humanity. Accomplishing these goals involves changing the language that people use to think and talk. Every activist realizes this to some degree. But this realization needs to become front and center.

To sum up: use language as a tactic for social change; use language that brings about the world you are seeking; and use language that evokes your desired reality.

Language and Communication

Language is often taken for granted because we use it all the time. But that suddenly changes when we cannot understand one another. We commonly say things in everyday conversation that are misinterpreted, taken out of context or obscure our intended point. We then say, "No, that's not what I mean," and scramble around for different words that better express our meanings and intentions. This common experience points to the fact that language doesn't always work. There's often a communicative impasse between our choice of words and the listener's interpretation. Activists and organizers want to avoid such impasses. This can be done by using language that enables rather than hinders understanding. Always strive for communication-friendly language. Below are five guidelines.

- **Be accessible:** Use language that is accessible to the widest audience possible. It may not always be exciting and sophisticated, but at least people will understand what you're saying.
- **Be clear:** Use language that clarifies your meaning and purpose. You're trying to facilitate rather than distort understanding.

If they can't understand you then they can't be moved and inspired.

- **Be respectful:** Avoid offensive language. This is always a judgment call because what offends one person does not necessarily offend another. But this comes down to your audience analysis. Read the audience and use language that is respectful to that community. If you're ever in doubt about using a certain word, then ask someone or simply avoid the word altogether.
- **Be provocative:** Use language that arouses feelings and emotions. Speak to the physical senses; speak to the human experience; speak to the heart; speak to people's desires, imaginations and visions. You don't want to overdo it and become melodramatic. But your language should be passionate and arousing — that helps people experience your (linguistic) reality.
- **Be interesting:** Use language that stirs interest and holds attention. This isn't always possible; some issues are simply cut and dried. But people like engaging, thought-provoking metaphors, analogies and descriptions. Again, this is helpful for evoking your reality.

Analyzing Language

Those who control language control the mind, and those who create language create reality. Anyone who has ever read George Orwell's classic novel *1984* understands these assertions. In Orwell's novel, a totalitarian government propagates a three-part slogan:

War is Peace; Freedom is Slavery; Ignorance is Strength.

These phrases not only invert commonly understood conceptions, but actually enable Orwell's totalitarian government to unleash a continuous war of infinite reach and endless duration. The citizens of that regime are besieged by linguistic power and never think to question the perversity of their sociopolitical reality. They are so enwrapped in their government's language that they have foregone the ability to think beyond their situations, enabling the government to act as it wishes.

While Orwell's novel eerily resonates with contemporary times, it does miss a key fact: every human being has the innate ability to think beyond every situation, no matter how oppressive that situation may be. It's not always easy, but it's always possible. The human mind is constituted by language, but that language is not static or locked. It's perpetually changing, with different words and meanings continuously emerging. Cracks and crevices are thus created, allowing for alternative ideas, insights, thoughts and actions. This allows us to outthink and overcome any and every language, no matter how ingrained and oppressive. But people must be motivated to do this. Just because they can does not mean they will. To question one's language is to question one's power, privilege, oppression and liberation. This isn't fun and people will resist the process. But you can use your persuasive, argumentative and invitational rhetoric to motivate people to question their language. Accomplishing that task delivers a major blow to present-day power structures. Propaganda, doublespeak, false ideologies, hierarchies, and inequalities cannot exist within a culture of critical thinkers. And that's the point — to foster a world in which people willingly investigate and analyze themselves, each other and their languages.

You can begin analyzing language with the five steps below. They provide general guidelines rather than a rigid method. That's because every analysis involves its own conditions and follows its own course. There's no one way to break down and think through the language; you can and should do different things at different times in order to execute the most effective analysis. The most important factor for a good analysis is systematic and detail-oriented thought. Take your time, be patient and be fair and accurate. Your goal is to critique the social, political and ethical aspects of the language and then provide a better, more socially just language. In the section that follows, we will analyze the language of identity, looking at cultural heritage, race, gender and sexuality. In one way or another, those analyses employ these five steps.

Identify the language. Designate the specific language you are analyzing. Literally circle or point out the specific words and language.

This is the raw material of your analysis; it gives you a concrete basis to begin your analysis from.

Address the context. Designate the time, place and occasion in which the language was used. Also designate the social, cultural, historical and political context. You're trying to understand why and how the language was used. You want to understand the contextual reasons for using that language. The context can justify particular uses of language. It can also delegitimize particular uses of language.

Draw out the social and political implications. Explain how that language affects our thoughts and actions. Explain how that language reflects and/or perpetuates specific aspects of society. Explain how that language is politically troublesome. Explain why that language is unethical, morally wrong, demeaning or distorting. And be sure to justify your explanations. Draw out the concrete connections between that language and its social and political effects. An analysis without justification is mere opinion rather than substantial critique.

Provide an alternative language. Suggest different words, phrases, descriptions or spellings. Replace the old language with a new language. Provide alternatives. Deconstructing language is helpful, but it doesn't give people the option of acting differently. Alternative suggestions do that, giving people the opportunity to change their ways.

Circulate your analysis. Sharing, discussing, debating and communicating your analysis with other people generates more ideas and alternatives. This helps you create a better analysis and helps others see their own linguistic blind spots.

The Language of Identity

Language and identity are inherently connected. As you think about who you are and how you define yourself, you think in a language. That language is tied to other people, like your friends, family and social peers. It's also tied to larger systems, like society, culture and history. And it's even tied to future generations who will be affected by the language of today. Because of these connections, your language and identity involve issues of power, domination, servitude, self-determination, social mobility, resistance, oppression and liberation. Investigating language thus becomes a tool for social change. The following sections do that by looking at some relationships between language and the identities of cultural heritage, race, gender and sexuality. These analyses do not represent everyone's wants, needs, and identities but they do provide a basis for further investigations.

Language and Cultural Heritage

Language and cultural heritage are interwoven, with each creating the other. My language expresses my heritage and my heritage expresses my language. This relationship is integral to the history of imperialism. One country invades another and strips the colonized people of their language. Their language and culture are then replaced by those of the imperialist power. We might be able to revive memories of that language and culture, but their living, breathing embodiments are gone forever. This issue is addressed in a famous quote by Malcolm X:

> What was *your* name? It couldn't have been Smith or Jones or Bunch or Powell. That wasn't your name. They don't have those kinds of names where you and I come from. No. What was your name? And why don't you know what your name was then? Where did it go? Where did you lose it? Who took it? And how did he take it? What tongue did you speak? How did the man take your tongue? How did the man wipe out your history?... [W]hat did the man do to make you as dumb as you are right now?[3]

Malcolm is referring to loss of a sociocultural birth name. He is specifically referring to the plight of African slaves who were either stripped of their names or lost them in the generations to come. Slaves no longer knew who they were or where they came from. An imposed and unrooted name replaced their tradition and they came to see themselves through the eyes of their white slave owners. This oppressive language erased self-knowledge and alienated the minds, bodies and wills of African slaves. It is not surprising that Malcolm Little became Malcolm X. Many others did the same, with Cassius Clay becoming Muhammad Ali and LeRoi Jones becoming Amiri Baraka.

Similar issues apply to the global use of English. The contemporary world privileges the English language. Travel destinations, commercial airlines, business deals and corporate call centers increasingly use two languages: an indigenous language and English. Conversing in multiple languages should be celebrated. But we should also realize that the English language is not inherently superior. In fact, it's more difficult to learn than many other languages and it's far less romantic than, say, Spanish, Italian or French. But then why is the English language so popular and important? Because of US imperialism. America's economic, military and media dominance has produced the need for others to learn English as a second, if not primary language. This process then replaces indigenous identities with Westernized, Americanized and English-ized identities. Altering the language alters the identity; the two go hand in hand. Many indigenous languages and traditions have been completely erased by this process. This erasure may not be intentional, but it still occurs and should be rightly understood as linguistic imperialism.[4]

Language and Race

Language plays a major role in the construction of race, race relations and racism. In North America, for instance, the words "black" and "white" are defined in part by linguistic subjugation. "White" usually refers to the good, the holy, the pure, the clean and the desirable. In contrast, "black" usually refers to the bad, the evil, the soiled, the dirty and the undesirable. These two words, alone, mean little. But these two words, when aligned together and read through the history of American race relations, encourage racist thought and action.

Think of the old Hollywood Westerns. The good cowboy always wears white while the bad cowboy always wears black. Think of the *Star Wars* movies. Luke Skywalker wears white and Darth

Vader wears black. Think of European depictions of Biblical stories. God is portrayed as an old white man with long white hair and a gray beard. Jesus is depicted as a white savior with blue eyes. This last one is quite puzzling since Jesus was born in Bethlehem and as far as I know, white males with blue eyes are not indigenous to that area. But so go the racist constructions of white Euro-American cultures. These racist constructions fund and are funded by the linguistic subjugation of "black" by "white." This linguistic subjugation then contributes to the ideas of white supremacy and to internalized feelings of racial inferiority and self-hatred.

The "N word" also speaks to issues of language and race. This is made evident by the fact that we say "the N word" rather than the actual word. The actual word is so wrought with negativity that its mere utterance evokes feelings of hatred, abuse, offense, guilt, rage and historical wrongs. We should also realize that no equally offensive word exists for the white race. No matter how hard we try, we cannot think of a word that equally offends the white population of the United States. Plenty of offensive words do exist, like cracker, whitey and honky. But none have the social, historical and emotional impact of the "N word." This example points to the non-symmetrical power relationship between white and black populations: the white race has the ability to utterly offend, while the black race lacks an equally offensive language. This non-symmetrical relationship emerges from the history of American racism — slavery, lynching, the KKK, Jim Crow laws, segregation, socio-economic inequalities, etc. People in power developed the ability to offend and oppress while those without power did not.

Race and language are not reducible to issues of white and black relations. There are potential tensions among all races and those tensions often involve language. Some of those tensions can be avoided by thinking critically about the language you use to address other people. This is tough because you never know which labels people prefer. But common standards are helpful, like using "Native American" rather than "American Indian," or using "Asian" rather than "Oriental." These standards are of course relative and always changing. The political implications of words, labels and languages change over time. People then choose different words to describe themselves, usually opting for ones that are more positive, affirming and up-to-date. Being aware as well as critical of these social norms helps you respect others' self-chosen languages.

Language, Gender and Sexuality

Gender and sexuality are commonly grouped together for historical reasons. For instance, second wave feminism and gay liberation both emerged during the 1960s and 1970s. Feminism was soon addressing same-sex relations, particularly lesbianism, and the gay liberation movement was soon addressing gender inequality, particularly male bias toward women. These early beginnings helped set the stage for today's affiliation between gender and sexuality. But gender and sexuality are commonly grouped together for another reason: because our society linguistically divides people into dichotomous categories of biological sex, gender and sexuality. For instance, many people assume that there are only two biological sexes, male and female. People also assume that each biological sex naturally exhibits either masculine or feminine characteristics. It is further assumed that sexual relations between these two opposing sexes are natural and normal — males and females "naturally" attract one another for procreative purposes.

These categories are problematic because they are reductive and oppressive. There are more than two biological sexes, two genders and two sexualities. Some folks are intersexed, meaning that their chromosomes and genitalia are not exclusively male or female. Our masculine and feminine characteristics are in no way biologically determined, but rather socialized into rigid categories. And finally, there are as many sexual orientations as there are people. Some people are heterosexual, some are homosexual, some are bisexual, some are pansexual and some are asexual. The idea that sexual attraction is determined by the innate need for procreation is simply unfounded. All kinds of sex goes on and very little of it actually leads to procreation.

These categories are not only dichotomous but also non-symmetrical. For instance, masculine women are more acceptable than feminine men. This is because masculinity is more valued than femininity. Our society literally supports the masculine over the feminine. Thus, women, even when living up to their feminine expectations, are valued less than men. Non-symmetrical relationships occur in other ways, too. Women are expected to compete for men's attention while men are expected to aggressively seek sexual relations. Men are thus given the freedom to actively pursue sex while women are supposed to passively wait for it. This double standard leads to the perception that aggressive women are promiscuous and passive men are sexually weak. Such relations perpetuate our society's heteronormativity. That means that heterosexuality is not only seen as natural and normal, but it's compulsory; males and females are obligated to follow these non-symmetrical heterosexual norms. Resisting these norms can often invite discrimination, derogatory labels and even hate crimes. Heteronormativity thus anchors homophobia and transphobia — fears of homosexuality and transgenderism.

Our language contributes to this situation because our gender and sexual identities are constructed through divisive and non-symmetrical language. Changing that language would change the categories, and changing those categories would change our gender and sexual identities. But that's tough to do. The language is so pervasive that most people are unable to think beyond these categories and because of this they inculcate themselves into gender and sexual norms. It's a wicked cycle that most people have difficulty getting out of.

This process can be better understood by looking at some basic, everyday words. The word "man," for example, often represents the human race. The canonical texts of Western society use "man" interchangeably with human, humanity, people and persons. But where are the women? They are written out of this *his*-story. The lineage of sexist language implicitly privileges men over women, setting a social-psychological-behavioral environment in which the lives of men eclipse the lives of women. Men are visible and empowered while women are invisible and disempowered. Look at the following list:

S/he
Wo/man
Wo/men
Fe/male
Hu/man
Hu/man/ity
His/tory

Each of these words contains the male counterpart, as if the female can only exist alongside the male. In contrast, the male counterpart can and does stand alone, which is why "man" designates humanity at large. Man is constructed as independent, superior and foundational to humanity. Woman, by contrast, is constructed as dependent, subordinate and secondary. This construction excludes women and establishes gender hierarchy within the individual mind, within personal relationships and within society. Many women then internalize this linguistic construction and subordinate themselves into lower paying jobs, less fulfilling careers and dependent relationships. Generations then pass, and it seems more and more "natural" for women to make less money, write fewer books, give fewer speeches, and follow rather than lead revolutions. This is sexism, plain and simple.

Similar issues occur with homophobic language. On the surface, such expressions as "fag" and "that's so gay" may seem like harmless catch-all phrases referring to any uncool, silly or foolish action or phenomenon. Such expressions are often uttered in locker rooms and on playgrounds and street corners without thought or concern. But these expressions perpetuate socially accepted homophobia, making it okay to dislike anything gay, queer or sexually suspect. The utterance of those phrases thus impacts people's lives, making if difficult for lesbian, gay, bisexual, queer and transgendered people to be themselves. Once again, that's oppression, plain and simple.

Despite all of these oppressions, positive social change *is* possible. For instance, many LGBT communities have appropriated the word "queer" as a self-affirming, open-minded sexual identity. Feminists have changed woman and women to womin, womyn, and wimmin. And African-Americans have used "Black is Beautiful" and "Be Black, Be Proud" to challenge racism. These actions empower people, groups, and communities to determine their own identities. The trick is to investigate language and create a more confident, independent and self-affirming identity.

Analyzing Propaganda

Propaganda is any communication that distorts or obscures people's understanding in the service of social, political or economic power. Basic deceit between two people is not propaganda. But that deceit becomes propaganda when it allows people and institutions to acquire and spread mass power. Propaganda can be intentional or unintentional. In other words, people may act in the service of propaganda without knowing it. Their lack of knowledge does not exclude them, their messages or their communication from perpetuating the effects of propaganda. This is not to say that everyone is equally responsible for propaganda. There's a big difference between conscious creators and unconscious perpetuators of propaganda. Patriotic citizens commonly support wars because they believe in the righteousness of their country, making little effort to determine for themselves if the wars are illegitimate and unjust. That type of patriotic blindness is different from the governments that lie in order build patriotic, pro-war sentiments. Despite these differences, patriotic dedication to ignoble causes is still propagandistic — it perpetuates false ideas and allows power structures to spread and proliferate. These enablers must assume some responsibility for the life and circulation of the propaganda. Each individual is somewhat responsible for acquiring accurate information, thinking critically and being self-reflective. Power-driven language and lackadaisical minds create conditions ripe for war, imperialism, ignorance, fear, hate, blind patriotism and the perpetuation of various oppressions and inequalities. It is the job of radicals to fight that tide and expose propaganda. This can be done by first understanding some basic techniques of propaganda, which include the following: repetition, association, omission, smear campaigns, false heroes and heroines, false testimonies, over-statements and card-stacking.[5]

Basic Techniques of Propaganda

Repetition: To constantly repeat an idea so often that people accept it even when it's unbelievable. *Example:* The war on terror is about democracy...the war on terror is about democracy...the war on terror is about democracy...the war on terror is about democracy...

Association: To fabricate a psychological or emotional association between two or more ideas, people, places, names or actions. *Example:* The Bush Administration's continual juxtaposition of Saddam Hussein and Osama bin Laden, with the implication being, of course, that Hussein was a terrorist like bin Laden and that he played a role in 9/11.

Omission: To consciously omit important information, usually crucial facts, dates or details. *Example:* The military's refusal to count and report civilian causalities; corporations' denial of sweatshop labor; politicians' refusal to discuss the negative impacts of free trade agreements; and the media's blackout of particular stories and events, like the fact that supposedly independent military analysts who appear on CNN, Fox News and MSNBC get their talking points from the Pentagon.

Smear campaign: To publicly smear, damage, ruin or discredit an individual, group, organization or movement. *Example:* The government smears anti-war movements; Wal-Mart smears union organizers; corporations smear whistleblowers.

False heroes and heroines: To fabricate heroes and heroines or exaggerate their accomplishments for the public to then support and rally around. *Example:* George W. Bush was cast as a savior after 9/11 when in fact he used the event to push through regressive policies. Private Jessica Lynch was turned into a war heroine who fought off Iraqi insurgents when in fact she was taken into an Iraqi hospital and cared for by Iraqi doctors. Army Ranger Pat Tillman was cast as a courageous soldier who was killed by hostile fire in Afghanistan when in fact he was killed by friendly fire.

False testimonies: To use fake or misleading statements by fake or misleading experts, authorities, celebrities or laypeople. *Example:* Religious conservatives who use doctors' reports that claim that AIDS is a "gay disease"; or politicians who use the reports of unspecified "secret service agents" to declare an imminent threat to national security.

Over-statements: To inflate or exaggerate the importance of a statement, report, study or issue. *Example:* Iraq is only months away from developing nuclear weapons! Osama bin Laden has released another videotape! National healthcare will lead to socialism! Regulating markets will collapse the economy!

Card-stacking: To exaggerate the importance of your side while downplaying the other side as frivolous, foolish or unimportant. *Example:* Political pundits who nonchalantly dismiss anti-war, anti-corporate and especially anti-capitalist organizations, protests, and sentiments as if these people and ideas are arcane, illogical and unworthy of discussion.

The Propaganda Model

The propaganda model of Edward S. Herman and Noam Chomsky is another helpful analytical tool. The model was originally developed in their now famous book, *Manufacturing Consent: The Political Economy of the Mass Media.*[6] This work investigates the structures of corporate media and how those structures lead to biased news and information. The book demonstrates how particular institutions, gatekeepers and ideologies create, shape and release news benefiting certain agendas and worldviews. Their model was developed during the Cold War era and thus focused on the media's bias toward capitalism: capitalism is good and Communism is bad; any views challenging this ideological double standard are quickly dismissed, ignored or attacked. This bias is perpetuated and socially ingrained through five basic filters.

- **Profit:** The media are corporations and are driven by a profit-seeking motive. Any news that threatens profit or the corporate agenda is dismissed or ignored.

- **Advertising:** Other corporations pay media outlets to run advertisements that attract viewers and that support capitalist ideology.
- **Unquestioned Authority:** The media rarely question the credibility of the US government or US corporations. These institutions are seen as reliable sources of information. Even if doubts do arise, the presumed benevolence of these institutions always remains intact — that's never questioned.
- **Direct Control:** The media exert a direct control over the range of social, political and economic discussion. Plenty of debate occurs to make the news seem legitimate, but the range of that debate is extremely narrow. The best example is the two-party system. The media regularly debate internal feuds and minor controversies occurring within the Republican and Democratic parties. But the media rarely if ever discuss the inherent problems, limitations and corruptions of a capitalistically driven two-party system.
- **Ideological Bias:** It is an unspoken (and unexamined) truth that capitalism is the very best system possible. This even continues after the Cold War, with the media perpetually smearing Fidel Castro's socialism and Hugo Chavez's Bolivarian revolution. We should realize, too, that terrorism now functions in the same ways that Communism did: Anyone tagged with the terrorist label is automatically deemed evil. It is becoming common, for instance, to label (and legally charge) radical environmentalists as eco-terrorists. This is quite puzzling since over-consumption, fossil fuels and corporate polluters are the ones actually terrorizing the environment.

The Language of Propaganda

The preceding model and techniques help us decipher lies, deceit and political agendas of powerful people and institutions. But given this chapter's focus, it's time to turn to the relationship between language and propaganda. The main purpose of this section is to demonstrate how the language of propaganda shapes consciousness, thus producing conformity of thought and action. We look at four aspects of language and propaganda: the language of false fulfillment, the language of association and coupling, the language of clusters, and the unintended effects of language.

The Language of False Fulfillment

The language of propaganda provides a false sense of fulfillment by telling people what they want to hear. We all want to feel good about ourselves, we all want to believe in what we are doing and we all want to feel proud of our country, culture and government. Propagandists know this and thus use language that fulfills our unmet desires. The logic works like this: you have a desire, the propaganda promises to fulfill that desire and so the propaganda rings true to the average person. Of course the propaganda does not reveal itself as propaganda. Instead, it is camouflaged as educational, informational, matter-of-fact or commonplace communication. In the end you feel as though your desires are being fulfilled and thus accept the propaganda as true and factual. This may seem like good old-fashioned rhetoric, but it's not. All propaganda is rhetorical, but not all rhetoric is propaganda. Both consciously shape language to maximize effectiveness, but propaganda is manipulative, distorting and power-driven. Propaganda seeks to *exploit* people's desires while rhetoric seeks to *liberate* people's desires.

The Bush Administration no doubt used the language of false fulfillment in the wake of September 11. The American people were in disarray and were looking for a way out. The Bush Administration stepped in with simplified, emotionally-laden, black-and-white language promising to fulfill the country's needs:

- "We did not choose this tragic event, but God has called us to respond."
- "Our loss will not go in vain for we are the chosen country."
- "This is a fight for freedom, and we will prevail."
- "You're either with us or you with the terrorists!"

This is exactly what the majority of Americans wanted to hear. The Bush Administration then went on to invade Afghanistan, invade and occupy Iraq and push through a whole slew of regressive policies like the PATRIOT Act, the Department of Homeland Security, Guantanamo Bay, racial profiling and domestic wire tapping. The Bush Administration has continued to use this type of language throughout its entire reign. In fact, the examples are so abundant that it would take an entire book to list and analyze the Administration's propaganda. Suffice it to say that the Administration undoubtedly used language of false fulfillment, exploiting the public's wants and needs.

It's not always easy to analyze the language of false fulfillment. It's even tougher to explain it to other people. That's because people don't want to see it as propaganda. Their desires are being fulfilled, so why would they want to analyze and thus reject that fulfillment? Breaking through that blindness takes time, patience and most of all evidence — you must provide thorough evidence that the language is exploitative. There are three main steps for doing this.

- Designate the language and then designate the unfulfilled wants and needs — lay those out side by side and literally point to the relationships.
- Demonstrate how that language promises to fulfill those wants and needs and how it actually accomplishes its goals.
- Demonstrate how the creators of that language are invested in the outcome of that fulfillment; explain how they have something to gain by fulfilling the public's desires.

This type of analysis usually takes a lot of time, work and space. You usually need extended essays or long conversations to convince people of your analysis. It's also difficult to summarize your analysis into a few sentences or a sound-bite. But that becomes easier with more practice and experience. For example, you might say something like this: "The Bush Administration exploited the events of 9/11 by telling the public what it wanted to hear. The Administration used specific language to fulfill the public's emotional void. Once gaining the public's trust and support, the Administration pushed through an illegitimate war. All this can be proven with a basic analysis of the Administration's September 11th language. Go back and analyze the speeches; the evidence is overwhelming."

The Language of Association and Coupling

Propagandists often pair words together in order to create a psychological association between the two. This is known as "coupling" and it occurs when two or more terms are aligned together. Aligning the terms creates an associative link in the public mind. The meaning of one term is transferred onto the meaning of the other. This type of propaganda is based on psychological association: if one term is bad, then so is the other; if the first is good, then so is the second. This technique is simple yet powerful because it short circuits thinking — it allows people to process and respond to information without reflection.

This technique was often used by the Bush Administration. In his 2002 State of the Union Address, Bush referred to the "axis of evil."[7] This axis included Iran, Iraq and North Korea. This grouping was quite ridiculous. An axis implies some group coordination, networking or cross-relation. In this case, that couldn't have been farther from the truth. Iran and Iraq were not allies but rather arch-enemies, and North Korea had absolutely nothing to do with either country. But that doesn't really matter to uninformed listeners. The three countries were already negatively perceived by the public. Linking them together simply intensified that perception.

This coupling served at least three purposes. First, it announced to the world that these three countries were on America's official watch list. They must obey orders or risk annihilation. Second, it foreshadowed the possibility of invading one or more of those countries — it basically prepared the public mindset for war. And third, it situated America's fight against terrorism within the language and history of World War II and the Cold War. Bush's phrase was catchy and forceful because it was culturally situated within these two sources. First, it was derived from the "axis of powers," a term that referred to the World War II alliance between Nazi Germany, Fascist Italy, and Imperial Japan. And second, it was derived from Ronald Reagan's reference to the former Soviet Union as the "evil empire." Bush's phrase thus aligns the post-9/11 war on terror with the "great ideological battles of the twentieth-century" — the war on terror thus becomes another manifestation of America's benevolent and peace-loving ways. Just as America was righteous and victorious in previous battles, America will be righteous and victorious in the war against terrorism. Just as Americans supported the Cold War, they will once again support the war on terror.

Coupling was also used in the Bush Administration's build up to the Iraq war. The Administration constantly coupled Saddam Hussein with Osama bin Laden and terrorism. The Bush Administration rarely said that Saddam was a terrorist or an ally of bin Laden. That was never *explicitly* stated. But every speech and every discussion implicitly aligned Saddam with either terrorism or bin Laden. The two names would appear in the same sentence or in the same paragraph or on the same page. The public sees this juxtaposition, knows that Saddam is already an evil bastard, and then thinks of him as a terrorist or harbinger of terrorism. It just seemed sensible that Saddam had something to do with 9/11. And if that's true, then invading Iraq is also sensible. You just have to go back and analyze the speeches to see how the Bush Administration used this ploy to consciously link Saddam with terrorism, allowing the public to draw a foregone conclusion: invading Iraq is an extension of the war on terror. There's only one problem: it was all a big lie. Saddam was not friends with bin Laden and he did not harbor terrorists. In fact, bin Laden's fundamentalism was diametrically opposed to Saddam's secularism. The Saddam and bin Laden connection was propagated through language of association and coupling.

This technique becomes pretty obvious once you know what to look for. First realize that coupling involves repetition — the coupling happens over and over. It isn't effective if it only happens once or twice. A few times will not catch any attention and infrequent occurrences are probably not propaganda. It only becomes propaganda when it's done over and over. Repetition is a major aspect of all propaganda, but especially with coupling. Having said that, here are a few guidelines for analyzing the language of association and coupling.

- Look for the couplings, especially for couplings that don't seem to naturally fit together.

- Pay attention to the repetition; excessive repetition usually means that something is in the works. Try to track how often the coupling appears.
- Do some research and see if there are any real connections among the words, names or terms.
- Try to figure out the associative purpose of the coupling. What purpose is being served by juxtaposing these terms, names or people? How is the public supposed to be interpreting this coupling? What outcomes are supposed to result from this coupling?
- Expose the coupling as propaganda. Make your case and argue your point. Always use concrete examples from speeches, essays, articles, etc. Cut and paste the examples into a list and demonstrate how often they occur. Use that evidence to prove your case.

The Language of Clusters

Clustering occurs when many peripherally related words are grouped together. Clustering is similar to but different from coupling. With coupling, a few words are directly aligned. With clustering, a whole string of words are *indirectly* bunched together. Many different words are indirectly related to one another, creating a cross-connected grid of understanding. You'll see a few words over here, and then a few more over there. Separately, the words do not have much influence. But that influence increases when the words are grouped together and repeatedly circulated through the mediasphere. Clusters provide a lexicon for the public to perceive and understand a particular social issue. These words are so abundant and occur so often that they become part of the overall cultural understanding. These clusters thus shape and constitute the public's consciousness of the world.

The following words and phrases serve as an example. These words and phrases regularly appear within the media's discussion and reporting of US wars:

- Collateral damage
- Surgical air strikes
- Smart bombs

- Precision weaponry
- Neutralize the target
- Military campaign
- Military engagement
- Spreading democracy
- Democratic campaign
- Peacekeeping
- Rebuilding
- Re-educating
- Reconstruction

Many of these terms started appearing during the 1991 Gulf War and continue to be used today. These words now permeate our political landscape, affecting if not severely altering the public's understanding of war. A specific pattern of understanding emerges from this cluster of words: American wars are humane; America fights for peace; America doesn't intentionally kill innocent people; people don't really die, they are only neutralized; technological sophistication makes old messy wars obsolete; war is no longer confusing but clear, precise and to the point; and American soldiers are peacekeepers and democratic missionaries rather than military grunts of a brutal imperialistic empire.

This linguistic patterning contradicts the hard facts of war. Yes, smart bombs are used and surgical air strikes do occur. But how "smart" are those bombs, *really?* How "surgical" are those air strikes, *really?* The Shock and Awe campaign of the 2003 Iraq invasion delivered annihilation, not precision. The US military was there not to "neutralize" targets, but to conquer a nation, and that involves murdering human beings. And the idea that America is "spreading democracy" seems pretty strange, given all the death, destruction and murder. That seems more like imperialism than democracy.

The purpose of clustering is to create patterns of understanding that shape the public mind. A cluster is wider and more involving than coupling; it's not just one associative link, but a whole way of seeing and understanding. Clusters frame, shape and literally create particular understandings that benefit the interests of particular people and institutions. Cracking clusters is difficult because they are so encompassing that people do not see beyond that frame or pattern. But cracking that cluster is liberatory — people suddenly see the world in new ways.

A cluster analysis involves three steps. First, you designate and group together the commonly used words. Basically, you're gathering your cluster. The words that you're gathering are not random. You're not picking a word from over here and another word from over there. You want to be systematic. You are looking for specific words that commonly appear in the media or are used by particular people or institutions. These words are usually used in conjunction with one another. Second, analyze the evoked thought-pattern of the cluster. You're analyzing the *combined meaning* of the words and deciphering the *pattern of understanding*. Every cluster creates a particular type of consciousness; you're trying to understand and expose that evoked consciousness. And third, provide an alternative understanding. Challenge the dominant cluster by introducing a different understanding that is more accurate, honest and truthful. Here you want to use hard facts, statistics, testimonies and a thorough analysis. You're trying to convince others that your alternative is more accurate than the dominant cluster. Here's a summary of the three steps.

- Designate and group together the commonly used words.
- Analyze the evoked thought-pattern.
- Provide an alternative understanding and demonstrate why your alternative is more accurate.

The Unintended Effects of Language

Propaganda is not reducible to a person's intention. Sometimes the unintended effects of language lead to propaganda. Let's assume, for instance, that a president steps forward and makes a public statement. That statement was not intended to deceive or confuse the public, it wasn't intended to serve powerful interests and it wasn't intended to acquire or spread mass power. But despite these benign intentions, the president's statement still accomplished those effects: the public was confused, powerful interests were served, and mass power was acquired. If this is the case, then the president's statement was propaganda.

This example highlights the unintended effects of language. Analyzing those effects allows you to understand how certain statements, words or phrases unknowingly serve propagandistic purposes. This approach to propaganda stops powerful people and institutions from claiming ignorance. Powerful people too often claim that they weren't intentionally deceiving the public or intentionally spreading propaganda. They are then let off the hook. Since we cannot assess their intentions, we cannot charge them with propaganda. Such rules benefit those in power, letting the same old people do whatever they want. But we don't have to play by those rules. We can create our own rules by analyzing the effects of their language and deciding for ourselves. Does their language have propagandistic effects? If so, then the case is over — it's propaganda.

The Bush Administration provides yet another example. The US occupation of Iraq is officially entitled Operation Iraqi Freedom. But it was originally named Operation Iraqi Liberation.[8] That name produces a very interesting acronym: OIL. It is astonishing that the Bush Administration overlooked this linguistic detail. Millions of activists were screaming "No Blood for Oil" and the international community was skeptical of US intentions. But yet, the Administration happened to label the invasion OIL.

All the analysis in the world will never truly reveal the actual intention behind that word choice. Perhaps it was a sincere mistake; a tiny error committed by an intern or part-time staffer. Perhaps it was a small joke intended to provoke laughter from the critics: "See, its all fun and games; no harm done." Perhaps it was a small but cynical wink at the world: "Yes, it is about oil and there's nothing you can do about it." Or perhaps it was a very sophisticated propaganda technique intended to thwart the war-for-oil charge. The rationale could go something like this: if the Administration really did invade for oil, it would not be so stupid as to entitle the mission OIL. The presence of that initial name thus proves that the war is not about oil, but about something else, like freedom or democracy. This theory seems a bit conspiratorial and I do not necessarily agree with it. But my hesitancy is with the intention, not the effect. We can never really know if the Bush Administration consciously used this acronym as a propaganda technique. But that doesn't really matter because the *effect* was the same: it helped circumvent the idea that the war is about oil. That move — that deployment of language — curtailed the public debate, massaged the public mindset and rhetorically altered a legitimate critique into a crazy conspiratorial theory. The OIL acronym may not have been intended as propaganda, but it had the same effects as propaganda. In the end, it's the effect and not the intention that matters.

Labeling the OIL acronym as propaganda may seem controversial to many people. But look at our contemporary society. Marketing, advertising and public relations companies use highly insidious techniques to get us to believe and enact all kinds of things. We no longer know who is intending what. It's one big sea of action and effect. The idea of "intention" is thus outdated; it no longer applies to the world we live in. Since intentions are no longer trustworthy, we must analyze the effects. If those effects turn out to be propaganda, then they will be labeled as such. This stops powerful people and institutions from claiming ignorance and places the power of analysis in the hands of the people. Below are some suggestions for analyzing the unintended effects of language.

- Designate the language to be analyzed.
- Trace out the effects of that language. To do this, you must explain the link between that language and the subsequent actions or behaviors resulting from that language. Designate the language and then designate the effects of that language.
- Be sure to use concrete examples. Literally show what has happened as a result of that language.
- Decide if those effects were intentional or unintentional. If you can prove that it was intentional, then fine. If you cannot prove that, then explain why the effects are important. Explain why the effects are propagandistic.
- Always be careful in how you present your case — highlighting the unintended effects can seem conspiratorial and can damage your credibility. Try to be fair in your analysis, recognizing that

you may be incorrect; avoid overstating the case or saying anything that cannot be supported; and realize that some people may think you're crazy — that realization should help you adapt your language, argument and analysis to your audience.

Political Correctness

Creating more ethical and socially-just languages leads to the issue of political correctness. Political correctness, or PC as it is often referred to, places activists in difficult situations. You're arguing for more socially conscious language, but conservatives are arguing that PC stifles thought, censors discussion and cuts off dialogue. This anti-PC argument carries social weight because it appears to represent the American truisms of free speech, democracy and constitutional rights. If PC hinders free speech, as conservatives say, then the PC advocates suddenly look like "liberal fascists." This logic is totally bogus, but it's still rhetorically effective for conservatives because it sways the general public toward anti-PC sentiments.

But the PC problem doesn't stop there. Sometimes activists opt for what might be considered *non*-politically correct language. We'll yell, scream, curse and speak from our hearts, calling it like we see it. This gets us past the liberal fascist claim, but it leads to another problem: our non-PC language is called angry and anti-American. This double-spin move sets up only two options — you're either a liberal fascist or an anti-American. Your radical rhetoric is thus quarantined, placing you in a lose/lose situation. But that doesn't have to be true. You can find ways out of this rhetorical problem, and that's what this section is about — responding to the PC dilemma. We begin by looking at some histories of PC and how it has morphed into the current liberal fascist charge. We then we look at some rhetorical techniques for dealing with and properly using politically correct language.

Histories of PC

The modern conception of political correctness began in the late 1980s and early 1990s, a time marked by diversity appreciation and multiculturalism. That agenda involved critiques of cultural representation, ethnocentricity and constructions of personal and group identities. That involved issues of language. Left-of-center constituencies focused on the political nature of language and considered the effects of particular names, terminologies and phrases. Right-of-center constituencies felt threatened and fought back. Many books were soon attacking the "liberal thought-police": Allan Bloom's *Closing of the American Mind* (1987), Charles Sykes' *Profscam* (1988), Roger Kimball's *Tenured Radicals* (1990), and Dinesh D'Souza's *Illiberal Education* (1991) are just a few of those books.

As the titles indicate, this battle was played out within the academy. This occurred for at least four reasons. First, many professors and academics of this time period had grown up during the radicalism of the 1960s and 1970s. Second, the investigation of language had already been an intellectual mainstay since mid-century — linguistics, semiotics and the philosophy of language had become part of intellectual culture. Third, academics, professors, teachers and intellectuals are often paid to think about such issues as language. And fourth, many schools and departments were seeking to expand curricula by including Black studies, women's studies, gay/lesbian/queer studies, and feminism. Such disciplines consciously investigate systems of power and language.

These academic conditions coexisted with wider events of the 1980s and 1990s: the rise of AIDS, the spread of crack cocaine and its effects upon poor urban people of color, the federal cutbacks by Ronald Reagan and George H. W. Bush, the rise of Hip-Hop and Gangsta Rap, the popularity of Public Enemy, a revived interest in Malcolm X, the popularity of androgynous male singers like Boy George, George Michael and Prince, the increasing visibility of LGBT professionals and the end of the Cold War. The last one is more influential than people think. The end of the Cold War eroded the traditional dividing lines of socialism and capitalism. Radicals were now focusing less on Marxian critiques of economic infrastructure and more on the hierarchies and oppressions of social, cultural and political identities. This motivated issues of multiculturalism, diversity appreciation, identity politics and language.

Conservative constituencies fought against this momentum and launched anti-PC campaigns. To the best of my knowledge, there was no monolithic and unified campaign. But various people generated enough cultural commotion to make PC a disparaging term. Today, PC is a catch-all phrase for just about all left-of-center critiques and inquiries concerning the political nature of language. But the present day form of political correctness is quite surprising once we uncover the historical morphology of the term.[9]

PC Timeline

- During the 1940s, political correctness was used as a term by socialists who disagreed with strict Communist party dogma. To be PC was to toe the party line without question. Open-minded socialists used PC to critique dogmatic Communists.
- Some years later, PC was used as an insult for people who acted radical, but were in fact liberal or moderate. The true radicals might say something like, "Just come off it! You're only acting radical so you can be politically correct!"
- In the middle to late seventies, PC was used by radicals to humorously mock one another's idealism. Dreaming of revolution was *so* PC. This use was both satirical and affectionate; it acknowledged and appreciated radical idealism.
- Then, during the late 1980s, conservatives began using PC as a disparaging term to discredit multiculturalists and diversity advocates. They used the term to smear *all* liberal and left-leaning critiques of language. Questioning the political nature of language became synonymous with laying guilt trips on people and stifling thought and discussion. In other words, conservatives successfully branded multiculturalists and diversity advocates as "PC thought police."

The newest use of the term is quite perplexing because it misses, or distorts, the intention of multiculturalism, diversity advocacy and critiques of language. In actuality, what conservatives call "political correctness" simply refers to interpersonal and intercultural respect. Politically correct language acknowledges the fact that my personal experience does not and cannot represent your personal experience.

What offends me may or may not offend you. My worldview is not the same as your worldview. Because of this we should mind our use of language. This seems very logical and even extends the basic tenets of human rights — each individual is due the proper respect and consideration of being a person in the world. That respect and consideration involves language — try not to offend others, think about the terms you use to refer to others, try to understand the traditions and heritages of others, etc. In a nutshell, PC asks us to recognize the political implications of language and to use the most ethical language possible. This understanding of PC allows us to reappropriate the term for our own uses and to respond to the conservative attacks on our demands for more politically correct language.

Responding to the PC Charge

Below are some guidelines for dealing with the PC double bind. These comments are intended to be used for face-to-face interaction, including conversations, debates, interviews, post-speech discussions, or online instant messaging. Despite this focus, many of these principles can be helpful for written and electronic communication. The overall approach can be applied to just about any rhetorical situation. These are not absolute tenets that completely safeguard you from the anti-PC quandary. They are just some basic ideas for navigating the PC playing field.

Know the game and know the rules. Be aware of the PC game and understand how the rules work. If you critique language then you'll be called a liberal fascist. If you speak from your heart and call it like you see it then you're called an angry Anti-American. This double-spin can silence you even before you speak. But knowing these rules helps you break the rules. If you're accused of being too PC, argue back that PC is actually a conservative construction intended to discredit multiculturalism, diversity and progressive ideals. Cite the genealogy above that outlines the history of the term. Point out that the current use was invented by conservatives and in no way reflects the real impetus of political correctness, which is interpersonal and intercultural respect. This type of response throws people off. They don't expect you to be so knowledgeable about the history of PC and they are not expecting you to meet the PC charge head on. People expect you to cower; when you don't, they are surprised. This enables *you* to control the frame of discussion. You then have more ability to question people's language and ask them to reflect upon is implications.

Read the context and break the expectations. Analyze the situation and then understand and break the expectations. The other person might be using offensive language knowing that you'll jump all over it. The person then gets to label you a PC fascist, making you look bad. If that's the case, then don't address the language. Just let it go and focus on the main issue of conversation. That may be tough to do, but it gets you out of the PC trap. But the situation might be different, with the person expecting you to be angry and non-PC. The person might try to bait you again, making statements that would normally anger you. Avoid that trap by doing the opposite — be calm and controlled as you speak in a politically correct fashion. This confuses the other person and allows you to have more control over the situation.

Sometimes the other person is prepared with both traps. The person might be pressuring you with both the liberal fascist charge *and* the angry anti-American charge. If that's the case, then stop, relax and call out the situation: "It's not actually PC or anger that stifles political discussion. Instead, it is narrow-minded thinking that inhibits dialogue and communication. We need to stop baiting one another and try to communicate on a person-to-person basis." Such a response locates the problem within narrow-mindedness rather than an individual person. This allows you to highlight what is going on without actually attacking the other person; it lets you make the critique without making the other person defensive. This clears space for more productive talk and debate.

Be fair and balanced and strive for credibility. Try to recognize and acknowledge the good within the bad. You might say, for instance, that the language of mainstream society is often sexist, racist, classist and homophobic. But despite these problems, American culture has made great strides over the years. People *are* more respectful and mindful and most people *do* try to avoid overtly offensive language. This is progress and everyone is better off for it. These kinds of comments, even when coupled with your more critical comments, earn you credibility in the eyes of others. People are then more likely to at least consider your ideas and less likely to label you as PC.

Use audience-friendly communication. Critiquing people's language often sounds preachy, snobbish, arrogant and condescending. Nobody likes that; it gets you nowhere. Take your time, think through the situation and patiently address the issues in audience-friendly ways. Straightforward critiques can often alienate people. If that's the case, then you need to use cautious, supportive and non-defensive communication. Here are four suggestions for doing that.

- *Suggest rather than assert.* Offering, proposing and suggesting alternative words and phrases lightens the situation, allowing for self-reflection without defensiveness.
- *Ask rather then tell.* Ask others how they feel about certain types of language. Ask them if they see any issues with that language. Ask them if other language might be more appropriate. These leading questions can spark discussion rather than heated debate.
- *Critique yourself rather than others.* Rather than critiquing others, turn the conversation back around and critique your own use of language. Give an example or brief story about your own journey toward linguistic awareness. Implicating yourself opens the floor for others to do the same. Rather than you pointing out their mistakes, they do it for themselves.
- *Assume the best rather than the worst of others.* Try to give people the benefit of the doubt and assume that they are doing the best that they can at this given time. You shouldn't excuse their language, but you should try to be understanding. This sets up a non-defensive situation in which people are more likely to think, reflect and discuss their use of language.

It's about effectiveness, not correctness. Your communication should be guided by rhetorical effectiveness rather than political correctness. Sure, you want to be understanding and supportive, and you want to avoid offending others, even those you disagree with or dislike. But sometimes you have to simply state the obvious by calling people out and laying it on the line. Some people *are* racist. Some people *are* homophobic. Some people *are* simply power-hungry imperialists without heart or soul. You need to think before you make these statements, hopefully using more effective language. But that's a judgment call on your part. There are no sure-shot rules for guiding your decisions to be PC or not. But the general goal is always the same: to make rhetorical choices that bring about positive social change. If you're ever in doubt, just remember that it's about rhetorical effectiveness rather than political correctness. Analyze the situation and make your decision.

Words of Change

This last section helps us create new words of radical change. For the sake of simplicity, we focus on "the word," which I define as a single word, term, phrase or utterance that expresses an ideological vision and a political identity and mobilizes people to action.[10] Some examples might include Communism, socialism, Bolivarianism, Pan-Africanism, anarchism, environmentalism, feminism and Zapatismo. Such words encapsulate and express political worldviews and define and anchor one's radicalism. We often see ourselves through these words, living out their meanings and political agendas. These words shape our understanding of social, cultural, political, historical, and economic operations. These words literally outline our political realities.

These words of change are discussed in the five sections below. First, we outline the basic nature of these words. Second, we discuss the life-cycle of words and the need to create newer, more rhetorically effective words. Third, we analyze the rhetorical effectiveness of two older words, "Communism" and "anarchism." Fourth, we review some newer words and discuss the changing nature of twenty-first century words. And fifth, we discuss five steps for creating new words of radical social change.

Understanding Words of Change

Words of change, as defined here, are not the same as mere slogans. Some slogans may eventually become words, but words are not reducible to slogans. Truly powerful words capture people's imaginations and withstand the test of time — they are more historically meaningful and more politically powerful than mere slogans. Words are also different than propaganda. Words could become propaganda if used to manipulate people and distort the truth. But that's a risk of all language, rhetoric and communication. Words, when properly used, empower rather than manipulate people.

Words of change consist of three key components: ideological vision, political identity and mobilization.

Ideological vision. The word encapsulates an ideological vision and political framework. It is a system of thought, action and direction. It could be a strict ideology, like Leninist Communism, or it can be a loose set of guidelines, like feminism. Either way, the word expresses a political agenda that guides and defines one's actions.

Political identity. The word expresses a political identity. That identity is developed by carrying out the political framework of the word. Communists become *Communists* by rejecting capitalism and fighting for better economic systems. Anarchists become *anarchists* by rejecting authoritarianism and fighting for voluntary relationships. And feminists become *feminists* by rejecting patriarchy and fighting for gender equality. Political identities emerge as people align themselves with the political actions of specific words. You can of course embody many different words, thus developing a decentered political identity, like autonomous-Marxist-feminist, for instance.

Mobilization. The word is also a mobilizing force that pulls people into political activities and creates conditions for social movements. Those conditions are produced by the word's rhetoricity: the word radiates an outward excitement that attracts people to action. That excitement grows and the actions become larger and more frequent as more and more people are attracted to the word. Soon a movement is born and the word becomes the catch-all expression of struggle and action. We thus get such historically powerful words as socialism, Bolshevism, women's liberation, labor, hippie, New Left and global justice.

The Lifecycle of Words

The rhetorical effectiveness of words doesn't last forever. Words are here today and gone tomorrow. They come into vogue, mobilize populations, and then fade away. Many words do linger on, but ineffectively so. These words had such impact in the past that many people hold on in the hopes of reviving that previous power. But that's often a losing cause. Words, like all human creations, aren't meant to last.

Feminist writer Lisa Jervis addresses this issue by questioning feminism's wave terminology. As she states: "What was at first a handy-dandy way to refer to feminism's history, present, and future potential with a single metaphor has become shorthand that invites intellectual laziness, an escape hatch from the hard work of distinguishing between core beliefs and a cultural moment."[11] She's basically arguing that the wave terminology perpetuates oppositional categories: First Wave is different from Second Wave, and those are different from Third Wave. For Jervis, these distinctions are troubling for at least three reasons: they fail to recognize the similarities across waves, they divide feminists and they perpetuate and are perpetuated by sexism, patriarchy and hierarchical structures. Jervis admits that there's no sure solution to the problem, but she does advocate for a context-based use. Sometimes you should refer to and identify with particular waves, and sometimes you shouldn't. It all depends on the context.

I believe that we should follow Jervis's lead and rethink the effectiveness of *all* current words. Personal investment makes this difficult because we *are* our words, and to question our words is to question ourselves. But we must face the music and reflect on the rhetorical force of our words. If that force is there, then fine; continue forward.

But if that force is absent or close to nil, then we must create new words. I believe that many of our words fall into the latter category; too many of them are timeworn, stagnant and overdone. That's a big statement, but I believe such constructive criticism is warranted. To substantiate my claim, I analyze two of our dominant words below: Communism and anarchism.

Examples of Old Words

I believe that the rhetorical effectiveness of Communism has passed and its revival, while possible, is unlikely. The Cold War has ended and so too has the mobilizing force of the word, "Communism." The same goes for "socialism." Both terms have been used, reused and *mis*-used by many authoritarian, murderous regimes over the last one hundred and fifty years. Those misuses undoubtedly damage the rhetorical effectiveness of "socialism" and "Communism." Other, more positive and accurate uses of these words have occurred. We have learned from, and we should continue to investigate the successes and failures of those uses. We should also recognize the credibility of Marx and Engels. Their work, along with that of Luxemburg, Gramsci, Lukacs and others, is brilliant and should continue to be read, discussed and applied. And, most importantly, the *call* of Communism remains pertinent. More ethical, equitable and socially just economic systems are still needed. That has not changed. But the word "Communism" lacks rhetorical effectiveness. Its overuse and misuse no longer stir revolutionary excitement.

I believe that "anarchism," as a word, suffers a similar fate. Too many people have too many preconceived notions of that term. The word is simply over-determined. The general public associates "anarchy" with chaos, disorder, violence and lawlessness. This type of political language alienates rather than attracts people. Such alienation obviously runs deeper than the word itself. Many people fear a nongovernmental, self-organizing system of life. Many if not most people believe in the inherent need for authoritarian rules, structures and governments. This prejudice obscures their understanding of anarchism. But convincing them otherwise must entail more than a long and detailed explanation. Explaining the actual meaning of the word can help, but that's unlikely to change their ingrained bias against it. Anarchism, to be effective, must undergo a linguistic upheaval. Anarchism, to be a social force, must cease being *anarchism* and start being something else.

Transforming these words involves more than a word replacement. A simple renaming won't do it. People are too smart; they will realize what you're doing and reject it. A true linguistic transformation involves an overhaul of thought, idea and application. The external packaging as well as the internal meaning of the word must be changed. Remember that language is the means by which we create worlds of experience. Re-evaluating "anarchism," "Communism," and many other words, must involve paradigmatic shifts. We must create systems that specify new realms of experience, new political agendas and new forms of action. We must create new words that express new ideological visions and political identities. Those words will then energize twenty-first century minds and bodies. This task is not easy, but it is possible. In fact, it's always in process. We simply have to take notice and consciously create more powerful, effective words.

The Potential of New Words

There are some contemporary words that point us in the right direction. These words may not be as powerful as, say, Communism or anarchism, but that is still to be determined. As time passes, some of these words may actually eclipse the power of previous words. But more likely, we will see a different type of wording. Rather than a single word speaking for many people, we will have many different words from many different people and agendas. Each word will express and encapsulate uniquely powerful constituencies. Those constituencies will then discuss and debate one another's words, generating a contentious yet supportive collective. The era of the single word will thus end, giving rise to an era of kaleidoscopic wording. I believe that this process has already begun. Reviewing the non-exhaustive list below supports my belief. As you'll see, no one word dominates. Instead, many words link together, forming a decentered lexicon of contemporary radical words.

Horizontalism: The use and construction of non-hierarchical relations, especially within activist and organizing efforts. Horizontal forms of organizing are used to create a horizontal society without leaders or followers; everyone equally participates in the creation of society.

Decentralization: Non-centralized forms of organization. People and groups act on their own with no centralized command or control. This occurs as a form of activism as well as a social ideal to strive for.

Networks: The inter-linking of decentralized points. People and groups act on their own but they are also connected to larger movements and/or communities. Those movements and communities are networks of people and groups.

Swarm: A form of decentralized, mass action. Collective action is stronger and smarter than individual action. Together, we can swarm the streets and overrun the power structures.

Precarity: The state of being uncertain and unsure, especially in relation to one's labor and work. It usually refers to the shifting face of the global workforce, much of which lives paycheck-to-paycheck and day-to-day. It also has existential underpinnings — to be unsure of one's place in the world.

Immaterial labor: A form of labor that uses and produces non-material phenomena. Immaterial laborers use information and communication to create feelings, emotions, symbols, languages and forms of knowledge. The marketing and advertising industries are common examples, but as this book argues, activism is also a form of immaterial labor.

Consensus: A type of group decision-making process. Usually, group members voice their opinions and then everyone gets to discuss the best option. No decision is finalized until everyone approves.

Participatory democracy: This is almost synonymous with consensus, but there are more implications with participatory democracy. Many activists seek to replace bureaucratic governments and voting systems with smaller, decentered neighborhood assemblies. This structure allows each person to directly participate in political decision-making processes. Participatory democracy is thus a vision for a different society as well as a tool for achieving that society.

Freeganism: An anti-capitalist, anti-consumerist lifestyle using alternative means of survival like dumpster diving, foraging, squatting, urban gardening, community bike shares and truly free markets in which everything is given away, shared or bartered. The word's use of "free" and "vegan" expresses a withdrawal from capitalist exchange and cruelty.

Hacktivism: A widely contested term that for the most part refers to forms of virtual civil disobedience, including virtual sit-ins, website defacement, software sabotage and the liberation of software codes as well as everyday political information.

Multitude: A self-constituting revolutionary class of various peoples, standpoints, worldviews and political agendas. This revolutionary class is based on the idea that every human being participates in the creation of local and global realities. If this is true, then we are all potential revolutionaries.

Global justice: The idea that *everyone* has the right to self-determination. This implies the abolition of all hierarchical relations and oppressive systems. No to representational government. No to corporate rule. No to capitalism. And no to racism, classism, sexism, homophobia, etc.

Bolivarianism: A form of quasi-decentered socialism. It was originally developed by nineteenth-century Latin American revolutionary Simón Bolivar and later updated and implemented by Venezuelan President Hugo Chavez. Bolivarianism uses decentered models of leadership, hands-on community organizing and self-empowering social programs to create a classless and unified society.

Zapatismo: A non-ideological political way of life as developed by Mexico's Zapatistas. Zapatismo combines aspect of Marxism, autonomism, liberation theology, indigenous culture, pacifism, militancy and modern Internet technology to create a self-determining yet collectively supported way of life.

Creating Twenty-First Century Words

The above list is exciting and energetic, but it's not enough. In fact, it's never enough. No word or group of words will say everything once and for all. New issues, events and experiences lead to new visions, and those visions need new expressions. We are thus compelled to create words and languages that evoke new and preferably better realities. Go out, look around and see what's happening. Touch the world and get a sense of your day. Then choose words and languages that express that experience. Think of words that enliven the world; words that bring to life details we have not yet seen. If you can do that, then you've just made your ephemeral experience concrete and livable for others. That is to say, you've just created a reality that we can experience, discuss and debate. That's the power of the word and this chapter ends with steps for creating such words.

Analyze the conditions of the day. Analyze the events and happenings of the wider world and figure out how people are thinking and feeling. Think about the words and languages that populate the public landscape. Think about the language being used to describe the current state of the world. Get a sense of the dominant metaphors, analogies and descriptions.

Analyze the current state of radicalism. Examine the events and happenings of your fellow activists, organizers, radicals, revolutionaries and social movements. Try to figure out what folks are focusing on right now. Try to assess the motivations and goals of today's radicals. Try to place your finger on the pulse of cutting-edge radicalism. This usually involves talking with people, doing research, living in the world of activism and looking around and taking note.

Brainstorm ideas. Think of some words that accurately describe the current state of radicalism. Don't overthink the process; just list the words as they come to you.

Use your imagination. Shuffle through your list and choose a few words that capture the heart of today's radicalism. As you do so, be creative and put those words to the imaginative test. See if you can tweak and refine those words, making them more powerful and attractive. The most powerful words do two things: they manifest details of the world that are commonly ignored or bypassed, and they help people understand their political visions, identities, desires and reasons for acting. Such words articulate what people are thinking but have not yet said. Those kinds of words are hot, edgy, sticky and vivid. They enliven collective dreams, bring people closer together and illuminate paths for action. Those words often have experiential impact — people immediately think, "That's it, I get it!" That won't always happen, but it's a good rhetorical guideline.

Share your words with others. Share your words with other people and see what they have to say. Some of your words may stick and some may not. Realize, though, that no word has the final say. You are one person among millions, so there's no way that a word or even group of words will fully capture the depths of the radical imagination. But that's not really the point. Instead, you are making a rhetorical contribution to a collective effort of radical social change. You're trying to create words that other people can relate to and identify with. This will help them understand and express their political goals and actions, and that will almost always be appreciated.

Body Rhetoric

Our discussion of rhetoric has so far focused on the verbal communication of language, speeches, writing, etc. This chapter expands our discussion to include body rhetoric. The basic idea is that our bodies communicate rhetorical messages. This often plays out through our choices and actions. For instance, many of us avoid specific stores, companies, corporations, brands and logos. We use bicycles and other eco-friendly methods of transportation rather than cars or other gas-guzzling vehicles. We choose organic and fair trade foods rather than genetically modified foods. We barter and exchange rather than charge for profit. We consider our daily behaviors and work past habits of power and privilege. At our meetings we encourage under-represented groups to step forward, and ask over-represented groups to step back. And of course, we engage in all types of protests, rallies and street activities. These political decisions are concretized and communicated through our bodily actions. Our physical enactments materialize our political views and beliefs. That's body rhetoric.

This chapter looks at four types of body rhetoric: embodied argumentation, street theater, rhetorical style and the vibe as bodily emanation. Embodied argumentation describes how our bodily actions actually make arguments. Street theatre describes political performances common to protests, rallies and marches. Rhetorical style describes the overall look and feel of our communicative gestures.

And the vibe, understood as bodily emanation, describes the energy that emanates from our bodies. In each case the body plays a rhetorical role in promoting or contesting political agendas.

Embodied Argumentation

Your body makes arguments. Those arguments are not always obvious, but the arguments are there, embedded within your bodily actions. For instance, you might resist arrest at a major demonstration. That resistance — regardless of what you actually say — argues against police authority and state control. You might also call off work as a protest against war. That bodily absence subtracts you from various systems and highlights the intersections of work, capitalism and war. You might even go on a hunger strike for higher wages. That action obviously argues for higher wages, but it's also a physical form of labor solidarity. You are sacrificing personal and temporary comfort for collective and long-term gain. That's an embodied argument.[1]

Bodily argumentation expands the realm of rhetoric in at least four ways. First, embodied argumentation is a call to action. You must literally do what you are saying. It's one thing to write a paper or give a speech, but it's another thing to give up your personal anonymity, stand out in public and physically resist the hands of power. Second, embodied argumentation provides more rhetorical options. You may be uncomfortable with conversations, speeches, essays or books. Perhaps you're more comfortable with non-verbal rhetoric. Embodied argumentation provides a framework for understanding that option. Third, embodied argumentation is empowering. You no longer have to wait for auditoriums, stages, lecterns or publishers. You can use your body anywhere and anytime to argue, debate, express, resist and liberate your views, ideas and political affiliations. This is risky, of course. But the trick is to maximize your self-empowerment while minimizing your risk. Fourth and last, embodied argumentation highlights the craft of everyday living. Although your body is continuously communicating, you want to craft that communication into well-defined arguments. This process involves time, patience, practice, craft, application and revision. In the end, your body becomes an ongoing site of radical rhetoric.

Embodied argumentation is further explained in the following sections. We begin by discussing three basic aspects of body argumentation. We next discuss the arguments of individual bodies and how to improve those arguments. And then we move to the arguments of collective bodies and how to improve those arguments.

Three Basics of Body Argumentation

There are three basic aspects to body argumentation: your body, your message and your audience. These three components are similar to those of public speaking. For instance, speakers use their bodies to further communicate their messages while adapting to the wants, needs and expectations of the audience. But this is also different from embodied argumentation. That's because embodied argumentation is much more fluid and ambiguous. The situation, time, audience and even your message are constantly changing. Understanding the basic principles of body argumentation can help you deal with these ever changing conditions.

Your body: Your body continuously communicates a message. The way you sit, stand, walk and gesture either emphasizes or downplays your political positioning. Being aware of your body as a rhetorical message grants you more control — you can begin moving and acting in ways that better communicate your politics. This allows you to align your internal politics with your exterior communication. Your body then becomes a political and rhetorical vehicle for social change.

Your message: Your body is a message that others constantly read and respond to. If that's true, then make embodied choices that highlight and strengthen your message. Wearing particular clothes, eating particular foods or using particular modes of transportation helps you communicate particular messages to others. But your bodily messages neither begin nor end with these specific choices. Your body is constantly on display. There's never a moment when your body is not communicating some kind of message. Thus, your body is a perpetual message. If that's true, then you want to craft every action, gesture and movement into a well-developed message. That's not truly possible; no one has such self control. But it's the awareness that counts. Understanding your body as a message helps you communicate more effectively.

Your audience: Your embodied messages should meet the wants and needs of your audiences. This is not about selling out or being fake or phony. Instead, you're emphasizing or downplaying particular aspects of your body rhetoric in order to persuade, move or simply communicate with others. What works for one audience will not necessarily work for another. This is true for all rhetoric, including body rhetoric. Just as you adapt your verbal communication, you must also adapt your nonverbal communication. This helps you create more effective arguments.

Individual Bodies

You can use your individual body to make all kinds of arguments. You can get tattoos or body piercings, wear particular clothes, display buttons and pins, create unique hairstyles, use particular handshakes, change your consumptive choices, choose particular living arrangements, use particular modes of travel, go on fasts or hunger strikes, remain silent, go limp, be loud and outrageous and reshape the way your body sits, stands and moves through the world. These bodily acts communicate social and political messages that others read and respond to.

Hairstyles are a good example. The long, often unwashed and scruffy hippie hairstyle of the 1960s embodied several arguments. It argued that the clean-cut values of the older generation were outdated; that the Protestant work ethic was a sham; that cleanliness was not Godliness; that gender norms and straight-laced sexuality were bourgeois constructions; and that personal and collective experimentation were revolutionary. The Afro hairstyle worn by Black Power groups was also argumentative. It denounced the brutality of white America and signified a Black insurrection, a politically-charged African-American identity and an affirmative Black Culture. The Afro was "Black and Proud," and it recovered and embodied one's cultural roots. In more recent times, some lifestyle anarchists wear all kinds of wild, unkempt and unwashed hairstyles. These anti-hairstyles highlight the wasted time, money and resources of personal vanity and cosmetic hygiene. These anti-hairstyles also mark a self-chosen exclusion from social normalcy, which argues against authoritarian social control and for personal freedom. We can also look to genderqueer hairstyles such as faux-hauks, mullets, shags and bleached tips. These do not distinguish between masculine and feminine identities and acknowledge that biofemales and biomales do not necessarily identify as women or feminine or as men or masculine, respectively. Such hairstyles undermine the assumed relationship between biological bodies and gender identities. That's an argument for gender liberation.

Personal consumption is another example of embodied argumentation. Take veganism, for instance. Vegans don't eat any meat or animal products, thus arguing against the exploitation of animals. But they also argue against the food industry, which is composed of international corporations that exploit animals, land, natural resources and human labor. Veganism calls attention to unreflective and wasteful consumption, personal and social irresponsibility and the systemic ills of the global economy. Veganism argues for a society of ecological sustainability, interspecies respect and personal responsibility. This embodied argument is a public act that potentially affects other people. People see not only the look of the vegan body, which is usually thinner, but they also see the vegan act of conscientious consumption. This leads to conversations about food, health, ethics, animals, politics and society. This embodied rhetoric thus segues into verbal rhetoric, which grants the opportunity for further social change as well as interpersonal dialogue and connection.

We can also understand personal sacrifice as a form of embodied argumentation. For instance, on March 16, 2003, Rachel Corrie, a peace activist working in Palestine, chose to stand between an Israeli bulldozer and a Palestinian family's home. The bulldozer did not stop, demolishing the home and killing Rachel Corrie. The tragedy of this story makes it difficult to understand the event in terms of "a body" and "an argument." But Rachel Corrie's actions did embody several arguments. First, that the Israeli military murders innocent people. Second, that world peace involves great risk and personal strength and courage. Third, that the entire Israeli-Palestinian situation is completely screwed up. Fourth, that people must be willing to place their bodies on the line in order to bring about peace. And fifth, that personal sacrifice, no matter how tragic the outcome may be, calls attention to serious political issues.

In each of the above cases, individuals use their bodies to make arguments. Most people probably don't think of their actions as arguments. But once you think about it, you realize that your body is a rhetorical device for influencing people's perceptions, thoughts and actions. This insight then helps you craft your actions for maximum effect. Next time you commit an action, realize that you are actually communicating a message to other people.

Creating Individual Arguments

Individual body arguments are about committing personal actions that evoke the meaning and spirit of your beliefs and views. This process is not the same for everyone. You and I might have similar beliefs, but we probably embody those beliefs differently. That's totally fine. You need to use your own experience and discover your own level of comfort. Below are four steps for doing that.

- First, reflect on your politics. Think about your personal beliefs, values and views.
- Second, turn your views into arguments. Begin by writing out your views as single-sentence statements: I believe in economic equality; I am against racism; I want universal healthcare; etc. Now turn these into declarative statements: economic equality balances the social playing field; racism is degrading and ugly; universal healthcare is a basic human right; etc.
- Third, embody your arguments. This can be done in many different ways. For instance, you can wear only sweatshop-free T-shirts, avoid racist language or campaign for universal healthcare. Some arguments are riskier than others. Embodying anti-imperialism might mean joining a protest, for instance. But it might also compel you to actually fight against an imperialist

power. The latter is a hell of a lot riskier than the former. Figure out how *you* can best contribute to social change and then embody those arguments.

- Fourth, continuously refine your embodied arguments. What works today won't work tomorrow, and what feels right now will feel wrong later. Try out different body arguments and make adjustments whenever needed. This allows you to embody different views and convictions. Your arguments will eventually become a way of life, helping you labor toward better realities.

Collective Bodies

Collective bodies also make arguments. This most often occurs through protests and actions, which might include: sanctioned rallies, marches and demonstrations; direct actions; silent die-ins; snake marches; street festivals; both militant and peaceful confrontations; a few people on a street corner or a million people across the globe. These collective actions rely on bodies rather than words, language or straightforward logical claims. Verbal communication is of course used, but it's peripheral to the embodied communication. Collective action relies upon the coordination and communication of bodies. Subtract those bodies and the collective action disappears. Below are three examples.

- In 1999, the Seattle protests shut down the World Trade Organization. People's bodies literally clogged the system. Speeches, interviews, talks and the Internet were obviously used. But the biggest factor was embodied argumentation. Take away those bodies and the WTO never gets shut down. But those bodies were there, and they made one hell of an argument: "The WTO is wrong and it must be stopped, now!" Those bodies made other arguments, too: that ordinary people can confront and beat one of the most powerful organizations in the world; that different political ideologies can work together and peacefully co-exist; and that many people are fed up with the devastating effects of neoliberalism and economic globalization.
- On February 15, 2003, somewhere between ten and thirty million people worldwide protested against America's potential

invasion into Iraq. It was one of the largest coordinated actions in global history. While this mass outpouring did not stop the Bush Administration's drive to war, it did make some very important arguments. First, that not all American citizens are deceived by their government's propaganda. Second, that worldwide populations have the means and drive to organize globally. Third, that geographical and cultural differences do not hinder but may actually enhance global movements. And fourth, that millions of people are willing to stand up to and denounce the most powerful and destructive regime in the world.

- In the summer of 2003, police and paramilitary forces violently repressed a peaceful demonstration in Oaxaca, Mexico. A popular uprising ensued and people responded by creating the Popular Assembly of the People of Oaxaca. This was a self-governing entity that rejected the authority of the Mexican government. This collective action embodied at least five arguments: that the Mexican government is brutal and oppressive; that the Oaxacan people have reached their breaking point; that governmental authority *can* be refused and rejected; that popular power is just as strong, if not stronger, than authoritative and institutional power; and that new forms of democracy are not only necessary but possible.

Critics may dismiss such collective arguments, saying that such actions are illegitimate forms of political discourse. They will tell us to give speeches, write letters or run for office. Such critics fail to recognize the restrictive nature of these socially acceptable acts. Speeches, letters and offices are easily controlled by corporate media, governmental bureaucracies, social biases and money, power and privilege. Collective actions cut through these contours and allow people to create the conditions of their own communication. We're not asking corporations for airtime. We're not asking congressional representatives for scheduled meetings. And we're not casting votes or asking others to vote for us. Instead, we are using our bodies to directly communicate with the engines of power. Embodied argumentation is not always the best or most effective form of rhetoric. But it is a form, and it can and should be used when appropriate. So, next time you are asked to defend the legitimacy of a protest or collective action, you can use some of the following statements:

- Protests and actions are alternative forms of rhetorical engagement.
- Embodied arguments are an immediate and empowering form of political communication.
- Embodied argumentation gives voice to those who are excluded from mainstream outlets.
- Embodied argumentation is a direct form of democratic debate.
- Embodied argumentation extends the bounds of civil dialogue.
- Protests and actions concretize political rhetoric.
- Collective action *is* communication, period.

Improving Collective Arguments

Improving collective argumentation is similar to but also different from good protest planning. For instance, traditional protests must secure permits, plan march routes, solicit powerful speakers, generate media exposure, create political spectacles and maximize the number of participants. More militant direct actions must strategically choose locations, decide upon the right amount of participants, create affinity groups, agree to the action's duration and, like above, gain media attention and create a spectacle. This logistical work relates to but is different from the *embodied* aspect of collective action. The embodied argument is a specific aspect of the action. The usual logistical planning is still needed, but the embodied argument deserves its own attention. You must consciously create an embodied argument that can be effectively communicated to the public. Below are four steps for creating and clarifying your collective arguments.

Clarify the actual argument of the action. Try to formulate your argument into one complete sentence. That sentence should be declarative and easy to understand. For instance: the WTO must be dissolved; the US must stay out of Iraq; the people of Oaxaca are their own self-governing system. Your declarative statement then serves as the foundation for your collective action. Build your action around that statement.

Create an action that embodies that argument. Design a collective action that evokes the meaning of the argument. That collective action could be a traditional protest, march or rally. But in all honesty, such traditional protests are outdated, no longer capturing the public imagination. This is even true for more militant direct actions — those too can be repetitive and humdrum. Strive for more creative and communicative actions. You're trying to collectively embody arguments that capture the public mind. For instance: have massive "love-ins" on the front lawns of homophobic politicians; create a five-thousand person exclamation point — ! — on dried-up, subsidized farmland; set up "No Border" camps across national boarders; recreate the battle of Fallujah at the Pentagon; reenact capital punishment in front of state courthouses; etc. These types of actions are by no means new, such protests are probably being enacted this very moment. But these actions are underused and that's a rhetorical mistake. These creative actions communicate messages that others can readily recognize and respond to. Embodying these actions often takes more time and effort than more traditional actions. But there's also more rhetorical punch, and that's the payoff.

Create a picture-bomb. You want to create picturesque actions that say, "Boom, here it is!" These "picture-bombs" need little explanation, capture the imagination and help people *en-vision* your embodied argument. Achieving that effect involves many factors. First, think of the number, placement, height and symmetry of the participating bodies. You don't always need thousands of people to make a good action, but the people — the bodies — need to be used and arranged in ways that make a powerful statement. Second, think of the clothes, colors, actions and nonverbal expressions of the participants. Dress people in strategic costumes, have them wear symbolic colors and ask them to coordinate their facial and bodily expressions. For instance, fifty people marching down the street in triangular formation, with each line of the triangle wearing a specific rainbow color, communicates gay pride and community. This visual action is more dramatic and memorable than five hundred people aimlessly marching down the street. And third, think of the participants' purposeful actions. Each person's body should be doing something very specific and purposeful. Each person's action should contribute to the overall meaning and effect of the larger protest. Such coordination is difficult to achieve at large protests, but it can be part of the preplanning, with instructions communicated via fliers, e-mails, websites or word of mouth. Your goal is to create a *visual argument* that others can read and respond to. That's a picture-bomb.

Don't forget the basic rhetorical issues. Always consider, for instance, your target audience; the social and political climate of your local, national and international situation; the length and duration of the protest; the effects of your embodied, collective message; the specific goal you are trying to accomplish with the protest; the anticipated counterattacks and criticisms that others may wage against your action; etc. Considering these details helps you create more rhetorically effective body arguments.

Street Theater

Using street theater has many advantages: it can easily communicate your politics to large crowds; it's accessible to wide-ranging audiences; it uses art rather than intellect, which is often more compelling and entertaining; it's spectacular, making for good media coverage; and it's usually fun and communal, which is extremely important for healthy activism. But these advantages are accomplished only when the street theater is done effectively. All theater does not automatically translate into *good* theater. Good theater takes time, thought and craft. Poorly done street theater accomplishes little; it could even hurt your political goals. You want people to remember your political message, not the bad theater. Also realize the purpose of street theater — it's a public enactment intended to communicate political messages. This usually (but not always) involves body rhetoric — people use their bodies to enact a political scenario. That scenario is the medium of the message. If the scenario doesn't work or doesn't make sense, then the audience walks away confused and turned off. Theatrical craft is thus essential to successful street theater.[2] The following sections focus on two basic forms of street theater and provide tips for improvement.

Two Basic Types: Staged and Improvisational Theater

Many forms of street or political theater exist: guerrilla theater, silent theater, multimedia performances, happenings, puppetry, spoken word, media hoaxes and stunts, theater of the oppressed, popular theater, billboard liberation, miming, dance, radical cheerleading, flash mobs, etc. All of these cannot be covered here. We thus cover two overarching forms — staged and improvisational theater. These classifications refer to the goals and structures of your performance.

Staged theater. Staged theater has a very specific goal and it tries to communicate a very specific message to a very specific audience. It's also very structured, with set movements, actions, timing or dialogue. Staged theater looks more traditional, like something you would see on a theatrical stage. Sidewalk skits, funeral processions, mock exorcisms, mock trials, image tableaus, reenactments, dramatizations of events and large, coordinated ensembles are examples of staged theater.

Improvisational theater. Improvisational theater is less structured. The movement, action, timing and dialogue are more freewheeling, festive, intuitive and interactive. Improvisational actors usually have a very loose plan of action and then read and respond to the reactions of the crowd or audience. The message of improvisational theater is also more fluid and open to interpretation. It's enough for the audience to get the general idea of the performance; the specifics of the message are not as important as those of staged theater. Some examples of improvisational theater include: political clowning, fun-loving antics, sketch comedies, spontaneous actions, flash mobs, improvisational marching bands and simply dressing up in political costume. These performances are usually briefer and more mobile than staged theater. While staged theater is usually more situated and set, improvisational theater is more roaming and sporadic.

Choosing your form. You should consciously choose which type of theater you want to use and then properly prepare. Too many people think that all theater is improvisational. That's not true. There's a marked difference between the two forms I've described. If you're going to do street theater, then you need to choose between staged or improvisational. If staged, then realize that *everything* needs to be staged. Every movement, action, gesture and look should be meaningful and purposeful. Every action and expression should point to a specific message. That's the whole point of doing a theatrical piece — to create a meaningful scenario that communicates a message. If you choose to do improvisational theater, then make sure the performers understand the general goal — to make fun of the president, to critique capitalism, to highlight educational inequalities, to spark political reflection, to laugh at political celebrities, etc. Each improvisational performer should then execute actions that reflect and communicate the general goal or theme.

The pros and cons. Realize that neither form of theater is superior to the other. There are pros and cons to each. Staged theater is usually longer and more crafted. This creates more psychological and emotional involvement for the audience, which can lead to greater audience reflection. This, of course, takes more preparation and rehearsal, which can be a drawback. Jobs, families and everyday living don't always allow for weeks of rehearsal. This can complicate the goals of staged theater. If you're doing staged theater, give yourself plenty of time in advance. This makes it less stressful in the long run and you won't be running around the night before. Also secure a rehearsal space. That can be expensive, but living rooms, basements, garages and even parks can serve as free spaces. If a number of people are involved, then you'll need to coordinate schedules. That's tough, but doable. Realize that everyone does not have to rehearse together at the same time every day. Break yourselves up into pairs or triples or whatever. Then, as the time gets closer, bring everyone together and run through it, making sure everyone is comfortable and coordinated.

Improvisational theater usually provides a quicker message. The audience — as well as reporters and journalists — don't have to do as much work to understand the message. Media blurbs and soundbites are then easily generated. But such blurbs and bites don't last; they pop up and then fade away. You can avoid this by creating and performing many different improvisational pieces on a consistent basis. Short pieces take low commitment on your part and they keep your message in the spotlight. But keep an eye on the overall effect of your message. Even short and varied performances can become old hat. At that point it's time for something new. Go back to the drawing board, brainstorm and come up with some new messages and new performances.

Street Theater Tips

Below are several tips for preparing and improving your street theater. As you read, keep in mind the difference between staged and improvisational theater. Suggestions that work for one form of theater do not always work for the other.

Message: Clarify your message before you perform. This will help you communicate your message to your audience. A performance without a message is simply bad theater. Performances that play off of ambiguity and multiple interpretations are fine, but that's not the same as having no message. Theater, especially political theater, is not reducible to entertainment and cheap laughs or smiles. It's about commenting upon, changing and even recreating the world. If you're doing staged theater, then you need a very clear and specific message. Try to summarize it into a single sentence or even a single phrase or word. You then need to translate that message into a staged performance. Also, the more concrete your message, the better. This allows the audience to walk away remembering your exact message. If you're doing improvisational theater, then your message can be more general, but you still need an overarching theme or goal. Specifying that theme or goal helps you interact with the other performers as well as the audience. Get together before the performance and make sure everyone understands the message. Then discuss what should be said and done to communicate that message to the audience.

Embodiment: Find ways to embody your message. Theater, like all art forms, is about showing rather than telling. You want to show — in other words, embody — your political message. You can begin with costume ideas. A dove represents peace. The grim reaper represents death. A gagged and handcuffed Statue of Liberty represents the loss of civil liberties. And an oil-stained, blood-soaked George W. Bush represents the geopolitics of war and oil. You then need to design your performative actions. *What are you actually doing to evoke the meaning of the performance?* You need to create actions that highlight the message of your performance: a mock torture scene, Mother Nature coughing from car exhaust, Mr. Dollar Bill buying Mr. Politician, a reenactment of a battle scene, etc. These actions embody and thus show the message.

Storytelling and narrative structure: Storytelling and theater are extensions of each other. As stated in Chapter Two, storytelling follows a five-part narrative structure involving characters, action, scene, conflict/resolution and plot. This structure can be used to create your street theater. Begin by creating a performance that will tell a particular story. Then create a plotline with a dramatic arch of conflict and resolution. Decide upon the imaginary scene of the action and create characters that can properly embody the story. Don't bypass that second-to-last detail. The narrative scene is very important — imaginary prison cells, battlefields or post-apocalyptic worlds help direct the actions of the performers. The scene is the place of action; without it, none of the actions make sense.

Physical setting: Street theater must be adapted to the physical setting. In fact, your performance should be created with the setting in mind. Consider the actual setting of the performance. Where, exactly, is it occurring? Each setting is different: office buildings, courthouse steps, elevators, bathrooms, street corners, coffee shops, subways, fast food restaurants and rural, urban or suburban settings affect what you can and cannot do. Subway cars are extremely small and bumpy while courthouse steps provide natural levels. These conditions must be factored into the performance. Also consider the symbolism of the setting: the White House, the Lincoln Memorial, Wall Street, the state capital building, an animal research center, a military recruitment office, Nike headquarters, a Wal-Mart parking lot, a McDonalds and so on. Find ways to highlight the connections between your performance and the symbolic setting. This adds an important layer of meaning to your performance.

Visual framing: Street theater should be crafted for visual effects. To begin with, everything must be bigger and larger than usual. All theater dramatizes life through exaggerated movements and gestures. Street theater does this tenfold. Street performances rarely have elevated stages or good house seating. The audience's lines of sight are usually constrained. Street performers must compensate by overexaggerating their actions. This is not the same as being melodramatic. You don't want to overact. Instead, you are adapting your bodily movements to the public conditions — you're making everything bigger, wider and larger. Street theater is supposed to be dramatic, emotionally intense and captivating. You are doing something unconventional and you are looking for attention. That's the whole point of your action. Step back during the preparation and rehearsal process and contemplate the visual framing of the performance. Find ways to make it larger than life and visually stunning — colors, costumes, props, height levels, synchronized actions, etc. The previous suggestions for creating picture-bomb protests can help with the visual framing.

Sound, voice, dialogue: Street theater acoustics are usually horrible. There are no walls or ceilings for your voice to bounce off. The performers must talk as loud as possible. Scream if you have to. But be careful; you can damage your vocal cords. As in public speaking, you need to project from your diaphragm — that little muscle that sits just above your stomach. If you're unable to generate enough sound, then create a performance without dialogue. This is very common with street theater, especially when performing in front of very large crowds. If you do have dialogue, even with a smaller crowd, try to keep the dialogue to a minimum. Use your body and props to communicate the message. (A note about props — these too have to be bigger than usual. Everything must be elevated and exaggerated during street theater.)

Body Placement: The front of your body should always face the audience. This is the "face" of emotion, action, meaning and drama. The audience cannot understand the message if they cannot see the front of your body. Sometimes this is not possible with large or circular crowds. In that case, move around the circle, allowing different sections of the crowd to see your front. This gives them enough to follow along and sustain their attention. Your head should point up and outward. Only look down if it's part of a performative gesture, and even then, your head needs to cheat upwards. If you are on the same level as the audience — like standing on street pavement — then your chin should point to the top of the audience's heads. This helps the audience see and hear you. If possible, find an elevated platform — stairs, a park bench, a monument, milk crates or even a curb can make it easier for the audience to see and hear the performance. And last, be aware of all the different environmental factors. Street theater is usually loud, chaotic and unstable. The "theater" is constantly changing. That means the performer has to also change. Pause for passing sirens, laugh *with* obnoxious hecklers, ebb and flow with the personalities of changing audiences, and ask audiences to pick up and move to better locations if needed. Adapting your body to the changing landscape is inherent to street theater.

Audience: Street audiences are not captive. They don't buy tickets and they are not necessarily interested in your performance. It's your job to get them interested. You can do this by either creating a spectacle or by literally soliciting their attention. The first involves creating a larger than life, visually stunning performance that attracts passersby. The second involves active solicitation, preferably before the performance begins. Announce that a performance will be starting soon. Passing out small announcement fliers is helpful. This also provides the possibility of adding your group's name, website, contact information, and/or political blurb to the flier. Interactive, improvisational performances make people feel implicated and put on the spot. This scares people and that's why most improvisational performances are humorous and lighthearted. Humor is less threatening than anger, outrage, or serious contemplation. Regardless of which emotion you're working on, try to be interactive, supportive and inviting rather than demanding and imposing. You want people to stay and watch. Like all rhetorical activities, street theater must be audience-centered.

Before moving to the next section, it's important to remember that not all forms of street theater are the same. Staged theater and improvisational theater involve their own forms of artistry and offer their own rewards and challenges. These eight tips are not exhaustive, but they should be helpful for choosing, crafting and presenting more politically powerful performances.

Rhetorical Style

Rhetorical style is the overall look and feel of your communication. It's the *way* you communicate. It's the *habit* of your gesturing, speaking and moving. Style is an embodied phenomenon, emerging from your enacted gestures and patterns of behavior that are noticeable to yourself and others. Style can be broken down into at least two categories: the style of your everyday, mundane communication and the style of your life. First, everyone exhibits a communicative style. It's part of your habitual way of acting in the world; it's part of the way you walk and talk. And second, each of us exhibits a personal style of life that is executed and carried out over an extended period of time — hence the phrase, lifestyle.

Style is commonly bypassed for negative reasons. We usually think of people who are overly concerned with style as superficial, egotistical, narcissistic and narrow-minded. These negative associations are understandable but misplaced. Rhetorical style isn't about gazing into the mirror or obsessing over fashionable details. Rhetorical style is about embodying *communicatively effective gestures* for the achievement of sociopolitical ends. If this is true, then rhetorical style is an ongoing issue of radical activism. Plenty of radicals are known for their styles: Mother Jones, Peter Kropotkin, Emma Goldman, Gandhi, Malcolm X, Dr. King, Cesar Chavez, Fred Hampton, George Jackson, Kathleen Cleaver, Angela Davis, Guy Debord, Edward Abbey, Howard Zinn, Leslie Fienberg, Subcomandante Marcos, Hugo Chavez, Vandana Shiva, Arundhati Roy, etc. These people are not known solely for their styles, but their styles are noticeable and memorable. This helps them push their political agendas. Take Subcomandante Marcos, for instance. His mask, pipe, slow and contemplative speech and witty humor have caught the world's attention. He is not reducible to these characteristics, but his charismatic traits help him communicate his politics. Marcos has style and he uses it for social change.

Style may seem glamorous and mysterious, but it's not. Every style, even the most provocative, is nothing more than a series of bodily gestures and acts. These acts, when repeated enough times, become second nature and habitual. These habits then become stylized. This understanding of style does two things. First, it reveals the basic nature of style: style is a consistent habit of acting in the world. That's all; it's really nothing special. And second, this understanding demystifies the process. Style is not given to some people and denied to others. Instead, we all have style; it's an ongoing aspect of our bodies. The difference lies in the effectiveness of the style: some styles are rhetorically effective while others are not. Some styles are simply too basic and average to catch the attention of others. Those styles are then bypassed and ignored. Radical rhetoricians want to avoid this; you want a style that stands out and attracts attention. This is *not* about an egotistical, "Hey, look at me!" Instead, it's about crafting your style to better express and reflect your political disposition. Doing this transforms your everyday habitual repetitions into a political aesthetic. That political aesthetic then becomes noticeable within the wider world of political affairs. Emma Goldman had good style. So too did Malcolm X, Stokely Carmichael, Che Guevara and Bernadine Dohrn. Certain groups have good style, like the Black Panthers. Even protest tactics like those of the Black Blocs have good style. Whether or not you agree with the Black Blocs' tactics, you must admit that the Black Bloc look and feel is memorable — it stands out and sticks in the mind. That's good style.

The following sections are organized around two main types of style — the style of everyday communication and lifestyles. Suggestions for improving these two types of style are also discussed.

Basic Communication

Good communicators have good style. Their essays, articles, books, speeches, talks, rants, raves, whispers, and ways are uniquely stylized. Their overall communication — whether it's spoken, written, embodied or otherwise — is interesting, attractive and charismatic. This helps us recognize and remember the words, ideas and actions of these people.

I can easily recognize the semi-scruffy yet crisp and concise voice of news reporter Amy Goodman. Her voice and her manner of speaking stand out from other radical news reporters. This is partly because I listen to her "Democracy Now!" radio show every morning. But it's also because of Amy's distinct style, which is smart, passionate, fearless, to the point and fair with a touch of good-hearted wit.

I can also recognize Ralph Nader's response to the latest World Bank rip-off. I can envision his drab-colored, slightly wrinkled suit; his hands flipping slightly into the air; his tall and hunched upper back; and his matter-of-fact responses. Nader has made thousands of television appearances, helping me remember and imagine his style. And while Nader is by no means the most charismatic speaker, his style is unique. Even people who don't like him know him as "that guy."

Mumia Abu-Jamal is another example. His speeches and writings are cold and detached yet highly impassioned. That tension or "contradiction" *is* his style. Mumia's voice — whether on paper or through a microphone — simultaneously echoes and transcends his death-row confinement. His style expresses his imprisoned frustration as well as his inner freedom.

Simone de Beauvoir, the great French writer and thinker, is an older but helpful example. Her highly intellectual prose combines autobiography, social critique, philosophy, poetry and all kinds of emotional ups and downs. Her style rides a dramatic tension between effortlessness and scrupulousness, with the two being held in check by a French sensuality. People have been reading her work for more than a half century, and not just for the poetic language, but for its stylized engagement with important social issues. De Beauvoir's style creates an air of attraction. People want to get closer to her and as they do, they become influenced by her thoughts and ideas.

Kalle Lasn, the famous culture jammer and editor of Adbusters Magazine, uses a bombastic style that prioritizes action: "We must act now or perish!" Not just the content, but his grammar, choice of language and descriptive writing provoke urgency. You may not always agree with what he's saying and you might critique his lack of strategic advice. But Lasn has a style that attracts people's attention.

While creating a radical style means different things to different people, the underlying issue is the same — to craft a style that both reflects your radicalism and attracts people to it. That's not easy to do. Coming off too radical alienates people. Watering down our radicalism doesn't attract any attention. The trick is to balance these two poles while adapting and adjusting to each and every situation.

Five Steps for Cultivating Style

Cultivating style is not an all or nothing process. It's not like you are starting from scratch. Instead, you already have a style; it just needs to be tweaked and developed. The trick is to reflect and then improve upon your more attractive and charismatic habits. This process of cultivation can be broken down into five basic steps: observe your own style and the styles of others, reflect upon those styles, experiment with different styles, apply your style and take chances with different stylistic choices.

Observation. First, take notice of your own and others' styles. Think about your own manner of moving, talking, laughing and smiling. Think about how you respond to questions or how you introduce yourself and say goodbye. Observe how others begin and end conversations; how they approach social and political issues; how they walk in and out of a room. Pay attention to the details of books you read. Notice the length of the sentences, the use of semicolons, ellipses and dashes. When watching a speech, consider how the person's gestures either strengthen or weaken their argument. When conversing with people, attend to the shape of their lips and the movement of their eyes. Look at their hand gestures and listen to the sounds of their voices. These observations should be done on a daily basis. Attune yourself to your everyday communicative interactions. See if people's styles reveal their political orientations. Think about what their bodies are doing to express their politics. All this is a bit obsessive, but you are trying to become more conscious of the styles that surround you on a regular basis. You don't want to objectify and judge anyone, and you don't want to drive yourself crazy. You're simply developing stylistic awareness.

Reflection. Second, reflect upon the pros and cons of the observed styles. Figure out if those styles work and if so, why. Consider how different people can improve their styles. Analyze the effects of people's styles on television, during interviews and during conversations. Think about the different types of people who are attracted to or turned off by those styles. Then, most importantly, think about how you relate to each style. How does your own style relate to and differ from that style? How might your own style be distinguished from that other style? Can you imagine yourself enacting that style? What, if anything, can you borrow from that person's style? Answering these questions gives you a better sense of your own rhetorical limits and possibilities.

Experimentation. Third, experiment with different rhetorical styles. Try on and try out different rhetorical choices and see what works for you. You need to learn what style works for each situation, among different people and with different issues. Such experimentation often leads to personal change and rhetorical growth. You can then use that rhetorical knowledge to expand, tease out and rearrange your stylistic technique. Such experimentation keeps you on edge, often providing greater energy and excitement to your communication. That makes for a better style.

Application. Fourth, choose and apply your style. This is tricky because you usually don't *choose* a style; instead, the style chooses you. Certain gestures and mannerisms will pop up, you'll take a faint notice and you will unconsciously repeat the successful ones and avoid the others. This process involves a small dose of conscious effort and a very large dose of unconscious repetition. But you're trying to become more conscious of the process. This will allow you to create your own style. But to do this you must apply and enact your style and then see what happens. You'll eventually recognize your own style; it will feel comfortable and natural. Achieving that comfort involves periods of experimentation, then application, followed by plateaus, and followed by more experimentation, etc. The process never really ends. Most styles ebb and flow with time, age, conditions, personal issues, wider events, etc. Many activists, organizers and revolutionaries have gone through this. The autobiographies and biographies of Emma Goldman, Gandhi, Malcolm X, Stokely Carmichael and others chronicle such changes. These biographical accounts are usually read as personal life journeys. But you can re-read these as stories of rhetorical changes — as chronicles of rhetorical development in which a person moves through different styles.

Chance. Fifth, take a chance and see what happens. You obviously need to think, analyze and rework your style. But in the end, it comes down to luck. You never really know which gesture, mannerism, accent or movement will work. You simply act and hope for the best. Learn how to let the process occur by itself. Don't interfere with it. Let it happen. Overthinking the process creates a flat and dull style. That's no good. You want to be fresh, alive and on your toes. You want your style to flow with the wants and needs of each situation. You want to embody steps one through four above, but you also want to be loose and fluid. That keeps you at the edge of your rhetorical potential, which is a good foundation for developing a radical style.

Lifestyle

Every person has a lifestyle, and that lifestyle affects the world in some way, shape or form. If that's true, then you can use your lifestyle to communicate radical messages of social change. Many activists do that already by avoiding sweatshop apparel, drinking fair trade coffee or volunteering at worker-run bookstores and cooperatives. All of this is great, but our lifestyle choices shouldn't be reduced to material effects, only. Realize that your lifestyle also produces immaterial effects. For instance, wearing Nikes and drinking Starbucks obviously affects the physical conditions of workers. We thus avoid those corporate products. But buying Nikes and Starbucks also normalizes capitalism, competition, hierarchy, exploitation, oppression and corporate control. These things become socially acceptable. That acceptance is a mindset, worldview, and orientation. These *immaterial* phenomena actually set the conditions for, say, worker exploitation. Many of us do realize this and thus avoid corporate products altogether. But we can take this to another level and realize that every aspect of our lives contributes to the ongoing creation of the world. From the clothes we wear to the food we eat, from the words we use to the gestures we enact, from the way we sleep to the way we walk: our lives continually affect the world. And the reverse is also true — everything in the world affects us. This reflexive relationship helps explain the importance of our lifestyles: we are always in the process of creating the world. Because of that, our lifestyles become a site for social change. We are thus compelled to fashion our bodily actions into rhetorically effective lifestyles.

Developing socially just and rhetorically effective lifestyles is much more challenging than learning how to speak, write, persuade or argue. The stakes are higher. A speech is over in a few minutes, but a lifestyle is constant and continual. People also judge your lifestyle. This isn't always fair, but it's common. We judge people by the way they live their lives. Lifestyle is not the be-all and end-all to social change. But most contemporary activists would agree that lifestyle is a major part of radical politics. We should be fair when addressing this issue and realize that we all live with contradictions. For instance, trying to live ethically within a capitalist system necessitates contradiction. How do you treat someone ethically if your entire life is based on exploiting others? Keeping such systemic issues in mind is helpful, but obsessing upon such contradictions leads to self-loathing. The trick is to do the best you can in the present moment, continually working toward self-improvement. That's a lifestyle worth pursuing.

Developing Styles of Life

This section provides some suggestions for developing more conscientious and rhetorically effective lifestyles. While we want to strive to be the best people possible, we also want to consider the communicative aspects of our lifestyles. If your style doesn't communicate well, then it's not as effective as it could be. Always keep in mind the rhetorical aspect of everything you say, do and live.

Looking into the proverbial mirror. Developing a rhetorically effective lifestyle involves a heavy dose of self-reflection. You must be willing to look into the proverbial mirror and change your less than desirable traits. You might begin by eliminating your sexist, racist, classist or homophobic traits. Making these changes is probably tougher than it sounds because such traits are part of your bodily fabric, most likely passed on to you through familial and cultural indoctrination. To overcome these traits you must re-craft your entire way of acting in the world. This takes time and patience. But your willingness to do that becomes part of your lifestyle — it becomes a stylized habit of acting against your own (and others') prejudices. Such self-reflection and re-crafting involves more than sexism or racism, or course. Redeveloping your lifestyle can involve anything you think needs changing, like eating habits, consumer choices, interpersonal habits, psychological outlooks, emotional responses, your self-image and self-esteem, short- and long-term goals, etc. The point is to develop a personally satisfying, socially just and rhetorically effective style of living.

Seeking role models for emulation. It helps to have role models to emulate. Seeking out people that you admire and identify with can help you develop your own positive lifestyle. The best models are those you know personally — friends, relatives, mentors and acquaintances. That's not always possible, though. If that's the case, then seek out more famous people — historical heroes and heroines. But avoid idolizing those people. No one is perfect; even the most famous and inspiring people have undesirable traits. Dr. Martin Luther King, Jr. was a womanizer, Che Guevara was homophobic, and Simone de Beauvoir often bowed to her male partner, Jean-Paul Sartre. Acknowledging such traits avoids creating false idols or unachievable ideals. Begin by embodying various traits of your role models. But understand that you can never be them. You must make your own daily choices and develop your own style of life.

Cultivating your style. Developing a lifestyle comes down to self-cultivation. In many ways, this involves the five basic steps mentioned above. Observe and reflect on your own and others' lifestyles. Experiment with particular lifestyle choices. Choose and apply the choices that work best for you. And always remain open to change and chance. This process takes time, patience, openness and courage. It's not a once-and-for-all final deal. Your lifestyle will ebb and flow with time, experience and circumstances. What you believe today will be different tomorrow. And your actions now will seem foolish later on. That's part of being human. The trick is to work on yourself in the service of social justice. Cultivate a lifestyle that effectively expresses who you are and what you believe. Be the most rhetorically effective radical that *you* can be.

Considering the rhetoric of your choices. Remember that your lifestyle is a communicative phenomenon. Every choice you make is communicating something to someone else. Rhetorical reflection is thus necessary. You want to make lifestyle choices with others in mind. This is not about living your life to please others and it's definitely not about fitting in or being socially accepted. Instead, it's about enacting your choices in ways that invite others to do the same. It's about using your lifestyle to induce change beyond your immediate situation. I realize that this is a highly controversial statement.

Many people would argue against what I am saying. But we're talking about the *rhetoricity of lifestyle*. This means considering how others will respond to your way of life. It's not about making different choices, but about executing the choices in favorable ways. Does your manner of living attract people to your politics? If yes, then great, but if no, then it's not rhetorically effective. This often comes down to personal attitude. People are attracted to inviting attitudes and they are turned off by defensive or over-righteous attitudes. Think of the most famous radical personalities. Many of them are upfront, confrontational, self-confident and even angry. But they're not defensive or over-righteous. They're radical without being interpersonally antagonistic or obnoxious. You're a person trying to affect other people. Your style should thus be interpersonal. That's a good guideline for enacting a communicatively effective lifestyle.

The Vibe as Bodily Emanation

We now focus on the human vibe, which is a form of energy that is felt between people.[3] This is a less commonly discussed form of embodied rhetoric. In fact, most people don't think of the vibe as rhetorical or embodied. Three clarifications can help us understand the vibe as a form of embodied rhetoric.

First, the vibe is a *bodily* phenomenon. Most people think of the vibe as mysterious, unexplainable or otherworldly and as something to do with the soul, spirit, or paranormal activity. But the vibe is felt through our bodies. We are embodied beings who transmit and feel vibrations. Those vibes don't fall from the sky or appear from nowhere. Instead, those vibes emanate from our bodies. It's an embodied experience. Because of that, I rearticulate the vibe as *bodily emanation*. Our bodies emanate feeling.

Second, the vibe is a communicative phenomenon. We can and do use it to communicate with one another. It may not be our primary mode of communication, such as language, but it is used quite often. We use it to express emotions and feelings, to gain the attention of others, to attract people to us or push people away, to better understand what people are saying, to feel out an audience, to find someone in a crowd, to protect and safeguard ourselves, to drift through a city landscape, etc. Bodily emanation is not something outside of your control; it can be used as a tool during your communicative interactions. If that's true, then you can improve your ability to use it more often and more effectively. It can become a dominant mode of your communication.

And third, bodily emanation is rhetorical. It plays a major factor in many face-to-face rhetorical situations. Think of charismatic speakers. Sure, they have effective gestures, bright smiles and well-written speeches. These things are obviously charismatic. But charisma is also vibrational. You can *feel* speakers' embodied vibrations, which makes you look and listen. Every good speaker emanates an attractive vibe. A speaker without a good vibe is an uncharismatic speaker. The vibe also functions persuasively. One person emanates a suggestive feeling that persuades another person to do or believe something. She or he was swayed in a particular direction; that feeling influenced the other person's choice. That's persuasion. A similar issue applies to rhetorical credibility. You must give off a particular vibe in order to create an air of credibility. The wrong vibe will actually hurt your credibility. Just as you build credibility by establishing common ground, you must also build it by establishing a vibrational connection between yourself and others. Without the right vibe people distrust you and thus walk away. The possible examples are endless and I assume the point is clear: bodily emanation is part and parcel of rhetorical practice.

The three sections below can help you improve your use of bodily emanation as a rhetorical tactic. The first section lays the groundwork for better understanding the nature of the vibe as bodily emanation. The second section discusses how to consciously use the vibe as a form of communication. And the third section further clarifies the vibe as a form of embodied rhetoric.

Understanding Bodily Emanation

Some people might dismiss vibes and bodily emanation, reducing such feeling to nonverbal sensitivity. They might argue that no actual vibe or emanation exists; that such feeling is simply a person's emotional or psychological sensitivity to another person's nonverbal communication. Nonverbal communication is no doubt a factor, but dismissing the vibe seems foolish to me. I cannot ignore my own and others' experience of human vibrations. There are countless songs, poems, pop cultural and everyday references to the vibe, and many people acknowledge their own vibrational experience. Despite this widespread acknowledgement, the word "vibe" gets thrown around too carelessly. People use the word to refer to everything and anything. That overuse hinders our understanding of the vibe. The vibe needs to be clarified, which is why I use the phrase *bodily emanation*. This phrase refers to the human vibe that is exchanged between human bodies. It does not refer to inanimate objects or non-human species. Those things may or may not give off vibes, but that's not what's being discussed here. Bodily emanation refers to the vibrational experience that occurs among human beings. With that in mind, bodily emanation can be broken down into three levels of experience: face-to-face interaction, the emanation of groups and crowds and global emanation.

Face-to-face interaction. We can feel each other's vibes while standing face to face. Vibes can be good or bad, attractive or repulsive, or even indifferent. But vibes are there — our bodies emanate them. The vibe can hit you, engulf you, enwrap you, flirt with you, seduce you, attract you or even repulse you. Regardless of the specific experience, it's there and detectable. You should also realize that your own body gives off a vibe. This is sometimes harder to detect, but it becomes easier with practice. You will sometimes feel your bodily emanation growing outward, literally getting bigger and wider and taking up more space. That's *your* bodily emanation. You can feel your own body and other bodies emanating vibes. It's a two-way process.

Groups and crowds. Bodily emanation also works in groups and crowds. Groups and crowds often have more feeling, more emanation, more vibe. That's because there are more bodies: more bodies equal more emanation. On one level, we feel the emanation of the group or crowd, while on another level, we contribute to it. Like above, it's a two-way process. You feel the crowd and the crowd feels you. This occurs at parties, concerts, gatherings, meetings, protests, spokescouncils, conferences and other events; and it occurs within classrooms, churches, stores, restaurants, auditoriums, and even within neighborhoods, towns and cities. People's bodies vibrationally respond to one another when placed in close proximity. Each body emanates a vibe and together the bodies produce a collective vibe. These collective vibes help explain the synchronicity of smart mobs, flash mobs, Black Blocs, snake marches, street festivals, etc. These events produce collective vibes that participants use to navigate streets, barriers, obstacles and police. The collective vibe is not the be-all and end-all explanation to such synchronized actions, but it does provide an insightful, if only partial, answer.

Global emanation. Detecting bodily emanation on a global level is much more difficult. In many ways this is a logical extension of what's been said already. If each body emanates a vibe, and there are bodies all across the world, then there must be a global vibe. But can we *detect* that global vibe? Yes and no. Many different people of many different backgrounds have talked about going with the flow or following the vibe. These statements imply a human vibe or global vibe — some type of vibrational flow spanning geographical space. We may not be able to consciously feel that global emanation, but we intuitively sense and understand it. For example, we often use the vibe to explain moments of coincidence or synchronicity. We experience those moments and aren't sure what happened. But later on we stop, think and chalk it up to "the vibe." In other words, the global flow put us in the right place at the right time. We didn't really feel the global vibe at a conscious level. It's not like face-to-face interaction or a group or crowd; we don't stand there and consciously feel it. Instead, it's like fish swimming in water. It's everywhere all the time and we simply take it for granted. It's so common that we never even question it. But yet it's there, all around us, constantly breathing, pulsating and self-producing a vibrational flow. If all this is true, then the global vibe can help explain such things as global uprisings, transcontinental synchronicities, the political upheavals of 1968, the events of Seattle, 1999, and the global intentions of the global justice movement. Global emanation can even be used to rearticulate a popular phrase from the 1960s, "You don't need a weatherman to know which way the wind blows."[4] In other words, just follow the vibe and let it happen — revolution is on the way! If that has any truth to it whatsoever, then we should find ways to consciously use the vibe for political purposes. Feel it, understand it and use it to generate revolutionary excitement.

Learning to Communicate with the Vibe

Learning how to use the vibe can be extremely helpful for activists and organizers. You can use it to help facilitate meetings and spokescouncils, judge and respond to rallies, solicit petition signatures, judge the intentions of riot police, participate in snake marches and flash mobs, avoid arrest, arouse or quiet audiences, empathize with others and increase and deepen solidarity. The vibe is helpful anytime you're communicating with other people. You can improve your vibrational communication by doing three things: attuning yourself to bodily emanation, correlating your bodily emanation and psychological and emotional intentions and learning to use the vibe ethically.

Bodily attunement. Communicating with the vibe begins with bodily attunement. This involves two sides: attuning yourself to your own bodily emanation and attuning yourself to the bodily emanation of others. First, become more aware of your own vibe. Feel your vibe moving from the inside to the outside of your body. Feel it pulsate when you get angry or upset. Feel it sink during moments of disappointment. Feel it jump out during surprise. Feel it heat up with passion. Feel it grow with inspiration. Feel it breathing as you move through the world. Becoming more attuned to your bodily being in the world helps you feel your own vibe, which is the first step to vibrational communication. You need to feel it in order to use it.

Then second, become more aware of other people's vibes. As noted above, this is difficult on the global level, but it's fairly easy with face-to-face interaction and groups and crowds. Next time you attend a protest or speaking event, see if you can feel the emanation of the crowd or the speaker. You'll obviously see and respond to people's verbal and nonverbal communication. But try to focus on the bodily emanation. The vibe won't be seen, but it will be felt. Feel the vibes coming off people's bodies and notice how your body responds to their vibes. Get in touch with your body's vibrational experience, allowing yourself to feel it. This becomes easier with time and experience. The more you train yourself, the more attuned you become to bodily emanation. You want to increase your vibrational sensitivity. This will enable you to consciously use it.

Psychological and emotional intention. Your psychological and emotional intentions are major factors of vibrational communication. On one level, your body constantly emanates a vibe, and that is unintentional. It simply happens. But on another level, your body communicates specific types of vibes. Those vibes are based on your intentions of being nice, mean, friendly, shy, standoffish, happy, supportive, defensive and so on. You want to correlate your bodily emanation and psychological and emotional intentions. Learning how to do this enables you to communicate your intentions through your bodily vibrations. Giving off the right vibe at the right time lets people know what you're feeling. This type of communication is rhetorically beneficial because it magnetically attracts people to you. People feel what you feel, and they are drawn to that experience. This helps during speeches, street theater and protests. It's also helpful for large, collective actions where everyone is giving off a similar vibe. That can be quite powerful.

You can also do the reverse and attune yourself to the vibrational intentions of others. This allows you to understand their intentions without them having to say anything. Such communication provides insights that otherwise are unavailable. It lets you know when to step up or step back, when to speak or remain quiet, what to say and how to say it, when to stand your ground and when to walk away and when to lend support or keep your distance. Realize, though, that your interpretation of someone's vibe can be wrong or inaccurate. You may think they are intending something when in fact they are not. Such vibrational miscommunication can be hazardous because the other person is not expecting or asking for your input. Keep that in mind and be cautious with your vibrational interpretations.

Ethical issues. Some people may question the ethics of vibrational communication. Is it ethical to use your vibe to persuade or mobilize people? Is vibrational communication too subliminal and thus shady? Is the vibe a form of trickery? All this depends on how and why you're using it. Using your vibe to convince people against their wishes is unethical, but that's true of any rhetorical device. However, using your vibe to open people's minds to the possibility of social change is perfectly fine. Just as speech and language can be used ethically and unethically, so too can the vibe and bodily emanation. Think of vibrational communication as a skill. Once you learn it you don't forget it. The ethics of that use is then up to each person and situation. Learning to use your vibe also helps you fend off the unethical intentions of others. It makes you more aware of vibrational tricks, which is empowering. That seems pretty ethical.

The Vibe as Embodied Rhetoric

As can be seen, the vibe is a form of embodied rhetoric that is used in many different situations. It's fairly common during spokescouncils and other large group discussions to designate a "vibe watcher." That person monitors participants' vibes, making sure that people don't get too upset or out of hand. Similar practices can be used in other situations. We can have "vibe watchers" and "vibe generators" at our protests, rallies and actions. These people can monitor the crowd's vibe and guide or, if need be, arouse that vibe. As group facilitators, we can attune ourselves to the group's vibe and use that awareness to move the conversation forward, speed up or slow down discussion and address issues people want to discuss but are afraid to ask. As public speakers we can use the vibe to increase credibility and charisma and to inspire and motivate action. As street performers we can increase the magnitude of our vibes, thus soliciting attention and increasing crowd size. During political debate we can attune ourselves to the vibe, thus increasing our own bodily presence and becoming more aware of the other person's intentions. If we're being arrested after an action, we can use our vibes to promote and maintain positive attitudes and to facilitate jail solidarity. During smart mobs, flash mobs, snake marches and Black Blocs, we can collectively attune our vibes to produce more synchronized and thus more powerful actions. As everyday people in the world, we can use our vibes to uplift the attitudes and spirits of our communities. And if enough communities do this, we can uplift the attitudes and spirits of national and international populations. We can even create a revolutionary vibe, leading to synchronized actions across the planet. Some of this may seem esoteric, irrational or over-imaginative. But if bodily emanation is real, then it can and should be used as a rhetorical device for changing the world.

Twenty-First Century Radical Rhetoric

The twenty-first century is just beginning and the future is unpredictable. Who knows what will be occurring fifty, sixty or one hundred years from now. But our current actions are hopefully laying the groundwork for a more radical, liberatory century — a century in which our dreams and visions become realities. To do that, we need to understand and then improve upon what we are currently doing, and then create new rhetorical approaches suitable for twenty-first century change. This isn't easy to do. We often get comfortable with rehashed ideas and overdone practices. Such familiarity then hinders our progress. But we must be conscious of these pitfalls and be willing to take risks.

The chapter begins with ten observations that help us understand some common rhetorical practices of contemporary activists. We then discuss how we can use these observations to mend the rhetorical gap between our actions and the public's reception of those actions. This issue was originally raised in the opening chapter. We now return to it with a better understanding of rhetoric. We then discuss the nature of network rhetoric, which is a paradigmatic figure of contemporary activism. We also discuss ways to improve our network rhetoric and the need to develop new forms of rhetoric that advance our radical projects. The chapter ends by proposing a new approach to radicalism based on the communicative labors of activism. This new approach is called "neo-radicalism" and it summarizes the intent and purpose of rhetoric for radicals.

The Rhetoric of Contemporary Activism

Social movements, political cultures and even small groups of activists exhibit rhetorical commonalities. For instance, the United States civil rights movement was laden with religious symbolism, urgency of the moment and calls to racial justice. European anti-nuclear autonomous groups of the 1980s embodied countercultural and anti-capitalist sentiments and prefigured the Black Bloc tactics. And third-wave feminism emphasizes anti-essentialist arguments, diversity of female identities and the micro-politics of gender and sexual relations. This section makes similar observations of anti-authoritarian, globally ambitious, post-Seattle activism since 1999. Based on my own experience as an activist as well as my knowledge of various books, magazines, websites, videos and so on, I provide ten observations for understanding the rhetoric of contemporary activists. These are by no means exhaustive and I am not trying to speak for anyone. Instead, I hope they resonate with your own experience. If that's true, then you can use these observations to improve your own rhetorical practice.

Our Rhetoric is Anti-Authoritarian

Contemporary, cutting-edge activism is heavily influenced by anti-authoritarianism. Some other possible descriptions might include non-authoritarian, non-hierarchical, horizontal, decentered and networked activism. Anti-authoritarianism tries to create a truly egalitarian society by eliminating hierarchical power structures. In terms of organizational structure, activists link themselves together into affinity groups. These affinity groups then execute autonomous actions that are horizontally linked to a wider plan or goal. Activists can act independently or in conjunction with the wider collective. Affinity groups can also create larger groupings, such as clusters and blocs. No actual leaders exist; only facilitators, organizers, point people or other temporarily designated roles. The anti-authoritarian structure is not necessarily new, but it has been revised and updated by contemporary feminists, anarchists, autonomists, anti-capitalists and global justice activists. Anti-authoritarian activism also engenders its own form of rhetoric that is non-hierarchical, decentered and dialogical. Ideally, no speaker, author, organizer or "body" is seen as more or less powerful; every person is given the opportunity to communicate; and people commonly dialogue until mutual understanding and even consensus are reached. This type of anti-authoritarian communication occurs at spokescouncils, social forums, conferences, organizational meetings, protests, and on websites, listservs and blogs. While anti-authoritarianism is commonly associated with younger Caucasian anarchists, it is found across the world, spanning different ages, races, cultures and political identities.

Our Rhetoric Promotes Diversity

It is difficult to find a publication, talk, speech or movement that does not in some way mention diversity appreciation. This is inherent to our times and movements; the plethora of actors, agents and agendas necessitates a discourse of diversity. But this is not diversity for the sake of diversity. Instead, our rhetoric highlights diversity as beneficial to the individual and to the collective. At the individual level, each person is a composite of multiple experiences, knowledges and actions. Each person is in a sense diversified. And encountering and experiencing greater diversity will usually make us worldlier, allowing us to become more knowledgeable and more appreciative of the world's differences. At the collective level, a multiplicity of individuals standing in relation to one another is more productive and powerful than single individuals standing alone. This collective power and action then necessitates an appreciation of diversity. We cannot work toward common goals of liberation if we do not respect and appreciate one another. In many ways this appreciation of diversity is something we value as activists. But as mentioned throughout this book, rhetoric and values cannot be easily separated. Our values can be identified through an analysis of our rhetoric, and our rhetorical practices materialize our values. The two are reciprocal. Thus, our valuing of diversity and our rhetoric of diversity are really one and the same. We talk about diversity and we invite and appreciate different types of talk.

Our Rhetoric is Idealistic and Prefigurative

Our rhetoric is idealistic in two ways. First, our rhetoric espouses social justice for all. This idealism permeates our protests, demonstrations, writings, talks, symbols, styles and actions. And second, our rhetoric is prefigurative. In other words, our words and actions try to invoke structures, practices, relations and values that do not currently exist. For instance, feminist rhetoric prefigures gender equality and matriarchal values while living in a patriarchal, gender-exclusive society. Racial justice rhetoric prefigures equal appreciation and opportunity for all races and racial backgrounds while existing within a racist society. And freegan rhetoric prefigures non-capitalistic consumption while existing within a capitalist consumer society. In each of these cases, prefigured realities are evoked not simply by what people do or how people organize, but also by our rhetorical approaches, ideas, symbolisms and communicative labors. Contemporary activist rhetoric leans toward the prefigurement of improved social and global realities. Such prefigurement imbues our rhetoric with hope, drive and a healthy belief that we can change the world.

Our Rhetoric is Multi-Historical

We reject the idea that any single history can encapsulate the antecedents of all people, of all places and times. We replace the *hi-story* with multiple and diffuse *low-stories*. Each culture, movement and idea emerges from a diversity of people, experiences and narratives. This perspective obviously relates to our rhetoric of anti-authoritarianism, diversity, etc. There is too much going on to rely upon or refer to a single story or a single author for understanding social justice and global revolution. This multi-historicism helps explain the difficulty of answering the commonly asked questions: Where's your representational text? Who is your spokesperson? What is your goal? Who and what do you represent? These questions are difficult to answer from a multi-historical framework. Our rhetoric looks for the manifold rather than a single or monolithic answer. We search for the intricacies of relationships and then complicate such questions. We refuse to accept that one narrative, or one person or one whatever can tell *the* story of our decentered struggles.

Our Rhetoric is Anti-Representational

Our rhetoric is anti-representational in two ways. First, we recognize that no rhetoric can fully represent another's experience; all personal, cultural and political representation is inherently limited. We thus avoid representing others and allow them to represent themselves. That's the whole point of direct democracy — to allow people to make their own political decisions. This is different from representational democracy in which people act and speak through proxies. Direct democracy is a cornerstone of our organizing practices. At meetings, we ask people of traditionally underprivileged or marginalized backgrounds to speak first and longest. We also rotate meeting facilitators and allow everyone's concerns and ideas to be heard. For our events, we invite a variety of people to help organize and speak, trying to generate a diversity of perspectives. These practices are anti-monolithic; no single representation dominates. And second, our rhetoric is creative rather than representational. This is a major theme throughout this book: language, symbols and embodied actions do not simply re-present but rather create reality and experience. There are obviously times when we narrate events and communicate messages in order to report and convey stories of crime, atrocity, liberation and struggle. But narrating an event does not simply represent that event. The form and content of the narrative helps to create a communicative experience of the narrated event. Our rhetoric creates rather than represents reality.

Our Rhetoric Privileges Complex Interrogation

Our rhetoric privileges complex interrogation rather than simple answers. This is evidenced by many of our practices. For example, our discussions challenge one another to reflect upon our own taken-for-granted assumptions. Our meetings commonly end with temporary and tenuous consensus rather than final answers. And we opt for informed, substantive analyses rather than quick, pre-packaged corporate answers. Our communication is not necessarily complex — we like to communicate in ways that everyone can understand. But we recognize the complexity of the world. Society, politics, and human experience are composed of manifold entanglements. Drawing upon one aspect unravels a web of relations. Our identities, knowledges, cultures, struggles and liberations are interconnected and systemic. We seek to break open and interrogate those relations. This worldview helps explain the public's skepticism of our actions and movements. Most people are unaccustomed to serious critical reflection and thus feel alienated by our complex interrogations.

Our Rhetoric is Symbolically Powerful

We seriously consider the use, effects and oppressive or liberatory powers of symbols. For instance, we often critique and reject particular logos, labels, brands and corporate symbols. We also practice culture jamming, adbusting and billboard liberation, and often investigate and explore the nature of mental ecologies, psychological environments and art and protest. Naomi Klein's *No Logo* and Kalle Lasn's *Culture Jam* have been best sellers within our communities. Guy Debord and the Situationists, with their emphasis on cultural and aesthetic *detournement*, are commonly referenced. And our demonstrations are saturated with symbols — the puppets, costumes, signs, slogans and placards are rhetorical forces. The same is true of our direct actions. Any good direct action strategically plots its symbolism: what is the action, where will it take place, at what time, for which audience and for what purpose? A direct action often seeks to physically intervene in the daily operations of an institution or group of people. We might clog a traffic intersection, occupy a building or shut down a business district. Such actions directly interfere with systems of power. But such actions are also symbolic, and that symbolism may be more important than the physical interference. A direct action will last for a few hours, maybe even a few days. During that time all operations of an intersection, city, business or even military regime will shut down. But those operations will most likely resume at some point. However, the symbolic force of that action carries on, circulating through the communicative engines of society. That message will hopefully catch wind, motivating other people to take similar actions.

Our Rhetoric is Confrontational

Our confrontational rhetoric often involves yelling, screaming, shouting, stomping, clapping, drumming, fists in the air, Black Blocs, loud slogans, passionate manifestos and declamatory speeches. *Clamor*, a now defunct post-1999 Seattle magazine, said it well: "An iconoclast among its peers, *Clamor* is an unabashed celebration of self-determination, creativity, and shit-stirring."[1] While this passionate and unapologetic attitude permeates our rhetoric, it should not be reduced to negativity or militancy. We might be loud and angry at times, but we are also quiet, solemn, cheerful, romantic, happy, celebratory and even festive. Many activists use silent die-ins, peace vigils, pacifism, meditation and humorous antics. Many activists are also approachable and inviting, preferring dialogue over verbal duel. These subtler attitudes are also confrontational, just in different ways. Confrontational rhetoric is about speaking truth to power and confronting and eradicating all forms of oppression. How we do that is relative to each activist and situation. Sometimes it's upfront and aggressive, other times it's laidback and subtle, but it's confrontational nonetheless.

Our Rhetoric is Visionary

Our rhetoric is driven by visions of a better world. We realize that what we do now creates a better and presumably more democratic future. We don't think of ourselves as actual visionaries. Such loftiness contradicts our decentered, diverse and multi-historical rhetoric. We're also not utopian. No one thinks we can right *all* the wrongs and live happily ever after. However, we do believe that we can do better; that we can replace current systems and structures with better ones; that we can become more ethical and humane social beings; and that we can do a better job of respecting ourselves, each other and our social and natural worlds. These are not simply ideals, but envisioned realities of the future. We can see these realities in our hearts and minds. Many of us have caught fleeting glimpses of this future during protests, conferences, gatherings, forums and festivals. Those glimpses may be brief, but they are there nonetheless — momentary experiences of something new, exciting and radically democratic. These experiences point to a different world, one composed of self-determination, interpersonal and collective support and egalitarian relations.

Our Rhetoric is Self-Righteous *and* Self-Critical

Our rhetoric is simultaneously self-righteous and self-critical. We want to change the world and we think we know how. Such righteousness is common to most activists, organizers and social movements. That's understandable — we obviously need to believe in ourselves if we want to change the world. But our righteousness resists over-inflated self-importance. There are no easy answers and there are no straight and narrow paths. Social justice takes many forms and posits no final or foreclosed utopian results. Our age of postmodern criticism balances our idealism with a brutal realism: we are fallible, everyday people, subject to the whims and mistakes of being human. While we are calling out injustice, we also realize that we might be perpetuating other injustices that we have not yet understood or recognized. We tend to look back upon previous social and political movements and analyze their particular wrongdoings: the self-destructive tendencies of the United States' Weather Underground and Italy's Red Brigades, the sexism of organizing in the anti-Vietnam war era, the racist exclusions of second-wave feminism, etc. But we also realize that future generations will look back on our movements and make similar assessments. They will ask, "How could they not have realized that they were…?" We cannot foresee how future generations will assess us, but such critical awareness humbles us nonetheless. So yes, we are self-righteous, but we are also self-reflective. Our critical righteousness is one reason why we are wary of vanguard parties. We all want a revolution and we all think we have the answers but we realize that our answers are specific to our own time and place. We thus conclude that each person and each community must revolutionize their own realities. We can and often do help each other whenever and however possible; but no one person, group or rhetoric holds the answer for all people of all places and times. Our self-righteousness is kept in check by our self-reflective criticality. This rhetorical tendency is evidenced by some concrete examples: John Holloway's *Change the World Without Taking Power;* Starhawk's distinctions among power-over, power from within, and power-with; and the call by Subcomandante Marcos to listen to rather than lead the indigenous populations of Chiapas, Mexico.[2] Critical righteousness obviously overlaps with many of the rhetorics mentioned above: anti-authoritarian, diverse, multi-historical, anti-representational, and complex interrogation.

Using these Observations to Mend the Gap

Chapter One discussed the rhetorical gap between our actions and the public's reception of those actions. The above observations can help mend that gap by allowing us to see our rhetoric in action. We can then figure out what works and what doesn't and then adjust to various situations. You might realize, for instance, that complex interrogation alienates some audiences. Particular audiences may not be used to it, so they shut down and tune out. Your message won't be heard. Understanding why they're tuning out helps you address and adjust to the problem. You don't have to eliminate your complex questioning; you simply have to adjust it to the wants and needs of your audience. Making it more attractive and less alienating reduces the gap between your actions and people's reception of those actions. Here are five suggestions for mending that gap.

Specify your audience. The "general public" sounds good but it's too broad. Yes, our actions often target the general public, especially with larger actions and protests. But specifying your target audience helps you communicate with actual people rather than an amorphous mass. For example, large anti-war protests often target four particular groups: policy makers, supporters of the war, people who are on the fence about the war and people who are against the war but not active. As can be seen, these four targets include just about everyone. In a sense, then, the protest *is* targeting the general public. But that classification is too loose and undefined; it doesn't help you create a rhetorically effective protest. Specifying those four target audiences concretizes your rhetoric; it gives you something specific to work with. Your protest now addresses actual people rather than amorphous masses. *Who exactly are you trying to reach with this specific rhetorical act?* Choose your audience(s) and adapt your rhetoric to their specific biases, wants, needs and expectations. This helps you create more effective actions and messages.

Make adjustments. Adjust your rhetoric to fit the wants and needs of your audience. This is not about eliminating your common tendencies of, say, diversity, multi-historicism or idealism. Instead, it's about negotiating your rhetoric. You want to find ways to attract rather than alienate your audience. For example, you might have an audience that is receptive to anti-authoritarian rhetoric but turned off by self-righteousness. Although you feel that your self-righteousness is also self-critical, your audience doesn't see that. If that's the case, then emphasize the anti-authoritarianism and downplay the self-righteousness. Feel free to create decentered, anti-hierarchical slogans, symbols and actions that tie together many messages, but do so with humility, modesty and reserve. Many activists missed this type of strategy in the wake of September 11. The social and political conditions suddenly changed, but the rhetoric remained the same. Many activists wanted to maintain the aggressive, in-your-face rhetoric of the global justice movement. That's understandable since we could see the majority of Americans following the Bush Administration into an era of imperialist domination. But American citizens were not ready for confrontational rhetoric. They didn't want to hear about their government's funding of the Mujahadin and theories of blowback. They didn't want to be confronted by notions of personal or national responsibility. They didn't want complex interrogation. Instead, they simply wanted to get on board and charge ahead. Adjusting to these conditions was (and is) absolutely necessary. I think the "Not in Our Name" coalition, which began approximately six months after 9/11, did a very good job of adjusting. That phrase, "Not in our name," is assertive and declarative without being accusatory. It makes a statement without making people defensive. This kind of rhetorical adjustment increases the chances of people actually stopping, thinking and hopefully changing their ways.

Name and explain your rhetoric. People often fear what they don't understand, and most people don't understand why activists do what they do. You can address this problem by naming and explaining your rhetoric. This is not the same as explaining your politics. The two are obviously related, but you're trying to explain your rhetorical choices of doing, say, a protest or action. Perhaps you're organizing a protest to stop animal testing. Your political explanation would then address the brutal and unnecessary treatment of animals. Your rhetorical explanation would address the importance of collective and public argumentation. You might explain, then, that a collective argument is more empowering and potentially more effective than writing letters to animal testing centers. Such rhetorical explanations should involve words, concepts, and phrases that properly label your rhetoric. Words like network rhetoric, embodied rhetoric, swarm rhetoric, collective argumentation, communicative and imaginative labor clarify your actions to others, helping them understand what they are seeing. This can reduce fear and attract rather than alienate people. You can also take the time to explain the nature and purpose of your rhetoric. This can be done in several ways. During a speech, take the time to explain your emphasis on diversity or multi-historical perspectives. Do the same in your essays, books, blogs and fliers. You can also do it during interviews, press conferences or opening plenary sessions of conferences. You can also designate people as "explainers" during protests and actions. These people can explain not just the political goals of the protest, but also the rhetorical choices of the protest. What is the rhetorical benefit of doing *this* protest? Why are there so many different messages present at a single protest? Why don't you lobby your congressional representative or run for office? These questions can be addressed during street conversations and interviews or through fliers and handouts distributed to onlookers and reporters. Also realize that designated explainers are not leaders or even spokespersons. The explainers can be democratically selected by protest participants and the explanations can be collectively drafted. The explainers then facilitate dialogue and understanding between protesters and observers.

Make more observations. The ten observations outlined in the previous section are by no means the final word. Other observations can and should be made by a variety of activists using various rhetorical approaches. I personally struggled with them: what type of groupings do I create and what do I include and exclude? I could have easily described our rhetoric as *processual*, meaning it seeks no final answers or destinations, and as *interpersonal*, meaning it privileges the personal and subjective voice over the scientifically detached voice. These struggles highlight the relativity of observations. You, too, can make your own observations. So go out, look around, reflect upon what you and others are doing and catalogue your observations. Then most importantly, *share* your observations. This helps other activists improve their rhetoric. Here are some brief guidelines for doing this.[3] First, be respectful. Realize that your observations are just that — your observations. Your perspective could be very different from others', so be reflective and cautious. Second, spend time in the world you are observing. Be an activist who observes rather than an outsider who simply watches. Experiencing the rhetorical rigors first-hand helps you understand and then communicate your observations. Third, be honest. Avoid exaggerating what you see. We sometimes want to romanticize our experiences. Such romanticism has its time and place, but here you're trying to help us improve our hands-on practices. Tell it like it is rather than how you imagine it. And fourth, provide supportive criticism. Don't be afraid to comment on what you see. Provide feedback, debate the utility of a message or rhetorical approach, etc. But also be supportive. We're all doing the best we can. Sometimes we succeed and sometimes we fail. Criticism without support is destructive rather than constructive. Your observations should be helpful rather than judgmental.

Take personal responsibility. We neither have nor want any rhetorical leaders. For this approach to succeed, each activist must assume rhetorical responsibility. What you say and do reflects upon other activists and organizers. Your own rhetoric can either strengthen or weaken the success of others. A poorly executed action in Canada travels through media channels and affects activists in Argentina.

We don't have to agree on every issue, message or tactic. But each of us should make concerted efforts to continuously improve our rhetorical labors. This is disputable, of course. For example, some activists may reject the whole idea that we should try to improve our communication and rhetoric. That's fine and simply enriches our activist discussions. But those activists who do agree that rhetorical improvement is important must take responsibility for their communicative effects. Each of us taking responsibility eliminates the need for rhetorical leaders. We thus take one step closer to a leaderless world.

Network Rhetoric

Network rhetoric is a paradigmatic figure of contemporary activism. It is very common for speakers, authors, movements, collectives, gatherings, periodicals, publications and websites to use versions of the following phrases: networks of activists, webs of struggle, nodes of resistance, interlocking systems of oppressions, wheels of influence and a movement of movements. These phrases are not exactly the same, but there is an underlying conception of contemporary radicalism as decentered, interconnected and networked. This structure also applies to our communication, giving rise to network rhetoric. Network rhetoric could have easily been one of the ten observations above. But due to its importance, it warrants extended discussion.

This section is divided into three parts. First, we discuss some examples of network rhetoric. Second, we discuss how to improve our network rhetoric. And third, we discuss the need for new forms of rhetoric. If network rhetoric is being discussed in a book such as this, then its end is already in sight. We need to move beyond our era of networks and create something new, fresh and exciting.

Examples of Network Rhetoric

Network rhetoric is composed of three parts: multiple and decentered messages, dialogue among those messages and the formulation of a public statement, message or action. Network rhetoric begins with different people voicing their perspectives. There is a discussion, issue, problem or concern that people respond to. This generates a plethora of messages. No single message trumps another. Instead, multiple messages are horizontally related to one another. There is then a dialogue among messages. Rather than a single dogmatic message dominating discussion and action, we have multiple and even contentious and contradictory messages dialoguing around a general theme. That dialogue then creates a public phenomenon — a statement, message, articulation or action that others can see and respond to, that the media picks up on, that generates more activist discussion, and so on. This type of network rhetoric is common to Indymedia sites, social forums, protests, spokescouncils and individual presentations.

Indymedia. There are hundreds of autonomously run Indymedia websites dispersed throughout the world. Indymedia exemplify network rhetoric in two ways. First, each site provides a clearinghouse for various messages, stories and dialogue. Anyone can leave a post and anyone can respond to a post. That's a decentered, dialogical network. And second, each site uses its own design and content to respond to the general theme of "be the media." In a sense, then, the different sites dialogue around the issue of independently run, user supported media. This dialogue has created the Indymedia phenomenon.

Social forums. Social forums allow different campaigns, strategies, problems, issues and ideologies to dialogue with one another. Each presentation or workshop provides its own message, but those messages are dialoguing around common themes of social change, community building and learning and listening. The dialogues are not always friendly and supportive; heated debates can easily arise. But those debates, no matter how divisive, are still a form of dialogue. Social forum participants then bring their experiences back to their communities, which generates more dialogue. Social forums, by their very nature, create public statements that people can recognize and respond to. There have been worldwide, regional, national, statewide and local social forums. Each one creates its own network and each one links up to create a larger network.

Protests. The most energetic and inspiring protests of today are decentered and dialogically networked. These types of protests bring together diverse groups and multiple messages, generating a fuller and more complex public articulation. The counter-summit protests of the global justice movement are the best examples, but most large protests of today follow the network structure. There is usually a general issue such as war, corporate control, housing or global warming. Each issue involves various factors affecting multiple communities. Organizers thus invite different groups who speak to different aspects of the protested issue. This generates internal dialogue among activists and external dialogue between the activists and the general public. The general public often misses the method behind the madness and thus criticizes these protests for being disorganized and incoherent. Our protests *are* organized, but they are organized according to the non-linear and non-dogmatic principles of network rhetoric. Onlookers too often don't recognize the structure of dialogical networks and the democratic impetus of many messages speaking to the protested issue. We'll discuss below how to deal with this common misperception.

Spokescouncils. Spokescouncils enable many different people to participate in their own collective decision making. Usually, there is a large circle with a facilitator. Individual activists and members from different affinity groups are given the opportunity to voice concerns and contribute to the conversation. While these conversations can range from friendly discussions to full blown arguments, participants usually strive for some form of consensus, however tenuous and temporary that might be. Spokescouncils often focus on strategic issues, like what type of action to take and when and how to execute that action. Spokescouncils are also used to draft collective messages like themes, slogans or communiqués that become rallying points for action. Similar forms of communication are found in neighborhood assemblies, autonomous gatherings and directly democratic procedures of organizational meetings. In each case, the communication is decentered, dialogical and networked, and it usually moves toward some type of public action.

Individual presentations. Individual speakers and authors also use network rhetoric. This occurs in different ways. Michael Hardt and Antonio Negri's *Empire* and *Multitude* conceptualize the world as an expansive network composed of ever-shifting nodes of power. David Solnit's *Globalize Liberation* is an anthology of diverse people, groups and movements trying to change the global system. Marina Sitrin's *Horizontalism* collects diverse and sometimes contradictory first-hand accounts of Argentina's push for direct democracy. And *Left Turn* and *Z* magazines provide analyses highlighting the interconnections among geographically, culturally and politically diverse oppressions and liberations. Generally speaking, networked presentations weave together diverse and even seemingly incompatible elements, factors, analyses, voices and people.[4]

Improving Your Network Rhetoric

Improving your network rhetoric helps bridge the gap between your actions and the public's reception of those actions. Generally speaking, the public is not predisposed to network rhetoric. Sure, they are used to multiple messages. But very rarely do people draw lines of connection among those messages. Everything is thus isolated and disconnected. It is your responsibility to make your network rhetoric intelligible and appealing to others. You don't have to cease or circumscribe your network rhetoric, but you do have to improve it. Articulating network complexities is not easy, especially within the limited time and space of contemporary sound-bites. But three basic steps can make your network rhetoric more appealing and intelligible: rhetorical framing, highlighting the connections and stressing clarity and accessibility.

Create a rhetorical frame. Use a slogan, statement, theme or title that ties all the nodes together. This is known as a rhetorical frame, and it helps people understand the relationship among the different factors, voices, people, ideas and analyses. Larger events such as forums, conferences and protests are inherently framed — the framing is created by the stated purpose or title. For example, the World Social Forum of 2001 used "Another World is Possible!" And the

United States Social Forum of 2007 used "Another World is Possible, Another U.S. is Necessary." These slogans inherently frame the forums, allowing people to understand the underlying relationship among individual workshops, talks and speeches. These frames can always be improved, but generally speaking, larger, collective actions are usually well framed.

However, individual presentations don't always fare so well. This is not always the case; good speakers and authors know how to frame their works. But less experienced activists miss the importance of framing. Many activists raise a plethora of issues without using a frame. This confuses the audience. Just because *you* see all the connections does not mean that everyone else does. Listeners and readers get lost in your cross-connections and start asking questions. How are all the pieces related? What's the underlying point? How does it all fit together? Why is this person jumping all over the place? Rhetorical framing addresses these questions *before* they arise. Below are two suggestions for creating a good rhetorical frame.

Rhetorical frames can be created by summarizing the connections among the different issues into a single word, phrase or title. So, for instance, you might be speaking about US foreign policy, international relations, war, capitalism and the Middle East. These issues can be summarized into "The Geopolitics of Oil" or something like that. This frame helps people understand the underlying connections of your presentation. Such frames should be created before you begin your presentation. That helps you structure your talk, speech, teach-in or essay. Then, during the presentation, continuously emphasize the relationship between the individual issues and the overall frame. This helps others follow along.

Your rhetorical frame should also be concrete, catchy and general enough to attract wide audiences but narrow enough to highlight the important issue(s). Using the above example, we might say: The Geopolitics of Oil; The US Empire; War and Oil; Oil, Capitalism and Empire; The Black Gold of US Policy and Empire. These frames are like good titles — they help prepare the audience and it keeps both the audience *and* the presenter anchored in something specific. Drawing upon many different ideas can get confusing, especially for people who are unfamiliar with the intricacies of the issues. A good rhetorical frame makes your network rhetoric more intelligible and accessible.

Use categories to manage the connections. Network rhetoric is based on highlighting the connections among diverse people, ideas, voices, issues, etc. Activists encounter three common pitfalls when highlighting these connections. First, activists sometimes forget to highlight the connections at all. You see the connections and assume that others will, too. But not everyone sees the world through networked eyes. It is thus imperative that you highlight the connections for everyone else. Explain how the different issues are connected. Second, activists sometimes overemphasize the connections. The audience then gets lost in the details. Highlighting too many connections confuses people; they're not clear on the purpose or focus of your rhetoric. And third, highlighting connections can take up a lot of time, thus testing people's patience and attention spans. People won't listen forever. They will tune out and walk away if it's taking too long. Thus, keep to the major connections and cut out all the secondary or minor ones. This shortens your time, keeping people interested and mentally alert. These pitfalls of over-highlighting, under-highlighting, and taking too long can be solved by using categories. These categories, also referred to as topologies, help you highlight and manage the connections.

For instance, addressing corporate globalization can be organized into the following categories: multinational corporations, transnational institutions, free trade agreements and political and economic ideologies. These categories can help you structure speeches, essays, workshops or teach-ins. These categories can also be used to organize protests, with different participants focusing on different aspects. This can obviously be done with speakers. But it can also be done with different groups creating different signs, performances or mini-actions that symbolize the different categories. While organizing the protest, put out a call asking affinity groups to take on different categories. These categories help onlookers get a better sense of the different connections that drive corporate globalization, thus creating a more audience-friendly protest.

Strive for clarity and accessibility. Your network rhetoric should strive for as much clarity and accessibility as possible. What constitutes clarity and accessibility is, of course, relative to each audience, but we all have some sense of what this means. Do whatever you need to do to make your rhetoric intelligible to others. That might involve some previously mentioned suggestions, like specifying and adjusting to your audience and naming and explaining your rhetoric. Or it may involve rhetorical framing and the use of categories. Whatever you do, try to make your rhetoric as clear, manageable and intelligible as possible. Again, these descriptors are relative to the situation. Clarifying the intentions of a protest is different than clarifying a three-point logical essay, which is different than a teach-in, etc. This is all true, but the bottom line is this: confusion alienates people, and due to the complexity of network rhetoric, you must work against confusion and work toward clarity.

Moving Beyond Networks

Networks are here today, but will be gone tomorrow. The fact that we are discussing networks means that the end is already near. That's neither good nor bad but simply part of the process. The most cutting-edge structures, ideas and actions exist long before anyone takes notice. The newest actions usually occur prior to any conscious realization of them. People eventually take notice, then catalogue what's happening and begin debating the utility and effects of those actions. This is not to say that networks are no longer useful. The network rhetoric of direct democracy is occurring all over the world — Latin America, North America, Western and Eastern Europe and parts of Africa and Asia. People are experimenting with different forms of politics and communication. They're creating new ideas and structures and pushing the limits of possibility. But that's why we don't want to limit ourselves to network structures. Sure, networks are currently altering how we understand the world. But our struggles and liberations should not be confined to a network frame of mind. That's too stifling. We must be open to post-network rhetorics — structures that we have not yet encountered. Who knows what they will be? Perhaps such structures are already occurring.

New structures and paradigms usually begin with conflicts, challenges or impasses. We encounter a problem and are forced to do something different. We then find a way to overcome that problem. That response then leads to new ways of acting and thinking. We shouldn't seek out new problems just to create new paradigms. Instead, we want to be open to the possibility of responding to current problems in new and innovative ways. This keeps our activism fresh and inspiring. Such excitement then generates discussion, dialogue, and debate about what should be done and how we should do it. That's rhetoric for radicals.

Neo-Radicalism: A Proposal

This last section proposes a new form of activism, referred to as neo-radicalism. Neo-radicalism approaches activism as a communicative labor that prefigures new realities. This approach helps activists close the gap between their visions of the future and the realities of today. This entire book has been moving in this direction — for instance, how communication and rhetoric create reality, how we can speak, write or argue more effectively, how we can improve our rhetorical skills to change the world and how communication is a tool for activism. These insights and assertions are now summarized into the theory and practice of neo-radicalism.

In many ways neo-radicalism is not new. That's because activists already use communication to improve the world. This is evidenced by the symbolic concerns of direct actions, the use of speakers at rallies, the writing of manifestos, the strategic designs of websites and fliers and the ongoing critiques of words, phrases, languages and discourses. These communicative and rhetorical issues are usually secondary, though, to more material issues like securing land and agricultural rights, fighting for higher wages and safer jobs, obtaining healthcare, eradicating poverty, ending wars, and shutting down capitalist institutions. These issues are obviously important, but this sharp distinction between material conditions and immaterial communication is outdated. Activists inherently use communication to create better living conditions. Talk, discussion, debate, negotiation, lobbying, speaking, writing, text messaging, blogging, postering, graffitiing, marching and protesting are forms of communication. Even the act of thinking, which seems so introverted and solitary, is a communicative process. There is nothing that activists do that is not communicative. If that's true, then communication should be the lens by which we approach activism, radicalism and social change. Communication should be at the very center of activism. But of course that "center" is actually a decentered process of ongoing, open-ended creation. There is no finite center to communication, and that's one reason why it fits perfectly with contemporary radical activism.

The following sections provide an overview of neo-radicalism. I begin by outlining the experiences and ideas that influence my understanding of neo-radicalism. I then explain the process of creating revolutionary realities, which is at the heart of this project. And finally, I close with some loose guidelines for developing a neo-radical agenda. These explanations are preliminary rather than comprehensive. Much more thought, discussion, and reflection are needed for developing neo-radical theory and practice. But due to the nature of this book, it seems appropriate to end with an account of this communication-based activism.

Understanding Neo-Radicalism

My understanding of neo-radicalism emerges from five sources: my experience with anti-authoritarian activism, my observations of activists' communication, my understanding of communication as the creation of reality, my knowledge of twentieth-century Western philosophy, and my appreciation for radical visionaries.

Anti-authoritarian activism. My own activism began right after the events of Seattle, 1999. As I mentioned in the Preface, it was the IMF and World Bank protests of April, 2000 that attracted me to activism. I saw the news reporting of those events and I immediately identified with what was happening — people standing up for their beliefs, placing their bodies on the line and trying to change the world. Something in that moment evoked my radical impulse. It's tough to explain, but something pulled me in and set me off on a path of radical activism. I soon began researching globalization and started participating in the global justice movement. The anti-authoritarianism of that movement was new and at times even scary to me. There were different rules, expectations and communicative styles that I had not before encountered. But it always intrigued me and I now realize that I was and am attracted to the prefigurative nature of anti-authoritarianism. I interpret that prefigurative approach through the lens of communication: prefigurative politics seeks to communicate different worlds into existence. This interpretation is no doubt influenced by my academic training. I was still earning my doctorate as I began my activism, not finishing until May, 2002, approximately two years after my initial attraction to activism. I was studying the philosophy of communication.

Activists' communication. My schooling trained me to observe and analyze people's communication. That observational and analytical eye follows me into the world of activism and I can't help but analyze the speeches, discussions, arguments and symbols of rallies, meetings, conferences and actions. I see people interacting and I automatically analyze their communication. Because of that, I constantly see how activists can improve their communication skills. I see activists trying to articulate messages, audiences trying to follow along, petitioners trying to solicit attention, passersby trying to avoid eye contact and the embodied power relationships between activists and bureaucratic authorities. But I don't simply see areas for possible improvement. I also see people trying to evoke certain realities; people trying to communicatively create different worlds. This relates back to my understanding of prefigurative politics and the relationship between communication and reality. Each person is an embodied reality and each activist is trying to create a better reality. In my mind, that creative, activist impulse is communicatively based. Everything the activist does communicates toward a better world.

Communication and reality. I am trained in the philosophy of communication, which is a field of study that approaches communication as the creation of reality. It argues that communication is not simply a conveyor of information. Instead, communication actually creates our perceptions and understandings of that information. Thus, I see activists' communication as the attempt to create new and better realities. The very large majority of activists (and people in general) don't readily see this relationship between communication and reality. Communication is seen as a tool for talking and reality is understood as a cold, hard fact. People in general and activists in particular obviously believe in social change. But the relationship between communication and reality is often excluded from the equation. It's more common for activists to talk about people's movements and social change or coordinated action and structural change. I totally agree with these equations, but I also see another one: communication is the creation of reality; change the communication and you change the reality. This is my take on human existence in general and radical activism in particular.

Western philosophy. Many twentieth-century Western philosophers support the idea that communication creates reality. Sigmund Freud and Friedrich Nietzsche, two major influences on twentieth-century thought, argued in different ways that human perception shapes our understanding of the world. Even Karl Marx, a hardcore materialist, argued that human beings are creators rather than receivers of the world. These ideas have been expanded, updated and changed by many different strands of thought: phenomenology, existentialism, pragmatism, structuralism, psychoanalysis, critical theory, poststructuralism, postmodernism, cultural studies, third-wave feminism, media ecology, etc.

Some of the post-1968 French thinkers are particularly relevant for understanding the political implications of how communication creates reality. For instance, Michel Foucault's notion of biopower highlights relationships among human bodies, social discourses and the organization of societies. And Gilles Deleuze and Felix Guattari use the concept of the rhizome to articulate the infinitely varied processes that create social systems. These thinkers were influenced by the French rebellions of May 1968 and sought to create proto-anti-totalitarian philosophies — ways of seeing and thinking that fundamentally excluded the possibility of despotic, absolutist and dogmatic politics. Many of these ideas are politically fleshed out by Italy's Post-Workerists. People like Antonio Negri, Maurizio Lazzarato, Paolo Virno and Giorgio Agamben personally knew many of the post-'68 thinkers and even lived in France. These Italian thinkers thus combine French philosophy and radical Italian politics to create concepts like empire, multitude and immaterial labor. This long tradition has affected my own thinking about communication, the creation of reality and the possibility of social change.

Visionaries. While many of the above ideas coincide with anti-authoritarian activism, many of them also fall short. In brief, many big-time Western thinkers are great for critiquing society but horrible at envisioning a better society. This may explain why many (but surely not all) activists shy away from philosophy and turn to, for instance, Marxism, anarchism and Zapatismo. These systems or "approaches" are rooted in the idea that we can and should change the world. They also provide hands-on steps or at least some guidelines for doing so. Marxism, anarchism and Zapatismo are thus visionary projects. But I believe the last one, Zapatismo, is the most pertinent for today's activists.

Zapatismo is a non-ideological, non-absolutist political way of life that responds to a major paradigm of today: neoliberal economics. In an age of absolute capitalism, the Zapatistas provide a globally conscious yet decentered and prefigurative response. This probably explains Zapatismo's popularity with anti-authoritarian activists. But it also helps explain the relationship between communication and radical social change. In short, the Zapatistas have labored communicatively toward the prefigurement of a better reality, one that directly challenges global capitalism. Their vision of a free, self-determining reality is not yet fully achieved and their reality is still under attack from a variety of powers. But they keep working and communicating toward an open-ended reality of Zapatismo. As Subcomandante Marcos once said: "In our dreams we have seen another world… This world was not a dream from the past, it was not something that came to us from our ancestors. It came from ahead, from the next step we were going to take."[5] In other words, they intuitively understand their desired reality and will create it by walking toward it. This visionary impulse resonates with my approach to neo-radicalism and the call to communicate new realities into existence.

Creating Revolutionary Realities

Neo-radicalism approaches activism as a reality-creating activity. It asks activists to use their communication skills to change currently existing realities and to create new and improved realities. This is not foreign to radical activism. Our social forums, conferences, protests, parades, carnivals, festivals and even small, intimate meetings and spokescouncils often evoke a sense of difference, a sense that something is happening here and now. From my own experience, that sense is the evocation of an alternative reality. We can feel and intuitively understand when these different realities are surfacing. That's because our perceptions, understandings and orientations shift, and we start seeing, thinking and acting differently. It's not that we become totally different people. Instead, our behaviors, thoughts and communicative styles adjust to the surrounding circumstances. Different desires and biases are suddenly accepted and even expected. For a brief time we are allowed and encouraged to *see* the intersections of different systems, to *envision* better societies, to *enact* anti-authoritarian characteristics, to *be* confrontational or self-righteous and to *talk* about and *demand* revolution. These experiences inevitably evoke — that is, prefigure — different realities.

These alternative realities could be understood as "temporary autonomous zones," a phrase that is often attributed to anarchist and theorist, Hakim Bey.[6] While this phrase is helpful and insightful, I prefer to use the phrase "revolutionary realities." There are three reasons for this. First, it accentuates the fluidity and ongoing nature of reality creation. While these alternative realities may be temporary, the process of creating reality is ongoing and perpetual. We're always creating realities, some of which perpetuate common and predominant realities while others are alternative or even revolutionary. Second, it highlights the insurgent, revolutionary nature of prefigured radical realities. These prefigured realities directly challenge the existence of all other pre-established realities. If prefigured realities are possible, then all current realities can be challenged, uprooted and usurped. And third, it attempts to alter and advance our approach to resistance, liberation, activism and revolution. In other words, my use of "revolutionary realities" tries to reconceptualize new possibilities for radical activity. That's also a motivation for my use of neo-radicalism: I am trying to create space for new types of thought and action.

If all of this is accurate, then we need to sharpen our reality-creating skills to the best of our abilities. This entire book underscores that idea in some way, shape or form, giving instruction on how to use your verbal and nonverbal communication to speak, write and embody different realities into existence. But these basic skills must be narrowed and focused into reality-creating tactics of neo-radicalism. For now, and in the little room we have left, how to do this will be divided into two steps: manifesting your desires and speaking to the desires of others.

Manifesting your Desires

You must embody the reality you desire. As you do so, your perception and understanding shifts and you begin to see the world differently. The hard, cold facts of the world still exist, but your orientation to those facts is different. For instance, you no longer see the United States of America as a benevolent caretaker of the world but as an imperialist superpower built on greed and self-preservation. You no longer see capitalism as an open and fair competition among self-interested individuals but as a vicious and brutal system in which the powerful feed on the less fortunate. You no longer see gender, race and sexual identities as natural and essential but as socially constructed categories involving issues of power, liberation and oppression. You no longer see homelessness, hunger and poverty as unfortunate mishaps of an otherwise ethical society but as direct results of inherently unjust systems, structures and institutions. You no longer see revolution as a crazy and impossible idea but as a possible and necessary movement toward a better, though never perfect, world. These perceptual alterations emerge as you embody your ideals and desires and become an activist bent on creating better realities. Seeing, thinking and acting differently evokes a reality that you then live out and create.

Living your politics means different things to different people. It can mean completely withdrawing from current social systems or it can mean doing the best you can within them. Regardless of which path you take, the underlying issue is the same: realities are created by embodying and living out your desires. You can, of course, change and live out different desires. This happens with beginning activists who start out seeking liberal gains, but over time become more and more radical. They start altering their lifestyles, taking more radical actions and demanding more radical changes as their understanding of social problems becomes more intricate. They are now living out different realities. This can go the other way, too. Long time activists can become burned out and worn down by overdemanding, low paying jobs. They then leave the grassroots for more secure and stable livelihoods. They are now living out different desires and creating different realities.

These scenarios underscore the labors of reality. Creating reality is hard work. We, of course, take it for granted because it's inherent to the human species. We do it without question or pause. It never consciously dawns on us that reality is a creative, belaboring process. But changing your reality or pursuing alternative and especially revolutionary realities spotlights that process. You suddenly realize the laboriousness of reality. That is perhaps one unconscious reason why most people avoid recreating their realities. They prefer to accept and live out the common and accepted realities of racism, sexism, capitalism, war, greed, control and institutionalized life. People don't necessarily like these realities, but resisting or changing them is hard work. It takes time, patience and conscious effort. It can also involve conflict. Realities are imbued with power relations, meaning that some people benefit and some people suffer. Those who are empowered don't want to give that up. They don't want to confront their personal privileges and they surely don't want to confront the privileges of others. Their lives are made easier by avoiding, denying or simply accepting these unjust realities. There are people, of course, who are open to confrontation and conflict. Those people are usually called radicals. Radicals don't necessarily *want* confrontation and conflict, but they are open to it because the possibility of social justice is worth the risk, trouble and labor.

Realize, too, that some desires and realities are riskier than others. For example, following a transgendered desire is often more difficult than following *just* a masculine or *just* a feminine desire. That's because wider populations misunderstand and fear transgenderism, which produces marginalization and discrimination. Transgenderism is thus a risky reality to embody. Similar issues apply to the pacifist's refusal to meet violence with violence. That desire exposes pacifists to potential harm, which is obviously risky. Likewise, anti-consumerist and anti-capitalist desires potentially expose you to arrest, social outcasting, inadequate healthcare, unreliable housing, irregular meals, etc.

These issues highlight the need for solidarity and collective support. We don't have to agree with one another, but we should try to support one another's desired realities. That ethic of support should be upheld as long as one person's reality does not interfere with another person's. Living out this ethic takes us one step closer to a truly decentered world in which all realities are accepted. In that world, no reality is better or worse than another. It's one big, ongoing cluster of desirous creativity, with our realities dialoguing, interacting and continuously pointing to better realities.

Embodying this creative process can be divided into three basic steps: understanding your desires, embodying your desires and being an activist for your reality.

First, figure out your deepest political desires. Try to understand what you want to do and how you want to live. Think of the world that you would like to inhabit. Think of the life you would like to live. Think of the society and culture you would like to live in. Think of the economic and political systems that would underlie those societies and cultures. Or perhaps economic or political systems would be obsolete. Perhaps you desire something else altogether. Okay, now you need to envision those dreams and conceptualize the details of those realities.

Second, start moving toward that reality. Figure out how to create that reality here and now. Think of what you need to do, how you need to live and how you need to communicate in order to manifest that reality. There are probably large gaps between your desired reality and the current reality. Don't let that discourage you. Instead, take it in stride and begin walking. Over time, those gaps will lessen and even close. You may also experience rough patches, difficult times and even serious conflicts. People may question your actions and even your sanity. Revolutionary realities are often, if not always, met with initial skepticism, ridicule and even suppression. This is where your hands-on rhetorical skills are helpful. Try to explain what you're doing and why. Try to explain that you are pursuing more socially just realities; that you are walking toward a better world, a world in which all realities are accepted and included. But of course, put this into a language that others can understand, relate to and identify with.

And third, be an activist for your reality. Strategically organize meetings, events, actions and campaigns that help bring about your desired reality. But this isn't about you, only. You're fighting for everyone's right to create self-determining and personally satisfying realities. Fight the oppressions, overturn the structures and eradicate the institutions that disempower people's reality-creating potential. Failing school systems, absurdly priced healthcare, genetically modified foods, worn down housing, media monopolies and corrupt and unresponsive governments impede everyone's ability to think, live and create differently. These things must be changed. This is where traditional radicalism and neo-radicalism meet — go out and be an activist who's trying to change the world.

Speaking to the Desires of Others

As previously noted, most people avoid recreating their realities, especially into radical or revolutionary realities. But you can encourage them to do otherwise. At the surface level, this involves using the rhetorical tactics and approaches addressed throughout this book. Use persuasion, storytelling, argumentation, invitational rhetoric and other skills and tactics to encourage people to pursue more radical realities. You obviously want to stress the liberating qualities and the personal and collective benefits of pursuing such realities. But this is a complicated process because you can never be sure why other people are not following their desires.

For instance, some people might desire radical realities but be afraid to take that chance. They live out commonplace, unsatisfying or liberal rather than radical lives. People's reasons for doing this will differ. Some people may feel that their radical desires are too troublesome to pursue. Other people may not know how to take the first step. And still others may cling to old desires, beliefs and behaviors. Regardless of their reasons, these people need support and encouragement to follow their radical desires. They need to believe that creating more socially just and democratic realities is worth all the work. Encouragement and support are the key issues here.

Other people may be pursuing their desires, but those realities are unjust and oppressive. These people need to be encouraged to investigate the politics of their desires. So, for instance, someone may desire a well-paying, comfortable corporate job. On one level this is fine. This person is not mean, hurtful or malevolent. But such a desire has unintended effects, like perpetuating classism and economic disparity, contributing to power monopolies and indirectly supporting various labor abuses. This situation is tough because most people prefer to ignore rather than confront the ill effects of their desires. Here, you need to stress their compliance with and perpetuation of inequalities, exploitations, sufferings and oppressions. But you also need to avoid accusatory language; that makes people defensive and they shut down. Using indirect approaches like invitational rhetoric, storytelling and first-person narratives is more helpful. These tactics allow people to come to their own understandings in their own ways. In time they will recognize the politics of their desires and hopefully make changes for the better.

Still other people need to be directly confronted. They know their realities cause direct harm to others and they are fine with it. They desire power, period. Indirect approaches are unlikely to work with these people. Different rhetorical tactics will be more or less effective with different types of people, but the bottom line is to get them to change. Such situations may necessitate more militant actions. As the famous abolitionist, Frederick Douglass, once said, "Power concedes nothing without a demand. It never did and it never will." Here, all options are on the table. Your approach to dealing with such power-desiring people is up to you. It could be more or less militant, but whatever it is, you're confronting power head on, looking to change or even abolish that desire.

Understanding different desires as in the above examples is helpful, but real life situations are not always so cut and dried. Teach-ins, workshops and large rallies often involve mixed audiences. Speaking to people's desires thus becomes more difficult. But in general, you're trying to do four things:

- Get people to acknowledge the political implications of their desires.
- Get people to pursue socially just desires.
- Get people to act upon those desires.
- Get people to envision and move toward better realities.

This type of talk is not really new. Every social movement speaks to people's desires — for instance, the desire for civil rights, global justice, gender equality, peace, etc. But a neo-radical approach centers this type of talk. You're trying to speak to something deeper and more profound. You're touching people's cores and unleashing their imaginations. You want people to actually envision and then walk toward radically different realities. This must involve desirous communication as opposed to plain old rational talk. Logical arguments and three-point essays rarely evoke that visionary, desirous appeal. You need to use languages, symbols, actions and ways of communicating that induce alternative realities. You're trying to awaken that sense of difference that we commonly experience at rallies, marches, forums, parades and festivals. But you're trying to do this on your own, without necessarily relying on the excitement of large protests or conferences. Ideally, you could do it any point in time and in any given situation by simply using the right words in the right way. It's you, your communication and your audience. Make it happen. This is difficult to do, but it's not impossible.

Similar arguments have been made by many other activists and thinkers. For instance, Stephen Duncombe, an activist and professor at New York University, asks us to tap into people's fantasies by spectacularizing our communication. Costumes, humor, charisma, bright lights, glitz and glam attract people's attention and get them involved in your politics. He calls this "Dreampolitiks." Likewise, David Graeber, an anarchist and Ivy League anthropologist, argues that such famous slogans as "All power to the imagination" and "Be realistic, demand the impossible" need updating. We need not only new slogans, but also new imaginary landscapes and new modes for communicating those landscapes. This resonates with the work of Alex Khasnabish, a Canadian-based sociologist of political imaginations. He argues that successful political insurgencies rely upon immaterial imagination as well as material struggle. Only by fighting on both fronts can political battles be won. The Argentinean-based group, Colectivo Situaciones, tries to do this by liberating thought and experience from the abstractions and constraints of language. They use open-ended, unfinished and entangled aphorisms, metaphors and theories to break past reified understandings. The US-based *Smart*-Meme Collective approaches the issue a little differently, using narrative techniques, culture jamming tactics and media trainings to help grassroots organizations create and package stories of social change.[7] And Patrick Reinsborough, a member of *Smart*Meme, writes about decolonizing the revolutionary imagination. As he states:

> In facing the global crisis, the most powerful weapon that we have is our imagination. But first we must liberate ourselves from the conceptual limitations we place on social change. As we expand the realm of the possible we shape the direction of the probable. This means directly confronting the myths and assumptions that make a better world unattainable.[8]

These calls and approaches to social change can be labeled different things — imaginative labor, affective labor, narrative labor, visionary labor or communicative and rhetorical labor. Regardless of what we call it, the power of desirous communication is obvious.

Neo-radicalism takes this to heart, seeking to mobilize people's desires and to create revolutionary realities. Desire, imagination and communication are the roots of neo-radicalism.

Guidelines for a Neo-Radical Agenda

Neo-radicalism's communication-based approach to reality and social change aligns with and is even a product of contemporary activism. First, it is based on decentered principles. Rather than marching lockstep under a single ideology or pursuing one vision or one world, we are free to move in a million different directions. Each individual pursues a unique reality and no reality is inherently better than any another. Realties are accepted or rejected based on issues of social justice. The question, "Is your reality socially just?" guides the evaluative process. This decentered approach concretizes the maxim, "one world, many realities." Second, neo-radicalism is based on a revolution of everyday living. Anarchists, autonomists and feminists have often said that revolution is not reducible to overthrowing governments or overturning systems. Large, widespread social revolutions are still necessary and welcomed, but we shouldn't wait for the great revolutionary crescendo. Your immediate life and your innermost desires are sites and vehicles for revolutionary activity. Third, neo-radicalism is based on collective action. Although you are seeking your own unique reality, no reality is an island. Your desires, visions and realities emerge from and contribute to the general lot of human interaction. Because of this, we are called to support, defend and help improve one another's revolutionary realities. Fourth, neo-radicalism is based on a plethora of tactics. There's no one way to do it. Yes, it is based on communication, but communication is multifarious and perpetual. The trick is to communicate with strategy, care and craft. And fifth, neo-radicalism is based on a well-reasoned idealism. Since the world is created and inherently pliable, radical social change is always possible. Hope and drive are thus part and parcel of the neo-radical project.

This section closes with some loose guidelines for developing a neo-radical agenda. These guidelines are intentionally broad and wide ranging, allowing for various interpretations and applications.

1. Neo-radicalism is based on the idea that human beings create their realities through communicative processes.
2. Neo-radicalism asks you to walk toward your innermost political desires and create whatever realities you so choose.
3. Neo-radicalism believes that every reality should be accepted, respected and appreciated so long as one reality does not impede another reality.
4. Neo-radicalism seeks to establish social systems that enable the free creation of our desired realities; this involves investigating, confronting and uprooting any social system that hinders this process.
5. This struggle continues indefinitely, for even if we create a world of truly decentered realities, there is no guarantee against the re-emergence of obstructive, controlling and oppressive forces.

Conclusion

Many aspects of neo-radicalism are not new. Activists have been talking about communication, vision, desire and revolution long before this book was written and they will continue to do so long after this book is forgotten. But rarely do activists dedicate the time to becoming better communicators. Communication is the creation of reality. You can use this reality-creating process to consciously create and recreate better, more radically democratic realities. I hope this book has given you some tools and tactics for doing that. I also hope that I have aroused something inside of you. That arousal is not so much about neo-radicalism or even about communication and rhetoric. Instead, it's about manifesting your innermost desires into concrete political realities. We all have those desires and visions and we all want better realities. I ask and even beg you to follow your heart and speak, write and act with a revolutionary desire so bright that it illuminates a path into and beyond the future. We don't know for sure what that future will look like, but we will know it when we see it. Eventually, the gap between this world and that world will close and we will have become the rhetors of the past who created the future.

Resources

The following sources are intended to further develop your knowledge and practice of communication, rhetoric and radicalism. This list is by no means exhaustive but rather an introduction to the material covered in this book.

Manuals and How-To Books

Albert, Michael. *Trajectory of Change: Activist Strategies for Social Change.* South End Press, 2002. Provides insights for improving the rhetoric of radical social movements. It's not a how-to manual, but it's a good discussion starter.

Alinsky, Saul. *Rules for Radicals: A Pragmatic Primer for Realistic Radicals.* Vintage Books, 1989. This classic was originally published in 1971 and is still widely used today. Alinsky understood the importance of communication and rhetoric.

Bobo, Kim, Jacki Kendall and Steve Max. *Organizing for Social Change: A Manual for Activists in the 1990s.* Seven Locks Press, 1996. A comprehensive and widely used manual for organizers. Includes sections on public speaking, using the media, designing workshops, facilitating meetings and fundraising.

Boyd, Andrew. *The Activist Cookbook: Creative Actions for a Fair Economy.* United for a Fair Economy, 1999. A great manual for street theater.

CrimethInc. Ex-Workers Collective. *Recipes for Disaster.* CrimethInc. Ex-Workers Collective, 2005. A comprehensive list of instructions for creating and carrying out subversive actions.

Cutting, Hunter and Makani Themba-Nixon. *Talking the Walk: A Communications Guide for Racial Justice.* AK Press, 2006. This is an excellent guide for handling mainstream mass media. It's written specifically for racial justice activists, but is helpful for all types of activists. Provides instructions for press releases, editorials, interviews, pitching stories, framing the issue, etc.

Kush, Christopher. *The One-Hour Activist.* Jossey-Bass, 2004. A general how-to manual for lobbying lawmakers. Helpful tips for writing letters, sending e-mails, making phone calls, etc.

Lakoff, George. *Don't Think Like an Elephant! Know Your Values and Frame the Debate.* Chelsea Green Publishing, 2004. Provides instructions on how to properly frame the conversation to win political arguments. Written for liberal democrats, but helpful for all activists.

Prokosch, Michael and Laura Raymond, eds. *The Global Activist's Manual: Local Ways to Change the World.* Thunder Mountain Press/Nation

Books, 2002. A collection of essays about global activism. Provides some practical tips for Internet organizing, doing research, fundraising, etc.

Salzman, Jason. *Making the News: A Guide for Activists and Nonprofits.* Westview Press, 2003. Provides excellent tips for contacting journalists, writing press releases, getting on television, securing radio interviews and publicizing your issues. Well organized and easy to read.

Shaw, Randy. *The Activist's Handbook: A Primer.* University of California Press, 2001. A general how-to manual for organizers. Covers, among other things, lobbying, coalition building, handling the media and direct action.

Books Related to Contemporary Anti-Authoritarian Activism and Movements

Callinicos, Alex. *An Anti-Capitalist Manifesto.* Polity Press, 2003. An overview of the global justice movement's anti-capitalism. Can be difficult to read, but its suggestions are very doable.

Day, Richard J.F. *Gramsci is Dead: Anarchist Currents in the Newest Social Movements.* Pluto Press, 2005. An excellent examination of present day anti-authoritarian activism.

Duncombe, Stephen. *Dream: Re-Imagining Progressive Politics in an Age of Fantasy.* The New Press, 2007. Makes a very convincing argument as to why activists should use imaginative communication. Written by a scholar-activist who knows his stuff. Easy to read and highly recommended.

Gordon, Uri. *Anarchy Alive!: Anti-Authoritarian Politics from Practice to Theory.* Pluto Press, 2008. A concise and informative look at the practice and theory of contemporary anarchism.

Graeber, David. *Fragments of an Anarchist Anthropology.* Prickly Paradigm Press, 2004. A very brief and insightful argument as to why anarchy is a legitimate form of social organization.

Holloway, John. *Change the World Without Taking Power: The Meaning of Revolution Today.* Pluto Press, 2005. Discusses creating an alternative world within the already existing world. It is difficult to read, but essential for anti-authoritarians, neo-Marxists and anti-capitalists.

Klein, Naomi. *No Logo: Taking Aim at the Brand Bullies.* Vintage Canada, 2000. An instant classic for anti-corporate and anti-consumer activists.

Lasn, Kalle. *Culture Jam: How to Reverse America's Suicidal Consumer Binge — And Why We Must.* Quill, 2000. A culture jammer's call to action by the editor of the famous AdBusters magazine.

Notes From Nowhere, eds. *We are Everywhere: The Irresistible Rise of Global Anticapitalism.* Verso, 2003. A great collection of essays by and for global justice activists.

Shepard, Benjamin and Ronald Hayduk, eds. *From ACT UP to the WTO: Urban Protest and Community Building in the Era of Globalization*. Verso, 2002. A very diverse collection of essays by activists focusing on a variety of issues, including but not limited to reproductive rights, community gardening, living wages, racial justice and the media. It focuses on the New York City area, but is applicable to everyone.

Shukaitis, Stevphen and David Graeber, eds. *Constituent Imagination: Militant Investigations/Collective Theorization*. AK Press, 2007. An excellent collection of anti-authoritarian theories, analyses and stories.

Solnit, David, ed. *Globalize Liberation: How to Uproot the System and Build a Better World*. City Lights Books, 2004. A great collection of essays by and for activists. Covers theory, analysis and how-to guidelines for changing the world.

Starhawk. *Webs of Power: Notes from the Global Uprising*. New Society Publishers, 2002. A collection of essays by the famous writer, activist and feminist.

Starr, Amory. *Global Revolt: A Guide to the Movements Against Globalization*. Zed Books, 2005. A concise and easy to read overview of global justice movements, tactics and concepts.

Classics and Compilations

Bey, Hakim. *T.A.Z.: The Temporary Autonomous Zone, Ontological Anarchy, Poetic Terrorism*. Autonomedia, 1985. Theoretical, poetic and polemic, it details many ideas common to contemporary radicalism.

Debord, Guy. *Society of the Spectacle*. Black and Red, 1983. A dense and theoretical critique of consumer society written by a leading figure of the Situationist International. Originally published in 1967.

Duncombe, Stephen, ed. *Cultural Resistance Reader*. Verso, 2002. Original texts by cultural radicals.

Goldman, Emma. *Living My Life, Volume One*. Dover Publications, Inc., 1970. The widely read autobiography of the famous anarchist, feminist and revolutionary.

Hoffman, Abbie. *Steal This Book*. Four Walls Eight Windows, 1996. Hoffman's classic manual on subversive activity. Originally published in 1971.

Katsiaficas, George. *The Imagination of the New Left: A Global Analysis of 1968*. South End Press, 1987. Written by a radical sociologist, this is a highly interesting explanation of an historical era.

Marx, Karl and Friedrich Engels. *The Communist Manifesto*. Penguin, 2002. The famous call to action that still influences radical politics.

McCarthy, Timothy Patrick and John McMillian, eds. *The Radical Reader: A Documentary History of the American Radical Tradition*. The New Press, 2003. A great collection of original speeches, essays and manifestos.

Vaneigem, Raoul. *The Revolution of Everyday Life.* Rebel Press, 2006. This book influenced the May, 1968 events in France and continues to inspire anti-authoritarian thinking and practice.

Theory and Philosophy

Butler, Judith. *Gender Trouble: Feminism and the Subversion of Identity.* Routledge, 1990. Butler is one of America's premier theorists on gender and sexual identity. This was one of her earlier books that put her on the map.

Cutting, Gary, ed. *The Cambridge Companion to Foucault.* Cambridge University Press, 1998. Provides a good introduction to the work of Michel Foucault, helping you navigate his indirect and cryptic writing style.

Deleuze, Gilles and Felix Guattari. *A Thousand Plateaus: Capitalism and Schizophrenia.* University of Minnesota Press, 1987. This is one of their most famous works, which includes an explanation of the widely cited concept of the "rhizome."

Gramsci, Antonio. *Selections from the Prison Notebooks.* International Publishers, 1971. This is the often-cited notebook of the famous Marxist theorist. It contains writings on hegemony and the organic intellectual.

Hardt, Michael and Paolo Virno, eds. *Radical Thought in Italy: A Potential Politics.* University of Minnesota Press, 1996. An excellent overview of Italy's post-Workerist thought. Discusses immaterial labor, general intellect, social factory and multitude.

Kaufman, Cynthia. *Ideas for Action: Relevant Theory for Radical Change.* South End Press, 2003. An excellent introduction to radical theory. Covers feminism, gender, race, ideology, Marxism, etc.

Laclau, Ernesto and Chantal Mouffe. *Hegemony and Socialist Strategy: Towards a Radical Democratic Politics.* Verso, 2001. A key text for post-Marxist thought, this book looks at class identity and hegemony from a discursive rather than deterministic perspective.

May, Todd. *The Political Philosophy of Poststructuralist Anarchism.* Pennsylvania State University Press, 1994. Combines anarchism and poststructuralist thought. Provides very helpful overviews of Marxist, anarchist, critical and poststructuralist theorists.

Activism and Social Movements: Academic Books

Bowers, John W., Donovan J Ochs and Richard J. Jensen. *The Rhetoric of Agitation and Control.* Waveland Press, Inc., 1993. Focuses mostly on older issues and examples of the 1960s like the civil rights movement and the 1968 Democratic national convention in Chicago.

Della Porta, Donatella, ed. *The Global Justice Movement: Cross-national and Transnational Perspectives.* Paradigm Publishers, 2007. A collection of essays examining the global justice movement from sociological perspectives.

Foran, John, ed. *The Future of Revolutions: Rethinking Radical Change in the Age of Globalization.* Zed Books, 2003. A compilation of sociological and political science essays on the nature of contemporary revolution.

Frey, Lawrence R. and Kevin M. Carragee, eds. *Communication Activism, Vol. 1: Communication for Social Change.* Hampton Press, Inc., 2007. A comprehensive compilation by leading activist-scholars within the communication field. Very helpful and insightful.

Morris, Charles E. and Stephen Howard Brown, eds. *Readings on the Rhetoric of Social Protest.* Strata Publishing, 2001. Contains some foundational essays for the scholarly examination of social movements and protest.

Reitan, Ruth. *Global Activism.* Routledge, 2007. Looks at the rise and nature of global activism from a political science and sociological perspective.

Stewart, Charles J., Craig Allen Smith, and Robert E. Denton, Jr., eds. *Persuasion and Social Movements.* Waveland Press, Inc., 2007. A well respected and often-used compilation of essays from communication scholars.

Communication and Rhetoric: Academic Books

Arneson, Pat, ed. *Perspectives on the Philosophy of Communication.* Purdue University Press, 2007. A compilation of essays by leading communication scholars covering major philosophical figures. Very readable and helpful.

Bizzell, Patricia and Bruce Herzberg, eds. *The Rhetorical Tradition: Readings from Classical Times to the Present.* Bedford Books, 1990. A comprehensive overview of the Western rhetorical tradition. Uses excerpts from original writings. Difficult to read but a great resource.

Herrick, James A. *The History and Theory of Rhetoric: An Introduction.* Allyn and Bacon, 2004. A concise and easy to read overview of the Western rhetorical tradition.

Radford, Gary P. *On the Philosophy of Communication.* Thomson Wadsworth, 2005. An easy to read introduction to the philosophy of communication.

Art, Performance, Storytelling and Culture Jamming

Ad Busters. The Canadian-based magazine dedicated to culture jamming, spoof ads and *un*commercials. The website provides instructions for your own culture jamming. adbusters.org.

Bread and Puppet Theater. A highly respected grassroots puppet theater troupe dedicated to radical social change. They've been around since the 1960s and are based in Vermont, US. breadandpuppet.org.

Chainworkers. Italian webzine using media and culture jamming tactics to unionize precarious workers. Very creative and effective. Chainworkers.org.

Clandestine Insurgent Rebel Clown Army. A decentered street theater troupe (mostly in Europe) using humor, sarcasm and political clowning. Their website provides hands-on tips and ideas. clownarmy.org.

Colectivo Situaciones. An Argentinean-based militant research collective. They weave together theory and practice in the service of liberation. situaciones.org.

CrimethInc. Ex-Workers Collective. A decentered collective of mythology makers spread across the United States. Their rhetoric is passionate and thought-provoking. Crimethinc.com.

d-i-n-a. A small collective of five international artists combining art and communication to create "radical entertainment." Guerilla art meets the digital age. d-i-n-a.net.

Reverend Billy and the Church of Stop Shopping. A larger than life performance artist who uses the persona of an evangelical preacher to spread anti-consumer messages. Based in New York City. revbilly.com.

*Smart*Meme. A non-profit collective helping grassroots movements communicate messages of change. They give workshops on story-based strategies like meme campaigns, branding, graphic design, etc. They have offices in different regions of the US. Smartmeme.com.

The Yes Men. Satirical political impersonators who infiltrate and disrupt the public meetings of corporations, government agencies and financial institutions. Their accomplishments are mind-boggling and absolutely hilarious. The two leading members are based in the US. theyesmen.org.

Yo Mango. A shoplifting movement based in Barcelona, Spain, that appropriates the excitement and appeal of popular culture and fashion to brand an anti-consumer lifestyle. Very exciting and energetic. yomango.net.

Publications, Journals and Media

Democracy Now! A long-running and highly acclaimed radio news program airing daily. Shows can be downloaded online. democracynow.org.

ephemera. An academic journal of radical theory and politics. Often covers some of the newest debates and concepts. ephemeraweb.org.

Journal of Aesthetics and Protest. Magazine of theory, art and analysis. Focuses on creative ways to change the world. journalofaestheticsandprotest.org.

Left Turn. Magazine dedicated to struggles against global capitalism and imperialism. Provides analysis, debates, reports and book reviews. leftturn.org.

Mute. A magazine of culture and politics that focuses on the newest issues of the day. metamute.org.

Paper Tiger TV. A twenty-five year old non-profit video collective that provides alternative coverage of issues often ignored by the mainstream media. papertigertv.blogspot.com.

US Indymedia. Participatory media in the US that uses open publishing. In other words, you post, read and respond to what you want. There are hundreds of local sites in America and across the world. indymedia.us.

Z Magazine: Long-time magazine of leftist politics. The website is updated daily and contains forums, videos, blogs, books, regional news, etc. A great resource in general. zmag.org.

End Notes

Chapter 1

1. Parts of this opening section were previously published in "Rhetoric for Radicals: A Call for Communicative Action," *Journal of Aesthetics and Protest,* June, 2007. journalofaestheticsandprotest.org/5/articles/Del Gandio/delgandio.htm. Cited February 1, 2008.
2. Here are some background resources that influence my description of twenty-first century radicalism: Alex Callinicos, *An Anti-Capitalist Manifesto,* Polity Press, 2003; John Holloway, *Change the World Without Taking Power,* Pluto Press, 2005; Jose Correa Leite, *The World Social Forum,* Haymarket Books, 2005; Stevphen Shukaitis and David Graeber eds., *Constitutent Imagination: Militant Investigations, Collective Theorization* AK Press, 2007; David Solnit, ed., *Globalize Liberation: How to Uproot the System and Build a Better World,* City Lights Books, 2004; Amory Starr, *Global Revolt: A Guide to Movements Against Globalization,* Zed Books, 2005; Notes from Nowhere, eds., *We Are Everywhere: The Irresistible Rise of Global Anti-Capitalism,* Verso, 2003.
3. For the concept of "communicative labor," see Ronald Greene's "Rhetoric and Capitalism: Rhetorical Agency as Communicative Labor," *Philosophy and Rhetoric,* 37.3 pp. 188–206, 2004.
4. For background on these and other theorists, see Paolo Virno and Michael Hardt, eds., *Radical Thought in Italy: A Potential Politics,* University of Minnesota Press, 1996. For cross-continental accounts and uses, see three helpful websites: Eipcp.net; Transform.eipcp.net; Rekomb inant.org. Also see the special edition of *Ephemera,* "Immaterial and Affective Labour: Explored," Vol. 7 (1), February 2007, Ephemeraweb .org/journal/7-1/7-1index.htm. All sites cited February 1, 2008.
5. Michael Hardt and Antonio Negri, *Multitude: War and Democracy in the Age of Empire,* Penguin, 2004. For debate over Hardt and Negri's work, see Gopal Balakrishnan and Stanley Aronowitz, eds., *Debating Empire,* Verso, 2003; and Jodi Dean and Paul Passavant, eds., *Empire's New Clothes: Reading Hardt and Negri,* Routledge, 2003.
6. From Plato's *Apology.* Quote found in James L. Golden, et al, *The Rhetoric of Western Thought,* Kendall/Hunt, 2003.
7. Here's the lineage: Socrates mentored Plato and Plato mentored Aristotle.
8. This information about Marcos comes from the documentary film, *A Place Called Chiapas,* directed by Nettie Wild, VHS, New York Films

Video, 1998. I highly recommend this documentary for its overview of the Zapatistas and insight into their rhetoric.
9. Ana Carrigan, "Afterword: Chiapas, the First Postmodern Revolution," in *Our Word is Our Weapon: Selected Writings*, Subcomandante Marcos, Seven Stories Press, 2001.
10. Emphasis added. Court transcripts found in Mark L. Levin, et al, eds., *The Tales of Hoffman*, Bantam, 1970.
11. Subcomandante Marcos, *Our Word is Our Weapon*.
12. Robert W. McChesney and John Nichols, *Our Media, Not Theirs: The Democratic Struggle Against Corporate Media*, Seven Stories Press, 2002.

Chapter 2

1. Che Guevara, "The New Man," in *Philosophy for a New Generation*, A. K. Bierman and James A. Gould, eds., Macmillan, 1971.
2. Sophia Delaney, "Anarchists Can Fly," in *We Are Everywhere: The Irresistible Rise of Global Anti-Capitalism*, Notes from Nowhere, eds., Verso, 2003.
3. Saul Alinsky, *Rules for Radicals: A Primer for Realistic Radicals*, Vintage, 1989.
4. Naomi Oreskes, "Most Scientists Agree that Global Warming is a Human-Caused Problem," in *Global Warming: Opposing Viewpoints Series*, Cynthia A. Billy, ed., Greenhaven Press, 2006.
5. Sonja K. Foss and Cindy L. Griffin, "Beyond Persuasion," *Communication Monographs*, 62, 1995.

Chapter 3

1. P. M. Bergman, "A Prefatory Note on Anarchism Today," in *The Anarchist Cookbook*, William Powell, Barricade Books, 1971.
2. See, for instance, Wilhelm von Humboldt, Ludwig Wittgenstein, Kenneth Burke, Edward Sapir and Benjamin Whorf, J. L. Austin and John Searle, Jacques Derrida and Eugene T. Gendlin.
3. *The Speeches of Malcolm X*, VHS, MPI Home Video, 1997. The speech "Democracy is Hypocrisy" is available online: Malcolmxonline.com/malcolm-x-videos. Cited February 1, 2008.
4. For some background sources related to linguistic imperialism, see selections from the following books: Marlis Hellinger and Anne Pauwels, eds., *Handbook of Language and Communication: Diversity and Change*, Mouton de Gruyter, 2007; Fredric Jameson and Masao Miyoshi, eds., *The Cultures of Globalization*, Duke University Press, 1998. Jerry Mander and Edward Goldsmith, eds., *The Case Against the Global Economy and for a Turn Towards Localization*, Sierra Club Books, 1996.
5. Two basic sources are: Charles U. Larson, *Persuasion: Reception and*

Responsibility, Wadsworth Publishing, 2006; Hugh Rank, "Persuasion Analysis," webserve.govst.edu/pa. Cited February 1, 2008.

6. Noam Chomsky and Edward S. Herman, *Manufacturing Consent*, Pantheon Books, 1988.
7. George W. Bush, "President Delivers State of the Union Address," January 29, 2002, Whitehouse.gov/news/releases/2002/01/20020129-11.html. Cited January 1, 2008.
8. Ari Fleischer, "Press Briefing by Ari Fleischer," March 24, 2003. Whitehouse.gov/news/releases/2003/03/20030324-4.html. Cited February 1, 2008.
9. The genealogy comes from Teresa Brennam, "Forward," in *Political Correctness: A Response from the Cultural Left*, Richard Feldstein, University of Minnesota Press, 1997.
10. My use of *the word* follows from several influences: Michael McGee's "ideograph," Doris Graber's "condensation symbol," and the general use of "meme."
11. Lisa Jervis, "Forward: Goodbye to Feminism's Generational Divide," in *We Don't Need Another Wave: Dispatches from the Next Generation of Feminists*, Melody Berger, ed., Seal Press, 2006.

Chapter 4

1. This section, and the title and theme of this chapter, are heavily influenced by Kevin Michael DeLuca's article "Unruly Arguments: The Body Rhetoric of Earth First!, Act Up, and Queer Nation," *Argumentation and Advocacy*, Summer, 1999.
2. Here is a helpful source as well as two popular street theater groups: *The Activist Cookbook: Creative Actions for a Fair Economy*, United for a Fair Economy, 1997; Bread and Puppet Theater, Breadandpuppet.org; and Clandestine Insurgent Rebel Clown Army, Clownarmy.org. Cited February 1, 2008.
3. Parts of this section were previously published in two sources: my doctoral dissertation, entitled *My Journey with Vibes, the Nexus, and Alteration: A Performing Philosophy*, Southern Illinois University, April, 2002; and "Visions of a Radical Life," *Lumpen Magazine*, January, 2008.
4. The phrase originated with Bob Dylan's song, "Subterranean Homesick Blues." It was later used by the Weather Underground and became popularized as a revolutionary slogan.

Chapter 5

1. "About Clamor," Clamormagazine.org. Cited February 1, 2008.
2. John Holloway, *Change the World Without Taking Power*, Pluto Press, 2005; Starhawk, *Truth or Dare*, HarperCollins, 1987.
3. For related guidelines, see Uri Gordon's "Practicing Anarchist Theory:

Towards a Participatory Political Philosophy," *Constituent Imagination*, Shukaitis and Graeber, eds., AK Press, 2007.

4. Michael Hardt and Antonio Negri, *Empire,*Harvard University Press, 2000; Hardt and Negri, *Multitude,* Penguin, 2004; David Solnit, *Globalize Liberation,* City Lights Books, 2004; Marina Sitrin, *Horizontalism,* AK Press, 2006. Leftturn.org, Zcommunications.org. Cited February 1, 2008.
5. Subcomandante Marcos, *Our Word is Our Weapon,* Seven Stories Press, 2001.
6. Hakim Bey, *T.A.Z.: The Temporary Autonomous Zone,* Autonomedia, 1985.
7. Stephen Duncombe, *Dream: Re-imagining Progressive Politics in the Age of Fantasy,* New Press, 2007; David Graeber, "Revolution in Reverse," nyc.indymedia.org/en/2007/10/9201; Alex Khasnabish, "Insurgent Imaginations," *Ephemera* 7 (4) 2007, Ephemeraweb.org/journal/7-4/7-4khasnabish.pdf; Colectivo Situaciones, "Something More on Research Militancy," in *Constituent Imagination. Smart*Meme, Smart meme.com. Cited February 1, 2008.
8. Patrick Reinsborough, "Decolonizing the Revolutionary Imagination," in *Globalize Liberation,* Solnit, ed., City Lights Books, 2004.

Index

About the Author

Jason Del Gandio teaches Public Communication at Temple University in Philadelphia, specializing in rhetoric, the philosophy of communication, and critical studies. He has designed and taught college courses such as *The Rhetoric of Globalization* and *Public Advocacy*. His current scholarship focuses on the performance, philosophy, and rhetoric of radicalism and is grounded in grassroots activism. He is a post-Seattle activist who has worked on globalization and free/fair trade issues, anti-war campaigns and Latin American solidarity. Some of his writings can be viewed online at Dissident Voice, Ephemera, Cultural Logic, Metaphilm, Re-Imagining Democracy, and the Journal of Aesthetics and Protest.